The Secret Mind
of Bertha Pappenheim

Also by Gabriel Brownstein

The Open Heart Club

The Man from Beyond

The Curious Case of Benjamin Button, Apt. 3W

The Secret Mind
of *Bertha Pappenheim*

The Woman Who Invented
Freud's Talking Cure

Gabriel Brownstein

PublicAffairs
New York

PublicAffairs
Hachette Book Group
1290 Avenue of the Americas, New York, NY 10104
www.publicaffairsbooks.com
@Public_Affairs

Printed in the United States of America

First Edition: April 2024

Published by PublicAffairs, an imprint of Perseus Books, LLC, a subsidiary of
Hachette Book Group, Inc. The PublicAffairs name and logo is a trademark of the
Hachette Book Group.

The Hachette Speakers Bureau provides a wide range of authors for speaking
events. To find out more, go to hachettespeakersbureau.com or email
HachetteSpeakers@hbgusa.com.

PublicAffairs books may be purchased in bulk for business, educational, or promotional
use. For more information, please contact your local bookseller or the Hachette Book
Group Special Markets Department at special.markets@hbgusa.com.

The publisher is not responsible for websites (or their content) that are not owned by the
publisher.

Print book interior design by Amy Quinn.

Library of Congress Cataloging-in-Publication Data

Names: Brownstein, Gabriel, author.
Title: The secret mind of Bertha Pappenheim : the woman who invented
    Freud's talking cure / Gabriel Brownstein.
Description: New York : PublicAffairs, 2024. | Includes bibliographical
    references and index.
Identifiers: LCCN 2023047264 | ISBN 9781541774643 (hardcover) | ISBN
    9781541774650 (epub)
Subjects: LCSH: Pappenheim, Bertha, 1859-1936. | Hysteria. | Nervous
    system—Diseases. | Psychoanalysis.
Classification: LCC RC532 .B77 2024 | DDC 616.85/24—dc23/eng/20231214
LC record available at https://lccn.loc.gov/2023047264

ISBNs: 9781541774643 (hardcover), 9781541774650 (ebook)

LSC-C

Printing 1, 2024

for Marcia, always

Contents

I felt a Cleaving in my Mind—
As if my Brain had split—

—Emily Dickinson

It is as if I were obliged to compare everything I hear about other people with myself; as if my personal complexes were put on the alert whenever another person is brought to my notice. This cannot possibly be an individual peculiarity of my own: it must rather contain an indication of the way in which we understand "something other than ourself" in general. I have reasons for supposing that other people are in this respect very similar to me.

—Sigmund Freud

I don't know much about medicine, but I know what I like.

—S. J. Perelman

About This Book

The night before he died, my father, Dr. Shale Brownstein, a retired psychiatrist and psychoanalyst, gave me an essay he had written about Bertha Pappenheim and Sigmund Freud and Freud's mentor, the great Viennese physician Dr. Josef Breuer. After my father died, Bertha Pappenheim became very important to me.

Pappenheim was one of the great feminists of the twentieth century, a writer, activist, and organizer, and the leading Jewish crusader against the *Mädchenhandel*, the "girl business," the sex trade in young women. All kinds of young women were forced into lives of prostitution, but of particular concern to Pappenheim were the Jewish girls. Jewish villages in eastern Europe were ravaged by pogroms and poverty, the unmarriageable women there were vulnerable, and many found themselves in desperate circumstances. On steamships and railroads, they were sent all over the world: including to Asia, South America, and the Middle East.[1] Pappenheim was the German-speaking world's loudest voice against this *Mädchenhandel*, and she did all she could to protect and defend Jewish women and girls. She was a controversial and well-known figure from the turn of the century until her death in 1936.

Her feminism is not what she's best remembered for. When she was younger and living in Vienna—well before she achieved any success as a writer, social worker, organizer, and activist—Pappenheim suffered a breakdown, a case that was diagnosed as "hysteria." She was treated by Josef Breuer, who sat with her and listened to the stories she told, and it was Pappenheim who named this process the "talking cure." According to Freud's acolyte and first biographer, Ernest Jones, it was Pappenheim who brought the idea of catharsis into psychoanalysis. One can argue that talk therapy was her invention as much as it was anyone's: she was the first to name the process, and the one who realized that by talking to a doctor, a patient might unburden themself of their problems.

She appears under the pseudonym "Anna O." in the book that Freud and Breuer wrote together, *Studies in Hysteria*, Freud's first book on psychology. Pappenheim's case is the first one in the book, and it's the eureka moment of psychoanalysis, the apple on the head, the kite and the key. Before he had a name for his treatment, Freud called it "Breuer's method." "This discovery of Breuer's is still the foundation of psychoanalytic therapy," he wrote in 1917. In the "Anna O." story, the patient confesses repressed, frightening memories, and as she does so, she is cured of her "hysterical" symptoms. By the end of a year and a half of treatment, so Breuer reports, Anna O. is left in "perfect health."[2]

There are a number of reasons to doubt the truth of Breuer's reported cure. He published "Fraulein Anna O." in 1895, more than a dozen years after his work with Pappenheim, and notes and letters of the intervening decade show that she continued to suffer terribly in the time after he treated her—continued depression, pain, difficulty speaking, rages, drug addiction, hallucinations, suicidality, and dissociative states, what her doctors continued to diagnose as "hysteria."

Breuer's treatment did not leave Pappenheim in "perfect health," and Freud and Breuer knew it. Throughout the decade after Breuer treated her, the two doctors corresponded about Pappenheim's continuing suffering. Freud's wife, Martha, was close to Pappenheim and the Pappenheim family. Martha and Bertha socialized, and in the years leading up to the publication of *Studies*, Martha wrote her mother letters about her meetings with Bertha, and about Bertha's struggles and symptoms. On at least one occasion, Sigmund Freud and Bertha Pappenheim were at the same dinner party. She didn't recover from her disability until she left Vienna, moving far away from Freud and Breuer to Frankfurt.

In the beginning of the twentieth century—in 1909–1910, when they both traveled, separately, to North America—Pappenheim was at least as well-known as Freud, and in many circles better known. The organization she ran, the *Jüdischer Frauenbund* (JFB) or the League of Jewish Women, devoted itself to the education and protection of vulnerable Jewish girls and young women, trying to give them skills so they could enter into jobs other than sex work. Pappenheim never let a psychoanalyst work with any of the girls she cared for. She also never acknowledged her years of illness or her connection to Sigmund Freud.

She was silent on the subject. Breuer didn't say much about it either. But Freud kept revising and retelling the story of "Anna O.," making it conform to his developing theories of psychoanalysis and psychosexuality. By some accounts, it's the case he referred to most often in his life.[3] As the years went on, Freud's descriptions of Anna O.'s problems became increasingly sexual, her relationship with Breuer increasingly sexualized. In the mid-1920s, Freud claimed to have "suddenly remembered" something Breuer had told him in the 1880s: that at the end of their work together, Anna O. suffered a hysterical pregnancy, calling out, "Dr. B's baby is coming," and that Breuer, unable to master his feelings of attraction for his patient, fled the scene.

The story of her hysterical pregnancy—a story of very questionable authenticity—has been inscribed into the history of psychoanalysis. Anna O. rolling on the floor, with open mouth and open legs: it's reported as if it were fact in Peter Gay's monumental 1988 biography of Freud, and in Melinda Given Guttmann's 2001 Pappenheim biography. It's there in Elaine Showalter's *Hystories* (1997), possibly the most widely read US feminist book on hysterical disorders.

After his death, my dad's essay fell like a stone into the still water of my mourning brain. My meditations spread in ripples, which widened out and deepened and spun. What was the trouble with Bertha Pappenheim?

At the center of this whirlpool is an absence. We know its shape but not its detail: a woman is seized by a self-destroying illness, an attentive doctor treats her, and an ambitious young neurologist takes this story and with it builds a theory that conquers the Western world. The story is set in Vienna between 1880 (when Breuer first saw Pappenheim) and 1895 (when *Studies* was first published), and we have very few solid facts. Pappenheim never spoke or wrote about her illness. Freud destroyed all his early letters and papers. Breuer's archive was lost in World War II. No one can tell you what happened, but there are many, many writers who have tried.

For over a hundred years, Pappenheim's case has been examined and reexamined. There's Breuer's story of her miracle cure, and Freud's story of her lurid relapse, and then stories in variation all around the core. She was raped by her father. She was in love with her father. She projected that love onto her doctor. Her life's work against prostitution was nothing more than an extension of her man-hating "hysteria." In the 1970s and 1980s, feminists turned these narratives on their head and argued that nineteenth-century hysteria was nothing but a construction of the patriarchy, that her sickness (for some writers) was a form of social revolt, and that her illness (for others) was the process by which she found her political voice. As "hysteria" fell out of fashion as a clinical term, psychologists, psychiatrists, and psychoanalysts proposed alternative diagnoses. She was depressed. She was schizophrenic. What kind of pill might have cured Bertha Pappenheim? In the 1980s and 1990s, writers intent on demolishing Freud's reputation—like Frederick Crews and Mikkel Borch-Jacobsen—argued that there was nothing really wrong with Bertha Pappenheim, that hers was essentially a case of medical bungling. All of her symptoms could be explained by drug poisoning. Or maybe Pappenheim was simply pretending to be sick, and Breuer was fool enough to believe her. Other scholars have applied post-structuralist readings to Freudian mythology. Pappenheim's illness was a language game, her symptoms symbols of what she could not speak. Or perhaps these symbols were "iatrogenic," a script that she was being fed by her doctor. Much of this writing is fiercely argued. Some of it is illuminating. Collectively it makes for a choose-your-own-adventure Anna O.

In Chimamanda Ngozi Adichie's TED talk "The Danger of a Single Story," she observes: "The problem with stereotypes is not that they aren't true, but that they are incomplete. They make one story the only story." What she says about stereotypes is true of ideological assumptions. These competing explanations aren't necessarily wrong, but they tend to be reductive, to present a single story.

For the last fifty years, these stories have been composed under the assumption that hysteria is not a real disease, that Pappenheim's mental and physical collapse was nothing but a historical relic, not legitimate but imagined, a kind of performance, and that people don't really get sick anymore in the way "hysterical" women like Anna O. once did. This is no longer the prevailing neurological view.

For much of the last century—and in many doctors' offices today—if you suffered from what was once called "hysterical paralysis," or "hysterical blindness," or "hysterical seizures," and you went to a neurologist, you would likely be told that your condition had no basis in biology, that it was "all in your head." After the dominance of Freudian thinking faded, pharmaceutically based psychiatry also backed away from the problem: no drug can make the blind see, can make someone rise from a wheelchair. The patients who suffered these things had nowhere to turn. Their problems, medically speaking, weren't treatable, weren't *real*.

Since the turn of the millennium, the neurological attitude has been changing. Now, at the leading medical institutions in the United States—in the offices of neurologists based in Brown, Harvard, Northwestern, Stanford Universities, at the National Institute of Health, and at Mayo Clinic—there are professionals and centers dedicated to the study and management of these kinds of disorders. These new treatments are connected with studies of brain biology, and they reframe 150-year-old questions about illness and health, mind and brain—about what used to be called hysteria.

When Freud came to Paris in 1885, he studied with Jean-Martin Charcot, the father of modern neurology. By then, Charcot had demonstrated the neurological basis for multiple sclerosis (MS) and amyotrophic lateral sclerosis (ALS), and he wanted to do the same for "hysteria," to discover the "dynamic lesions" in the brain that caused the condition.

"We're beginning to identify the dynamic lesions that Charcot was looking for," says Massachusetts General Hospital's Dr. David Perez. Perez, a Harvard neurologist, psychiatrist, and neuroscientist, would never call his patients "hysterical." The current preferred diagnostic language is "functional neurological disorder," or FND.

Read the medical literature and you'll see that "functional neurological disorder" and "hysteria" are sometimes used interchangeably, particularly when describing the history of the condition. In a March 2023 case study in the *New England Journal of Medicine*—a study of a young man who falls into seizures, who intermittently loses his ability to speak, and whose leg sometimes becomes paralyzed—Perez's colleague Dr. Jonah N. Cohen writes, "Treatments for Functional Neurological Disorder have evolved from the late 19th and early 20th century writings of Freud and Breuer." A 2021 statement coauthored by Perez and thirty other leading international brain researchers—including the chief of the Neurology Branch at the National Institutes of Health, and the chair of the Department of Psychiatry at Mayo Clinic—begins by announcing, "Functional neurological disorder (FND), also known as conversion disorder and previously termed hysteria, is a prevalent and disabling condition at the interface of neurology and psychiatry." Reframed as FND, "hysteria" is no longer seen as a historical relic—it's a problem that has been studied for centuries, and a condition being taken seriously in the leading hospitals in the world.

At his busy FND Unit at Mass General, Perez's team includes four neurologists, and two psychiatrists, as well as a speech therapist, a physical therapist, two occupational therapists, and two psychotherapists. He has recently received a $4.1 million grant from the NIH to perform structural and functional brain imagining studies to better understand the neurophysiology that underlies his patients' symptoms.

This does not mean that "FND" is strictly synonymous with the old term "hysteria," or that the diagnosis can be applied backward in time. The nineteenth-century diagnosis "hysteria" was broader than FND; it included symptoms—hallucinations, for instance, or suicidality—that are not considered aspects of functional neurological disorders. The current diagnostic criteria for FND didn't exist in the 1890s, and you can't go back and apply these criteria to long-dead patients. Still, neurological diagnosis and treatment of FND reframes the historical debate.

For decades now, academics have argued that "hysteria" was never a legitimate medical diagnosis, never an actual physical disease. Edward Shorter's 1992 study, *From Paralysis to Fatigue: A History of Psychosomatic*

Illness in the Modern Era, is a seminal text arguing that such disorders are psychologically driven and culturally defined. "In psychosomatic illness," Shorter writes, "the body's response to stress or unhappiness is orchestrated by the unconscious." For Shorter, the old symptoms no longer occur. "Hysterical paralysis," he writes, "was quite specific to the late eighteenth and nineteenth centuries."

A 2007 article in the *Journal of the Royal Society of Medicine* rebuts Shorter directly and by name, offering photographic evidence of the persistence of the "dragging gait" of functional leg paralysis: patients in Paris in 1888, London in 1895, Berlin in 1991, and Edinburgh in 2004, all trapped in the same postures. The authors write, "Anyone who thinks that hysteria disappeared with the death of Charcot cannot know what goes on in neurology outpatient clinics."

At a 2022 FND Society conference, a PowerPoint slide flashed across the screen—the cover of Shorter's *From Paralysis to Fatigue*. "There's lots of this stuff out there," said the physician at the podium, and without further comment, he moved on.

"Those people who say hysteria doesn't exist," I was told by another neurologist, "I'd like them to come to my clinic any day of the week." This doctor would never call her patients "hysterical"—the word is laden with too much baggage—but for her, as for her colleagues, the terms "FND" and "hysteria" can be used to refer to a single field of study, centuries of clinical research into a specific, serious, and not uncommon diagnosis.

Clinical neurologists and academic theorists occupy parallel, independent spheres. They speak different languages and ask different questions. Academic theorists look at an illness as if they were studying a text. They ponder meaning, they theorize motivation, they situate terms in their historical and cultural milieux. Neurologists don't do that. If a patient is suffering from dementia or migraine or MS, they don't ask, "What is the meaning of this?" (Or, as early twentieth-century German psychosomatic healers once asked, "Why this symptom? Why now?") The questions at Perez's FND Unit at Mass General are more along the lines of "How can we help you?"

"Functional" is a word doctors have used since long before Freud's time. Its antonym, classically, is "organic." Patients can go into functional seizures, though they do not have epilepsy. They can suffer functional leg paralysis, though their muscles and nerves seem perfectly intact. They can go functionally blind, even though there's no discernible deficit in their eyes, optic nerves, or visual cortex. They can suffer functional paralysis. Their symptoms can move around their bodies just as Pappenheim's did, in ways that seem "incongruous and inconsistent" (as the neurologists say) with any specific physiological diagnosis.

For Jon Stone, the Scottish neurologist who is among the world's leaders in FND diagnosis and treatment, the history of neurological interest in these symptoms and these disorders is "U-shaped"—that is, lots of research in the nineteenth century, dwindling to almost nothing in the late twentieth, and then resurgent attention in the twenty-first.

The new attention paid to these illnesses came into stark focus in the United States when, in 2006, the eminent neurologist Mark Hallett, chief of the National Institute of Health's Medical Neurology Branch, and chief of its Human Motor Control Section, wrote an influential paper declaring that functional neurological symptoms and disabilities had to be taken seriously, that their neglect amounted to a "crisis for neurology."[4] In 2013, the fifth edition of the *Diagnostic and Statistical Manual of Mental Disorders* (*DSM*) of the American Psychiatric Association, the *DSM-5*, the index of diseases of American psychiatry, adopted neurological language to describe the condition: FNSD, functional neurological symptom disorder (the "S" for "symptom" has, since 2015, been dropped from most neurological and psychiatric discussions of the disorder). In 2018, the International Classification of Diseases adopted a neurological approach to the condition, and in 2019 neurological terminology was approved by the World Health Organization. FND is not a marginal diagnosis—it is the conviction of the most advanced brain scientists considering the phenomenon. "A core neuropsychiatric illness"—that's the language you see in the literature. Still, in hospitals all over the world, FND patients face stigma and poor treatment. Many clinicians—like many academic historians—don't believe their patients' symptoms are genuine or biological or legitimate.

If you go onto websites where FND sufferers discuss their experiences, you will see the same stories again and again: patients being bounced from neurologists to psychiatrists and back again, patients who cannot walk being discharged from hospitals, patients being told to "stop it" while their bodies are wracked with convulsions. W. Curt LaFrance of Brown University and Joel D. Mack of the Oregon Health and Science University (psychiatrists specializing in FND at, respectively, the Providence [RI] and Portland [OR] Veterans Administration Hospitals) write that doctors too often react to these patients with "a sense of therapeutic nihilism."[5] In *Hysteria: The Biography*, the sociologist Andrew Scull calls these patients "modern medicine's untouchables." Doctors can say the problem isn't "real," that the patients are only pretending to be sick, but that doesn't do much to resolve the patients' pain and suffering, and it doesn't stop the patients from showing up in emergency rooms.

Every day, on Twitter, there are voices attacking the FND diagnosis: emergency room doctors who prefer the term "non-specific"; psychotherapists who trust in the old Freudian paradigm; patients who fear that the term "functional" may be used to dismiss the actuality of their symptoms; and anti-vaxxers who think that the FND diagnosis is a dodge, used to explain away the side effects of what they believe to be pernicious injections. But within the neurological community, FND is accepted as the current term for an age-old problem.

The British medical journal the *Lancet* reports that functional neurological symptoms are the second most common reason for outpatient neurology visits, after headache, and according to a recent volume of *The Handbook of Clinical Neurology*, FND is about as common as multiple sclerosis or Parkinson's disease, accounting for roughly 6 percent of neurology patients overall. (As Jon Stone points out, this is roughly consistent with numbers of patients diagnosed with "hysteria" in nineteenth-century France.[6]) Though FND still largely affects women, who make up about two-thirds of those diagnosed,[7] the condition can strike all kinds of people, and it can ruin lives. fMRI (functional magnetic resonance imaging) exams reveal that something seems to be happening in the intersections of brain networks of FND patients, often around the patients' temporoparietal junction, or TPJ, and in the past decade, neurologists have developed diagnostic protocols so that FND is now a "rule-in" diagnosis: they no longer want doctors to say to patients, "There's nothing wrong with you, it's all just psychosomatic."

"This can happen to anybody," I was told by Dr. Kathrin LaFaver, a German-born neurologist who trained at the NIH and the Mayo Clinic, who directed the FND clinics at Louisville and at Northwestern University Hospitals, and who is co-editor of a recent textbook on the treatment of functional movement disorders. "This can happen to you."

New neurological thinking posits FND as an embodied illness that lies in the borders between psychiatry and neurology, an illness whose symptoms are no more or less symbolic or intentional than are the symptoms associated with vertigo or Tourette's.

Stone, the pathbreaking Edinburgh neurologist, often uses the analogy of a computer when describing the condition to his patients: FND is a like software problem, not a hardware problem, he tells them. All the wiring of the patient's neuroanatomy may be fine, but the programming is off. Brain networks have become entangled, messages are not getting through, and so the patients can become deaf as Pappenheim sometimes did, or their arms can become as useless as hers did, or their legs can get paralyzed, or they can go into seizures—all of these are things that befell Anna O. I have met these patients, and they have described to me their suffering and recovery. I have spoken with their doctors and read the literature of their field. FND is not a new kind of illness. It's a new way of considering one of the oldest medical conundrums. "How is it that in all civilized countries," asked Pierre Janet in 1906, "hystericals have agreed to simulate the same thing from the middle ages to the present day?"

FND doesn't compete with the contradictory arguments of the theorists who have retroactively diagnosed Pappenheim, but it offers a new way of organizing their stories. No one story has to be right. It's perfectly plausible that Pappenheim was abused as a child, depressed as a teenager, suffered from physical ailments and drug poisoning, put on shows of her unhappiness and need, was oppressed by her culture, and suffered symptoms that were similar to those around her. All of this can happen to FND patients, but none of it makes their suffering intentional or unreal. Her arms and legs and hands and eyes and ears didn't work, that's what Breuer tells us. Her consciousness split in two, she suffered a *condition seconde*," a state of dissociation that matches up pretty well with what contemporary FND patients suffer (some call it "brain fog").

These kinds of breakdowns happen to people all the time—so the neurologists argue—and in that view, Pappenheim's ailment can be seen not as something peculiar or antique, but as something that continues to be a problem faced by patients and their doctors. New medical thinking can help sort through the various stories told about Pappenheim's illness. Academic scholarship can put neurological arguments in context.

What Breuer did was radical. The way he treated Pappenheim—the way the two together invented a treatment—was freewheeling, improvisational, and undogmatic, very different from the codified practice of Freudian psychoanalysis. He sat down with a young woman who had lost control of herself and he paid attention to what she said. He worked doggedly and devotedly. He did it without the psychoanalytic theory that Freud would build, or the diagnostic language of present-day neurologists. He paved the way for both. The talking cure, for Breuer, was as much as anything else a listening cure, and most doctors who take a serious interest in FND agree that listening to patients, and affirming their experience of the disorder, is the first step in the patient's diagnosis, treatment, and rehabilitation.

For the new doctors studying FND, the way to heal these patients is not to get them to confess their repressed secrets (secrets that may exist more in an analyst's dogma than in a patient's subconscious) or to separate them from their social conditions; the way to treat them is to help them reprogram their brains and regain control of their bodies, a transdisciplinary approach that crosses borders between psychology, psychiatry, neurology, and various modes of physical, occupational, and speech therapy. There is no single, agreed-upon, one-size-fits-all approach, but all the doctors I spoke with told me that it was crucial at first to listen to the patients, to attend to them, to help them understand that their symptoms are real, common, and treatable, and in this way to work with them to construct an understanding of their illness, "a narrative that has healing power,"[8] as one neurology paper I read described it.

From the long-damped ashes of Pappenheim's work with Breuer, we have arrived at a new kind of talking cure, a new kind of listening cure, practiced by doctors whose primary field of study is the neuroanatomy of the brain.

I found the FND doctors I spoke with to be heroic, not because they have come up with a new unified theory of the disorder, but because they are helping people who for so long have been mistreated and ignored. In his 2022 John Walton Prize Lecture to the Association of British Neurologists, Stone reminded his audience he had no magic authority on his subject, that there was no Wizard of Oz: "We're just ordinary people, standing behind a curtain, trying to do our best." Current neurology presents an unsettling image of the mind, something less substantial than we're accustomed to: the mind as a thin crust that floats precariously on the magma of our lives. What we imagine as the firm ground of our identity is in fact a precipitate, something that sits on top of a roiling mass of neurons, history, and culture. What is underneath can explode, volcanically, and can wreck us. What I learned, sorting through all this, was how crucial it is to listen to patients' stories, and how difficult.

The years in which I worked on this book were years of enormous personal pain, the worst years of my life. I began to conceive of the book when my father died. I was deep into writing it when my wife, Marcia, the one person to whom I was closest in the whole world, was diagnosed with pancreatic cancer. She more than anyone urged me forward in writing this—no one believed in my writing more than Marcia did—and with her encouragement I kept on working on it through her sickness, decline, and death. Between my dad's death and my wife's, the world—and my city, New York City—was seized by the COVID-19 pandemic. It was a horrible three years.

"We tell ourselves stories to live," wrote Joan Didion in *The Year of Magical Thinking*, her book about the deaths of her husband and child. These words are often quoted as if they're a heartwarming exhortation to storytelling, but I think her meaning isn't far from Shirley Jackson's horror story observation, "No live organism can continue for long to exist sanely under conditions of absolute reality." Absolute reality, traumatic reality, isn't something that any of us can stomach. So we tell stories. This is a story I wrote while my world became too much to bear.

"The mechanism of poetry," Freud wrote (and by *poetry*, according to Charles Bernheimer, he meant *creative writing*), "is the same as that of hysterical phantasies."

I do not claim to have solved any great mysteries here, to have discovered what Anna O. *really* suffered, or to be able to tell you what FND *really* is. In imagining this lost medical history, I have accepted the best current medical language for the disorder that Breuer (a groundbreaking neurologist) diagnosed in his patient. In imagining Pappenheim's life and illness, I have based my writing on what few facts we have, on the most plausible explanations I have found in the diverse and contradictory commentary, on the work of powerful historians, and on the stories and expertise of contemporary FND patients and doctors. As Freud wrote in one of his case studies: "Like a conscientious archeologist, I have not omitted to mention in each case where the authentic parts end and my constructions begin." The nonexistence of this common, age-old condition—and the persistence in calling it hysteria—was a super-sophisticated attempt to explain away a deeply, deeply troubling and persistent phenomenon.

"What is left over," asked the philosopher Ludwig Wittgenstein, "if I subtract the fact that my arm goes up from the fact that I raise my arm?"

It's not so easy to describe this illness, because it is a problem that attacks the borders of some of our favorite words, like "mind," "body," "voluntary," "real," "healthy," and "sick." This is an illness that messes with our fundamental understanding of the world, and maybe that's why its current neurological descriptor—functional neurological disorder, or FND—can feel a little mushy.

"What's really new and different now," Jon Stone told me, "is the voice of the patients, incredibly eloquent patients who know the history of their condition."

It has been my honor to talk to some of these people, and I am grateful that they have allowed and trusted me to tell their stories. The lives of these patients have helped me imagine something of what Pappenheim's illness and recovery might have been like, and the work of contemporary FND doctors—who see themselves attacking the same problem addressed by Breuer, Charcot, Freud, and Janet—can help illuminate a strange and muddled story.

The nineteenth-century English physician James Paget described one of his patient's functional (he called it "hysterical") paralysis this way: "She says, as all such patients do, 'I cannot,' it looks like 'I will not,' but it is 'I cannot will.'" In his contribution to *The Handbook of Clinical Neurology*, Jon Stone quotes this approvingly as a description of FND.

I kept writing this book through years of trial and pain. Writing it was my way through, that's what Marcia kept saying to me, and after she was gone I kept working on it with her voice in my head, and I began to think of FND not as an act, but as the loss of an ability to act according to a script the rest of us have learned and memorized, a script that says we have control over our bodies. We all go around willing ourselves forward, telling ourselves that we are autonomous creatures, that our legs and mouths and lungs are really our own, to do with as we will. For me, my dad's death, the COVID-19 pandemic, my wife's cancer, and her intolerable loss put the lie to that story. My father's was the strongest body I ever knew, and I watched aghast as it betrayed him. The coronavirus moved across New York City as if all its citizens were a single body, a fertile field on which to grow. And Marcia's cancer was narrative chaos, a glimpse of the pandemonium inside us all. The cells of our guts and skin and bones and blood and brains and gonads are all dividing and dividing, and for no reason they can mutate and turn and become malevolent and deadly. Her death revealed my life as unstable, and her loss made the world seem unreal. The progress of time became a cruel joke, a nasty prank played on me.

"Freud even defined hysteria as narrative incoherence," Elaine Showalter wrote in her book *Hystories*, but maybe narrative chaos is closer to actuality than any human storytelling can ever be.

In this book, I have tried to imagine the story of Bertha Pappenheim—how her life might have been—and also to understand the myths of "hysteria," a history in miniature of the ways we have tried and failed to understand our bodies and our selves, as well as the bodies and minds of others.

PART ONE

Imagining Pappenheim

1

I had dinner with my father the night before he died. I drove to the Upper West Side on October 8, 2018, and there he was at his apartment door, eighty-five years old, smiling, stooped, freshly shaved, white hair combed carefully back, and dressed only in a pair of underpants—Dr. Shale Brownstein, retired psychiatrist and psychoanalyst.

I kissed him. He kissed me.

"Hello, hello!" he said. "I'm doing great!"

The doctors didn't know shit. No more catheters for him, he said, and no more diapers. Sure, he said, there had been a few accidents. But in just a week at home, he had learned again how to hold it in, how to let it out.

"I'm cured!" He moved without a cane or a walker, showing off gingerly. He pressed upon me an article from the *New York Review of Books*, David Oshinsky on the history of mental hospitals. "I wrote to him. I said, 'Put me to work!' I can't sit around like this all day."

In the kitchen I took the lid off a pot, and there was my mother's beautiful beef stew.

"She knows I can't eat that shit," he said.

I fixed myself a bowl, grabbed a beer from the fridge, and made my way to the dining room table. My father followed, carrying in one hand a cantaloupe and in the other an enormous carving knife.

"She treats me like I'm a dangerous lunatic," he said, as he settled into his chair.

I said, "That's because you act like a dangerous lunatic."

This made my dad laugh—eyes squinting, naked shoulders going up and down, the whole business—and that was my cue to deliver my message, the one I had been rehearsing. All the rage between my parents (it had been going on for months), all of their fighting, was papering over terror. There was a great unspeakable fact lurking in all their arguments. Their craziness came from their inability to speak it, I hazarded, to face it rationally. Neither he nor my mother could face the fact that my father was—but here I could not get it out of my mouth either, could not muster the word *dying*—so instead I said that neither of them could admit that he was so sick.

"Not so sick," my dad said, cutting the melon in two.

"Pop," I said.

He quartered the melon. He pointed his knife at me. "You put me in that hearse."

He meant the ten-thousand-dollar ambulette we had hired in August to move him from the hospital in Vermont near his summer house to the rehabilitation facility on Amsterdam Avenue just blocks from my parents' apartment on Riverside Drive, where the windows overlook the Hudson.

"It was dark in there," said my father. "It was like death." He munched melon. "The lynch mob," that was his new name for my mom, me, my brothers, our wives, and any old friend, doctor, nurse, or therapist who tried to help him.

He had no memory of the summer: months of hospitalizations, misdiagnoses, ambulance rides, emergency rooms, and sudden, mind-altering fevers. We came home one sunny summer day from the Vermont hospital and before we even got out of the car, he had turned delirious. I had tried to carry him, all his two hundred pounds of feverish deadweight, up the stairs and into the house, and meanwhile he shouted the single worst one-syllable obscenity he could muster, the name of the President, like a bitterness he could not rid from his tongue: "Trump! TRUMP! TRUMP!!!!!!" Then, it was right back to the emergency room, where on the hospital gurney he thrashed like a hooked fish, trying to escape his IV tubes.

"I just hurt my tushy a little bit," he said while he ate his melon. "And she"—he meant my mother—"put me in that hospital."

I was confused by this and then remembered the first days of his crisis, when in late July the neighbor in Vermont had found him in the backyard, unable to get off the ground.

"When you fell," I began.

"I didn't fall!" he barked. Then quietly, slicing a crescent of cantaloupe into fourths, he said, "I just sat down a little bit. I bruised my tuchus."

My friends told me that he wasn't really himself anymore. I said that he was the guy I always knew. The truth, as with so many cases of dementia, was that the breakdown of his mind was warping his personality, pushing it to its extremes.

My dad had loved taking care of people. He had spent his life doing it. He'd been a great doctor. At Harlem Hospital, he'd worked to save raped girls, and desperate boys, and spent hours and hours holding infants infected with AIDS, singing to babies no one else would touch. In private practice, he had been therapist to much of the 1980s avant-garde: the sculptor Richard Serra, the performance artist Spalding Gray, the photographer Peter Hujar; these are the names I can say, either because these people acknowledged their treatment publicly, or because they are now dead. The names I can't drop include a tennis champion, a notorious child abuser, and one of the greatest composers of our time. One time, my dad came home with a stack of Lou Reed records, and I said, "Him?"

My father had clear blue eyes and a mischievous smile, and he could produce a lot of ambiguity within the single syllable "No."

The truth is, he did more than I will ever do to ameliorate the world: to rid it of suffering and to fill it with beauty. He was a bully of a dad, but he loved us fiercely. My dad was a big, strong man, a yeller and a hitter, and the only person I know to have hauled off and punched a uniformed, armed New York City policeman. He did it to protect my brother Daniel. His dominant emotion was a loving, protective rage, a rage that all his life he never quite got control over. Taking care of people was, for him, a way of taking pleasure and a way of having power. People speak of liberal guilt. I don't think my dad, child of lower-middle-class Jews from Buffalo, New York, ever for a second felt guilt about his wealth or his skin color or his drinking or his violence or really *anything* he did, and he did some pretty crazy shit. But he felt injustice bitterly, was outraged by it and took seriously the Jewish admonition to *tikkun olam*, to repair the world, and while he liked to think of himself as a peaceful man, he indulged in righteous anger. All his life seemed a work of Sisyphean labor. In Harlem, they called him Dr. Whitestein, and he turned that resentment back on his colleagues bitterly, and also inward on himself. Freud, hero of my dad's youth, was the villain of his later years. Mulling relentlessly in his long retirement, my dad despaired over the value of psychotherapy, talk therapy, his primary avocation and livelihood. His eyes would tear up, and he'd ask awful questions. Had it ever helped anyone? He was tough to console. He was a very learned man.

After dinner, we caught his socialist news broadcast—*Democracy, Now!* on CUNY TV—and then he raised a finger. "I got something for you." Unsteadily, he pulled himself up from his chair. He toddled through the apartment, a big man on little withered legs.

"Here," he said, handing me a fat padded envelope. "I reread it again and I think it's perfect. My masterpiece."

The envelope contained two piles of paper, each in its own binder clip. One was the masterpiece: an essay he had written years earlier, "Josef Breuer and Psychoanalysis." The other was more eclectic. On top was a single-paragraph letter to the editor, blown up, so that the words *Bertha Pappenheim* were pixilated and falling apart at the edges. It was from the *Times Literary Supplement*, written by Allen Esterson, and it began, "Shale Brownstein's reference to Bertha Pappenheim's supposed phantom pregnancy as a 'recovered memory' (letters, April 26) may lead some readers to believe that Freud had a recollection of being told of the incident by Breuer." The next photocopy was a letter in response to Esterson's, by Alan C. Elms, of the University of California, and it read, in part, "I recommend 'The True Story of Anna O.' in John Forrester's *The Seductions of Psychoanalysis*." Next to that, my father had written, heavily underlined, *all FALSE!* I looked for my dad's April 26 letter. It wasn't in the packet, but my brother Daniel found it later on the internet:

Sir—Paul Lerner's review of *The Enigma of Anna O.*, by Melinda Given Guttmann (March 22) should have explicitly stated that the story of Bertha Pappenheim's alleged pregnancy was a "recovered memory" which Freud developed late in life. More importantly, he failed to mention that Pappenheim, like her friend Martin Buber, had a deep antipathy for anything and anybody related to psychoanalysis.

SHALE BROWNSTEIN

When my mother found a photocopy of the letter in his desk among his things, it had a note scrawled at the bottom: "I called this a 'recovered memory' as a dramatic gesture. It worked! SB."

The next page in the binder clip was a photocopy of a review of the book *Freud's Women*, in the same periodical, and it had another spindly annotation from my dad: "!All as you say *BEFORE* the October trip to Charcot! Certainly Ambroise Tardieu, already dead in 1879, was left out of Freud's thinking. Big failure!" Then, in a separate binder clip, there was a copy of a long article, "Aristotle and the Effect of Tragedy," by Jacob Bernays.

"Who was he?" I asked.

"A *chochum*," said my dad.

I didn't recognize the word.

He wrote it on the back of the envelope, in Hebrew and in English transliteration, and then the translation, "Wise man." On the photocopied page near Jacob Bernays's name, my dad had written:

Martha Freud's uncle, Rabbi
1) a seminary in Breslau
2) librarian at BONN
Did Bertha use catharsis ideas??
SB

I was sitting in an armchair in the living room, and he was standing over me in his underpants, and he began to lecture, very emphatically and not entirely coherently, waving a finger and sometimes a fist, and I did what I have done since I was a small boy whenever my dad started in on one of his lectures—that is, I let my mind drift and waited politely for him to finish.

"Josef Breuer!" he corrected himself. "Jacob Bernays!" I had to understand about Bertha Pappenheim. "She must have known! She loved the theater!"

"Freud was shit!" said my father, who had driven up to Vermont sometime in the early 1990s with his multivolume hardcover standard edition of the master's collected works and had destroyed all of them. I always imagined a burning, a private bacchanal involving an outdoor grill, lighter fluid, and a bottle of vodka, but probably he just dropped them into a bin in the dump.

My phone rang. It was my mother. She was on her way home. I took the envelope, shoved it in a pile of papers in my backpack and headed back to Brooklyn. I kissed my dad goodbye. When I saw him the next day, he was lying on the carpet where together we had stood. He was dead, and I was crying.

———•———

There had been years in his life when my father had been enthusiastically engaged in Judaism, when he had studied Talmud at the Jewish Theological Seminary. We called old friends and neighbors, trying to track down a rabbi he had worked with, but all those rabbis were dead. The morning of the funeral, my brother Ezra was in Queens, trying to negotiate a price on a plot in a Jewish graveyard. The only spot he'd found was one set aside for the residents of a single apartment complex—immigrants who had all come over together from the same Eastern European town and lived together in the same buildings in Queens. I imagined my dad among them in some spectral condominium of the afterlife, alone by the ghostly shuffleboard courts, surrounded by hunched, kibbitzing, poolside shades. As I dropped my last shovelful of earth on his coffin, I remembered him telling me that he didn't want a Jewish funeral. He wanted his ashes spread in the backyard of his country house in Vermont.

I heard his voice. "You fucked it up!" It was something he said often.

The night before his funeral, I had tossed and turned in the sheets. I had cried out, "Daddy, daddy, daddy, dad." I woke up at four a.m. and sat at my desk and scrawled out memories, but come daytime, I had no idea how to mourn him. Day after day I sat down at my desk and wrote. The pages had no focus. They went everywhere. There was too much to remember. I started going to synagogue on Saturdays. I rose from my seat to say the mourner's kaddish, and then all of us mourners had to speak the names of our beloveds.

"My father, Shale Brownstein."

It was the same congregation where my youngest had celebrated a bat mitzvah, and it happened that one Saturday when I came to mourn that another girl was getting bat mitzvahed. That day, all the assembled eighth graders must have wondered: Who was that dude in the back row sobbing?

Right before the end of the service, I ducked out. Somewhere in the blocks between synagogue and home, I remembered the envelope, the one that contained his masterpiece. It was the key, I thought; it would lead me to him. I got home. I looked for it. I couldn't find it anywhere.

———◆———

For weeks, I went through fits of sorting through drawers and folders and piles of paper. I looked for it in my office at work. No luck. I gave up. Then I started looking again.

At that time, my mind was full of holes and absences. I kept forgetting things—names, errands, meetings. I'd open a kitchen cabinet and ask myself, *What was I looking for?* Each morning I sat at my desk and scribbled compulsively, filling notebooks. Between fits of writing, there were fits of looking for that envelope. I had declined when he was alive to listen to his story about Bertha Pappenheim and Josef Breuer and Sigmund Freud. Now I wanted to hear it.

So I went to the Community Bookstore in Park Slope and got a copy of *Studies in Hysteria*, the Penguin Classics edition (the Standard Edition is titled *Studies on Hysteria*—no English preposition can match the martial triumph of the original German's *über*), and I sat down and read. It was like peeking into my dad's sock drawer when I was a kid and getting that whiff of cedar and pipe tobacco and paper money.

Studies in Hysteria was published in 1895, and it's Freud's first book on psychology, and the book that launched Freud's career as a theorist of the human mind. "I can give no better advice to anyone interested in the development of catharsis into psychoanalysis," wrote Freud, "than to begin with *Studies in Hysteria* and thus follow the path which I myself have trodden." Freud cowrote *Studies* with his mentor, Josef Breuer, and it's a contentious, complex book, a collection of three essays on the nature of hysteria, one by Breuer, one by Freud, one (a preliminary statement) written by both of them, and five case studies, one by Breuer, and four by Freud. Breuer's essay "Anna O.," the one about Bertha Pappenheim, is the story of the discovery. It is the founding myth, the genesis of the theory and practice of psychoanalysis, and it is she, the patient—Anna O., Bertha Pappenheim—who names it "the talking cure." She says this in English because her hysteria at that point in time prevents her from speaking German.

In his case studies, Freud practices this "talking cure," what he calls "Breuer's method," and what Breuer calls "the cathartic method," and in his final essay, after the discovery and the practice, Freud sets out to describe his new theory of the workings of the mind.

Ernest Jones worked closely with Freud, and in his Freud biography Jones wrote that Pappenheim was "the real discoverer of the cathartic method"—that is, she was the one who conceived of the curative property of talk therapy, that one could to some degree expiate one's problems by talking them out. (Pappenheim's friends were appalled that Jones had revealed that she had been Breuer's patient.) According to Breuer, her other name for the "talking cure" was "chimney sweeping" (she said this in English, too), and the etymological root of the word "catharsis" is in defecation. That's how I experience talk therapy: getting out all the crap that's stuck in the tunnels of my mind. If you (like me) have ever gone to a therapist and talked out your problems and so felt unburdened by them, then you are following a path first set out by Bertha Pappenheim.

The thesis of *Studies* is expressed most succinctly and famously in its first chapter: "Hysterics suffer for the most part from reminiscences." Freud and Breuer's patients suffer from seizures or paralysis, loss of speech or loss of sight, problems with their gait or sense of smell, but in each case these strange physical symptoms are not a result of any physical injury or disease or organic breakdown of the body. The functional disabilities, Freud and Breuer argue, are caused by a failure to remember, caused by some disturbing painful fact lurking just below their consciousness. The psychical trauma, unable to be expressed in language, is converted into sickness of the body. Through the discovery in the case of Anna O.—which is to say, Breuer's work with Bertha Pappenheim—and through repeated experiments in analysis by Freud, the two authors declare that they have found a way to cure these problems:

Individual hysterical symptoms disappeared immediately and did not recur if we succeeded in wakening the memory of the precipitating event with complete clarity, arousing with it the accompanying affect, and if the patient then depicted the event in the greatest possible detail and put words to the affect. [Italics theirs]

The symptoms of hysteria can be cured, they tell us, by narration—it's not simply the memory of the traumatic event, but the repressed trauma's conversion into storytelling, that cures—they need to tell a tale that is clear, detailed, emotional, and arousing.

In the collaboratively written "Preliminary Statement," Breuer and Freud seem to agree in this assessment of hysteria and its cure. In the two independently written essays later in the book, they seem to disagree. Freud thinks "hysteria" always comes from repressed sexual impulses, and for Freud studying hysteria is a way of looking into the roiling conscious-and-subconscious brew of the human psyche, the things we refuse to admit to ourselves. For Breuer, hysteria is a kind of stunned state; he calls it "hypnoid hysteria," and it's a state that exists outside of ordinary consciousness. (This is not dissimilar from Pierre Janet's later notion of hysteria as a state of "dissociation.") For Breuer, hysteria is not necessarily caused by sex. Breuer seems to have a larger sense of the things that can cause this split in consciousness, and his notion of "hypnoid hysteria" is that it can stem from a variety of kinds of repressed, unresolved trauma. Toward the end of the book, Freud seems to argue that "hypnoid hysteria" doesn't actually exist. For Freud, there is only hysteria caused by sexual repression and sexual desire, the mind's linguistic surface at war with the preverbal urges that lie beneath.

Studies is the book of Freud's becoming. He wrote it in his late thirties when he was a practicing neurologist, intellectually isolated in the hard-science world of Viennese medicine, with five little children in his house, and with very little money, and with a bad habit of dosing himself with cocaine. The struggling doctor in early middle age plugged into his gifts for narrative and his fascination with psychology—and shazam! The book is loose and half-baked and argumentative. This Freud is full of curiosity, uncertainty, and questions. He makes crazy leaps and bounds all around Breuer, his mentor, collaborator, and antagonist. The two men are coming at the same problem from different directions. Breuer was a serious bench scientist, Freud a radical theorist.

I picked it up hoping for a glimpse of Bertha Pappenheim, wondering, *Who was this woman who had obsessed my father?* But that was a mistake, for two reasons. First of all, Breuer does his best to hide Bertha Pappenheim's identity—he conceals any information that might allow someone to find out who "Anna O." really was. Secondly, much of what Breuer does tell us is a lie.

Breuer writes that her illness was "resolved in its entirety," that upon conclusion of the "talking cure" his patient lived in "perfect health" ever after. Breuer treated her between 1880 and 1882, and he did not publish the book until thirteen years later, and she spent those intervening years in and out of sanitariums. Breuer visited her often in those years, and he found her suffering so awful that at one point he told Freud that she would be better off dead.[9]

Freud, too, knew all about her struggles. Pappenheim was his wife Martha's intimate friend. Bertha's father was appointed Martha's guardian after Martha's father's death—so Pappenheim was Martha's almost sister, Freud's almost sister-in-law. Pappenheim visited the Freud apartment both before and after the birth of the Freuds' first child, in 1887, and she was a regular guest at Martha's kaffeeklatsch. Martha wrote letters to her mother worrying about Bertha, that she was not herself, that the light had gone out of her eyes, that she was still sick, still suffering, still hallucinating. When *Studies* was published, Pappenheim had left Vienna, was living in Frankfurt, and it was while she was away from those Viennese doctors, after a decade of suffering, that she began to put her life back together again. Over the course of the following decades, Pappenheim became perhaps the most prominent Jewish feminist in the German-speaking world.

In the early twentieth century, many Jewish girls from Russia, Poland, Hungary, and Galicia worked as prostitutes. These were girls from impoverished, patriarchal societies, despised communities routinely set upon by antisemitic pogroms. In the years before and after World War I, many young men left these villages, looking for work. The young women who remained were desperate and at risk. Thousands of girls were caught up in this trade, and they were transported all over the world, from Asia to South America. Pappenheim's *Jüdischer Frauenbund*, the JFB, was the single largest Jewish women's group in the German-speaking world. At its height, more than one in every five eligible women (that is, Jewish women in Germany and Austria) belonged, and Pappenheim traveled to Russia and Romania and Jaffa and London and New York and Toronto, lecturing and raising money and trying to save young Jewish women. Pappenheim's JFB supported girls' schools across Eastern Europe, some 250 schools that served some 38,000 students. In 1907, in Neu-Isenburg, near Frankfurt, Pappenheim built a home for rescued Jewish girls and unmarried mothers. By 1937 it had cared for 1,500 women.

"A volcano lived in this woman." That's how she was eulogized.[10]

The sex trade always preys on poor, urban, vulnerable young women, and at the turn of the twentieth century, in the cities of eastern Europe, the poor, urban, vulnerable women were disproportionately Jews. The old statistics are not entirely reliable, but in 1890, by one count, Jewish women made up roughly a fifth of Warsaw's registered prostitutes. In Minsk, in 1910, one estimate indicated that roughly two-thirds of the prostitutes surveyed were Jewish. The men who employed these girls were, from Pappenheim's view, all too often Jews. There was a congregation of Jewish pimps in Constantinople. There is a graveyard for Jewish pimps in Buenos Aires. There was a widespread pernicious stereotype, equating prostitution and Jews. "All the business of prostitution in this city is in the hands of the Jews," wrote the American consul in Odessa in 1908—expressing prejudice and overstating the facts.[11] Contemporary historians argue that many of these impoverished women had no other option but prostitution—that theirs was, in a phrase of recent scholarship, "a choiceless choice." (According to new research by Aleksandra Jakubczak, a prostitute in Warsaw could earn eight rubles in two nights, the same wage a domestic servant would make in a month and a half.[12]) Antisemites played up the stereotype of the Jewish pimp and prostitute. This is how Jews are drawn in Hitler's *Mein Kampf*, as vermin, spreading disease—so this trade, this *Mädchenhandel*, was a forbidden subject among respectable Jews in Europe. Bourgeois Jews, seeking to acculturate and assimilate in modern Europe, were embarrassed by the subject of prostitution. Religious Jews recoiled. Isaac Bashevis Singer wrote of Jewish prostitutes, "The mere sight of them is defiling."[13] But Pappenheim stood up for them.

This is the thread that connects her two lives, the suffering young woman who invented talk therapy, and the powerhouse fighting the sex trade: Bertha Pappenheim all her life sought to speak the unspeakable. But no one in Pappenheim's care—no one she rescued from the *Mädchenhandel*—ever saw a psychoanalyst.

"Psychoanalysis is, in the hands of a doctor," she wrote, "like confession in the hands of a Catholic priest—whether it is a valuable tool or a double-edged sword depends who is using it and for what." Anna Freud said that Pappenheim was an opponent of psychoanalysis for all of her life.[14]

That's, I think, why my dad liked her so much—because she was pragmatic in her treatment of trauma and violence and oppression, and because she was opposed to Freud and the Freudian theory that had swept my dad up when he was young, and to which my father as an old man had become apostate.

What happened to Bertha Pappenheim in 1880? What was the nature of her illness? We can't trust Breuer's story about her cure, but what about his diagnosis of hysteria? What robbed her of her language and her control over her body? How did Pappenheim and Breuer come up with this new kind of treatment in which she told stories and he listened? And how did the bedridden young woman of the late nineteenth century become the powerhouse activist of the early twentieth? Did her storytelling really help her?

These questions are unanswerable. The body of commentary around the Anna O. case is almost infinite. Go searching for an explanation of her sickness, and it's a little like pornography on the web: whatever you want, it's out there.

The contentious discussion around hysteria, the disease that afflicted her, is even larger. For most of the second half of the twentieth century, the consensus among doctors and historians was that as a disease it did not exist, that hysteria was a strange cultural phenomenon of the late nineteenth century, but over the last two decades, neurologists have been treating patients whose problems once would have been described as "hysterical." These doctors have been scanning their brains and rewriting history. This redefinition of an ancient disease is probably the best justification for a new book about Bertha Pappenheim. There is a new neuropsychological way of seeing patients like her that is being articulated even as I write.

This book will attempt to apply new science to an old problem, and to animate a story that is profoundly obscure. I know, as I write this, that I'm an amateur, in over my head. But I will do my best to tell you what I've learned. In sum, our minds are not as stable as we think they are, and we ought to listen to what these patients are telling us.

———————

We know very little of her early life, beyond what's in *Studies*. The story is that in middle age Pappenheim went back to Vienna to erase all records of her past, and that she destroyed all her early correspondence and writings. She did collect an archive of her adult life's work, and when she was dying and the Nazis were in power in Germany, she tried to get a friend to smuggle her papers out, but all these pages were lost.

Freud also got rid of most of his early letters and journals. In 1885, he wrote to Martha (then his fiancée): "I have destroyed all my notes of the past fourteen years, as well as letters, scientific excerpts and the manuscripts of my papers. . . . I couldn't have matured or died without worrying about who would get hold of those old papers." Breuer's archive, too, was lost in World War II. What we have in terms of documentary evidence of the Anna O. case are just a few scattered letters and medical records.

What a strange and sexy name they gave to her: the palindrome and then the round open O, an orifice, a mouth open wide. There she is in the night sky of psychoanalysis, the constellation by which the master trimmed his sails.

2

I fixed myself a cup of tea, I sat down in my recliner, and I opened up *Studies in Hysteria*. The book begins with a short, four-paragraph preface, which more or less announces that the authors will avoid close description of the women they're writing about:

> Our experience was gathered in private practice among an educated and literate social class, and its subject matter touches in many ways on the most intimate life and fortune of our patients. It would be a severe abuse of confidence to publish reports of this kind, with the risk of patients being recognized and facts which had been entrusted to the doctor alone spreading among friends and acquaintances. We have had, therefore, to do without observations which are highly instructive and offer powerful evidence. This, of course, applies above all to those cases in which the sexual and marital relations have an aeteological significance. Thus we have been able to supply only very incomplete proof of our view that sexuality, as the source of psychical traumas and as the motive of "defense," of the repression of ideas from consciousness, plays a major role in the pathogenesis of hysteria. Precisely those observations of a strongly sexual nature had to be excluded from publication.

Studies, which in many ways is about the sex lives and sex drives of young bourgeois women, begins by announcing that, for the purposes of propriety, any discussion of their actual intimate lives will be avoided.

After the preface comes the "Preliminary Statement" coauthored by Freud and Breuer. The disease is called "hysteria," and it's defined by a set of strange and variable symptoms that seem to have no discernible physiological cause:

> All kinds of neuralgias and anesthesias, which have often persisted for many years, contractures and paralyses, hysterical attacks and epileptoid convulsions, that all observers have taken for genuine epilepsy, *petit mal* and tic-like affections, persistent vomiting and anorexia to the point of refusing all food, a great variety of visual disturbances, constantly recurring visual hallucinations and so on.

When I first read the book, this weird and changeable illness seemed very antique to me, but as I talked with the doctors who are currently studying conditions very much like these, and as I met the patients who are suffering paralyses, contractures, seizures, tics, and visual disturbances, the problem became vivid and urgent. Go to the website of the Functional Neurological Disorder Society, the international society of medical professionals studying and treating FND, and you'll find doctors from the NIH, the Mayo Clinic, Harvard, and Stanford all discussing patients with similar conditions, and you will find them explaining that—though the terms are not synonymous—the roots of this new diagnosis, FND, is in the study of an old illness, hysteria. People suffer attacks very much like the kind Bertha Pappenheim suffered—failure to walk, to talk, to see, to move—and doctors are still trying to understand the psychology and biology of the condition.

"Although largely neglected for much of the 20th century," David Perez, Jon Stone, W. Curt LaFrance, and several of their colleagues write in the *Journal of Neuropsychiatry and Clinical Neuroscience*, "FND is among the most common conditions encountered by neurologists and clinical neuroscientists." Common triggers for FND include pain, illness, surgery, grief, and stressful family settings. Histories of sexual abuse are reported in up to 36 percent of the patients—in the general population, 18 percent of women report histories of sexual abuse. About a third of FND patients suffer depression, up to a quarter, anxiety.[15] The patients that I talked with often described a set of escalating stressors—extreme pain, for one patient, after repetitive hospitalizations. For another, it was a history of anxiety and medical misdiagnoses, spiraling out of control over decades. For still another, an even more complex cocktail: a history of abuse, a period of unemployment, unfortunate combinations of prescription drugs, and the general difficulties of childbirth and motherhood.

Much of the most current physiological and imaging research is focused on the way stress and trauma can alter the interconnectivity of the brain networks. The hypotheses are forming, the ultimate explanation is unclear, but the suspicion among those who study the subject suggests that, in FND patients, the limbic system, where our emotional processing takes place, connects in unusual ways to the salience network, where the brain decides what information is important, or to the motor control areas, which allow us to gain agency over our bodies. Much of this happens at the temporoparietal junction, the TPJ—a spot under the temple, which, if you stimulate it experimentally, will cause out-of-body experiences. In the brains of these patients, there are no wounds, no lesions, no breakdowns. The neurons are all fine. It's the connectivity and pathways of information that seem to be out of order—on an fMRI, neurologists can observe unexpected trajectories in the neurological currents running in the patients' brains.

In *Studies*, the first example of a hysterical patient comes in the "Preliminary Statement." She is not named, but we can see that she is Anna O., that she is Bertha Pappenheim, sitting by the bed of her dying father.

A girl, who, tormented by anxiety, is watching over a sick bed, falls into a twilight state and has a terrifying hallucination, while her right arm, which is hanging over the arm of the chair, goes to sleep; this develops into a paresis of the arm with contracture and anaesthesia. She wants to pray and cannot find the words; finally she manages to say a children's prayer in English. Later, when a difficult and highly complex hysteria develops, English is the only language that she can speak, while her mother tongue is incomprehensible to her for eighteen months.

Again, at first reading, this sounded less like science than like gothic fiction, but according to neurologists I've spoken with, caring for a sick relative is a relatively common triggering event for a functional breakdown. Very frequently, FND affects the mouth—speaking, drinking, swallowing, eating. The "twilight state" is also a typical symptom—a *condition seconde*," Breuer called it, "time-missing" for Anna O., or a "splitting of consciousness," as Oliver Sacks describes it in his book *Hallucinations*.

When describing FND to their patients, modern doctors reach for our most current technological metaphor, computers—hardware and software. In their "Preliminary Statement," Freud and Breuer use the most urgent and exciting medical language of their moment—bacteriology and virology. (Koch's work on tuberculosis was published between Breuer's treatment of Pappenheim and the writing of *Studies*.) "The psychical trauma, or more precisely the memory of it, operates like a foreign body" in the patient's subconsciousness.

In Breuer and Freud's view, repressed trauma works like infectious material lodged in the patient's mind. The talking cure exorcises the foreign body and thereby cures the patient: "The method removes the effectiveness of the [repressed traumatic] idea." *Studies* does not present a single, unified argument. It's a debate, several essays along the way toward a conception of an idea. The language they're using is fairly new, and Breuer and Freud seem anxious that not all their readers will accept it: the word "unconscious" often sits in quotation marks, and when Freud writes about "*the existence of hidden, unconscious motives*" he puts the words in italics. In this first book of Freudian psychology, words like "denial" are grasped gently, as though with heat-proof tongs.

After the "Preliminary Statement" come the five case studies: Breuer's "Fraulein Anna O.," and then those four dazzling essays by Freud, "Frau Emmy von N.," "Miss Lucy R.," "Katharina," and "Fraulein Elisabeth von R." Breuer's marks the eureka moment, the technical breakthrough; Anna O. is the foundation on which everything else is built. Freud's cases tell the story of how he learned to employ the techniques invented in "Anna O.," talk therapy and the cathartic method, and in his case studies Freud begins to build a theory around Breuer's work. At the end there are two essays, Breuer's long and windy "Theoretical Issues," mapping out the state of the medical theory of hysteria and possible future directions for study; and Freud's "On the Psychotherapy of Hysteria," and it's in this essay that Freud breaks with Breuer explicitly and makes his claim that he's never seen "hypnoid hysteria," and that hysteria is always related to sex and sexuality, and that both trauma and hysteria allow us to observe the dynamics of the human psyche.

On my first time through, I found Breuer's case history, "Fraulein Anna O.," to be tough sledding. That was true the second time, the third, and the fourth time. The story is full of gaps and repetitions and implausibilities. It's impossible to know exactly what's going on. Freud is a great narrative artist, a born storyteller, brilliantly evoking his patients and their struggles. Dramatic narration is not Breuer's strong suit. In "Anna O.," the sequence of events is twisted and tortured. As I read, I kept flipping the pages back and forth and drawing question marks in the margins. The story's fundamental premises—what happened when and where—kept eluding me.

I read the essay again and again, and I still didn't know what to make of it, so I went to my computer, and then to the library, and I found that scholars on the subject shared my confusion. "On each successive rereading of 'Fraulein Anna O.,'" wrote the psychiatrist and historian Walter Stewart, "I am struck by how much remains a mystery." Or as Max Rosenbaum and Melvin Muroff put it: "Breuer described a new technique. Anna O. helped him. That might be all we can say."[16] Peter Gay begins his discussion of "Fraulein Anna O." this way: "There are contradictions and obscurities in successive versions of the case, but this much is more or less beyond dispute: In 1880, when Anna O. fell ill, she was twenty-one"—after that, Gay moves into the contradictory and various accounts and commentaries.

"There is no Freudian historiography only mythography," Mikkel Borch-Jacobsen writes. "The official history of psychoanalysis is a vast anthology of tall tales."[17]

I wanted to read "Anna O." to learn about Bertha Pappenheim. This was a fool's errand. The opening paragraphs are the most stylish and fluid parts of the case study, and they offer the most compelling description of the main character. Some suspect that Freud, not Breuer, wrote them, and they are worth quoting at length:

> Of considerable intelligence, remarkably acute powers of reasoning, and a clear-sighted intuitive sense, her powerful mind could have digested, needed even, more substantial intellectual nourishment, but failed to receive it once she had left school. Her rich poetic and imaginative gifts were controlled by a very sharp and critical common sense. The latter also made her *quite closed to suggestion*. Only arguments had any influence on her, assertions were without effect. Her will was energetic, tenacious, and persistent, sometimes heightened to such obstinacy that it would give way only out of kindness and consideration for others.
>
> One of her principal traits was a sympathetic kindness. Even during her illness, she benefited greatly from the care and support she gave to some sick and poor people, for it allowed her to satisfy a strong drive. Her spirits always tended slightly to exaggeration, whether of joyfulness or grief, and as a consequence she was somewhat moody. The element of sexuality was remarkably underdeveloped: the patient, who became transparent to me in a way that seldom happens between two people, had never been in love, and not once in the mass of hallucinations that occurred during her illness did this element of the inner life emerge.

These first paragraphs feel like a fiction writer's construction of dramatic irony—the kind of short story in which the doctor (blind to his patient's love for him, and to his love for his patient) realizes (too late, and heartbreakingly so) that he has lost her. Breuer could see right through her, he writes, but her erotic life was invisible to him. You can't help wondering what he's trying to hide.

The whole essay feels this way: like something is lurking behind the words, as if the essay is not so much a lens through which to see Anna O., but a screen to keep us from perceiving her real identity. Sometimes she's deaf. Sometimes she can hear. Now her hands are paralyzed. Now they're ripping buttons off a nightdress. Breuer marches forward in time, but then circles back. "Before I describe the further course of the case," Breuer writes, "I need to go back once and depict a peculiar characteristic that I have as yet only touched on in passing." Later, he writes, "On another occasion, which I cannot find in my notes and have now forgotten, there was in addition to the contracture of the arm a contracture of the right leg." It's like his memory is faulty. On account of his strong desire to guard her privacy and not to reveal her identity, he discards and distorts basic narrative facts. Breuer doesn't tell his readers that Pappenheim was rich, or Jewish, or that her parents were immigrants to the city. Where in fact Pappenheim was moved to a sanitarium in the summer of 1881, Anna O. is moved to "a house in the country." Breuer barely mentions the drugs he prescribed her. There's is a whole subcategory of Anna O. studies, trying to guess when Breuer started her on which addictive medication.

Martha Freud thought Pappenheim was head-turningly attractive. In Breuer's case study, we do not get his patient's height (about four-eleven), her eye color (blue), her complexion (fair), or the color of her hair (dark). She's mostly a collection of symptoms, and the symptoms come and go, but what's most painfully obscured in "Fraulein Anna O." is not her body or her family or her life, it's her voice. This is a case study that's ostensibly all about her talk, but we don't get to hear much of it. She drops astonishing two-word phrases like "talking cure," or "chimney sweeping," or "time missing," or "torment torment," but when it comes to the stories Anna O. told Breuer, we get just the foggiest outline.

> These stories were always sad but sometimes very pretty, in the style of Hans Christian Andersen's *Bilderbuch ohne Bilder [Picture Book Without Pictures]*, and this was probably her model: the starting or central point was usually the situation of a girl sitting anxiously at an invalid's bedside, but other quite different motifs were also worked into the composition.

What were those motifs? We cannot know. Mostly, Anna O. talks to her doctor at sunset, when she is in that state that Breuer describes as hypnoid—she spaces out, every day, at around suppertime, and

tells stories that echo back to that moment described in the "Preliminary Statement": the sick old man in the bed, the hallucinatory visions of
snakes and skulls, the attempt to say a Hebrew prayer, the English rhyme
coming out in its place. Toward the end of "Anna O.," Breuer tells us that
in the last months of treatment he hypnotized her repeatedly, drawing
memories out of her to draw out her symptoms. But there's no mention
of this period or practice of hypnosis in Breuer's contemporaneous notes,
and there's some reason to believe that the way Breuer describes hypnosis in "Anna O." is not the way it happened in real life. Hypnosis as
a treatment for hysteria was fringe medicine in Vienna in 1881—in the
late 1870s Breuer told his colleague Moriz Benedikt to stop hypnotizing
patients[18]—but by 1895, hypnotism was part of the conversation around
hysteria, and Sigmund Freud (the German translator of much French
neurology) was among those who had helped bring the foreign medical
practice of hypnosis from Paris to Vienna. It's as if Breuer were revising
his memories as he was writing them, working out the story so it would
fit with Freud's developing theories.

Pappenheim didn't talk to Breuer about her parents or her sex life or
her childhood, as a contemporary talk-therapy patient would. Mostly, on
the one hand, she sorted through memories of her dying father's sickness and decline, and, on the other hand, she invented fairy tales. Breuer
sat and listened. He came almost every day, sometimes twice a day. His
"talking cure" is really, on the part of the doctor, a listening cure. Toward
the end of his treatment, her consciousness split, according to "Fraulein
Anna O.," so that in the daytime she is living in 1882 with everyone else,
but each night her mind reverts back, one calendar year exactly, to the
same date in 1881. Breuer comes each morning and hypnotizes her, and
then comes again at night and does the same, and in her hypnosis he
throws her ever backward in time: For each symptom—her deafness, her
loss of speech, her paralysis, her anorexia, her insomnia, her time-missing,
the paralysis of her limbs, and the weakness of her neck—she has to recall
each occurrence, and she has to name them backward in time, back to
the origin moment. Each time they strike on that first occurrence of the
symptom, the symptom vanishes. Finally, on the last night—the anniversary of her transportation to the "house in the country"—Breuer casts her

years back in time, and all the way to that hotel room in Bad Ischl where her symptoms first occurred, and at last she tells her story: the paralysis of her arm, the hallucinations, the inability to speak German or say Hebrew prayers, the English children's song that she said instead, and the train whistle that broke the spell. The awful, repressed night recurs to her in all its horror, and then the hysteria was done.

"She spoke German immediately afterwards," Breuer writes, "and was from that moment free of all the countless individual disturbances that she had displayed before. . . . Since that time she has enjoyed perfect health."

If the diagnosis is antique, the cure is like magic—it's a Gothic tale with an implausibly happy ending.

There's a single word Breuer uses several times in the case study when describing his patient, *transparent*. At the beginning, this word connotes the intimacy that developed between him and Anna O.: she "became transparent to me in a way that seldom happens between two people." Later it's the scientific justification for the project itself: "The interest of this case seems to me to lie above all in the extensive transparency and intelligibility of [her 'hysteria's'] pathogenesis." But toward the essay's final paragraphs, the word takes on a new meaning.

> Although I have suppressed many details which were not without interest, the case history of Anna O. has become more extensive than a hysterical illness which was in itself not unusual would seem to merit. But the account of the case was impossible without going into detail, and its peculiarities seemed to me sufficiently important to justify this extensive presentation. In the same way the eggs of the echinoderm are important for the study of embryology not because the sea urchin is a particularly interesting animal but because the protoplasm of its eggs is transparent, and what can be seen in them allows one to draw conclusions about what may also happen in eggs with cloudy plasma.

If, in the opening paragraphs, she's like a romantic heroine, by the end she's a protoplasmic mollusk. Breuer apologizes for even writing so much about her.

I set *Studies* down after reading "Fraulein Anna O." I looked again for my dad's envelope. I was ransacking my mind, trying to remember what he had told me about the case. There was something there, I felt, which I could only dimly perceive. The story of hysteria—a disease that had always existed, or maybe never had existed, that rampaged through a continent of women and gave birth to a science of mind, a science that like the illness was discarded by late twentieth-century medicine—Jews and women, codes and counter-codes, information and misinformation and half-understood messages full of latent power, and Vienna at the end of the nineteenth century—the story haunted me as if it were a novel I needed to read, like some combination of Margaret Atwood and Philip Roth and Italo Calvino.

The insight and the confusion, I thought, the stories Pappenheim told Breuer, the stories Breuer wrote down, and the theory that Freud created, and the slander that Freud told about Pappenheim after Breuer died, a story that—along with its substantiating details—has now been mostly debunked. According to Freud, on that strange night when the last of her hysterical symptoms vanished under Breuer's hypnotic spell, Anna O. fell to the floor suffering abdominal cramps, cried out, "Dr. B.'s baby is coming!" and Breuer, unmanned, grabbed his hat and fled. Bertha Pappenheim is a toothed vagina, Anna O. with her legs opened for the dream baby, and her mouth opened wide to scream at her doctor.

In *Freud: The Secret Passion*, John Huston's 1962 movie, Freud (Montgomery Clift) is present with Breuer while his patient (Susannah York, here called "Cecily") goes into her imaginary labor pains, and Larry Parks as Breuer confesses: "It's Matilda—she believes there's something between Cecily and me . . . that . . . I'm in love with the girl." In *When Nietzsche Wept*, the 2007 film starring Ben Cross as Breuer and the sometime Israeli children's television host Michal Yannai as Bertha (baby doll skin, kitty cat features, exotic-dancer orange hair), Pappenheim, laughing demonically, falls into her phantom pregnancy right in front of Mathilde Breuer and her friends, and when Bertha cries out that Dr. B.'s baby is coming, all the Viennese ladies gasp and stare. She's the prettiest ghoul of psychoanalysis, beautiful and terrible, sexy and sexless, pregnant and barren, never fucking but always castrating, clinging, desperate and needy.

I went to the library. I went to the internet. I found so many articles. "Anna O. Had a Severe Depressive Illness," "The Case of Anna O.: A Neuropsychiatric Perspective," "The Unmirrored Self, Compensatory Structure, and Cure: The Exemplary Case of Anna O.," "The Rescue Complex in Anna O.'s Final Identity," "Revisiting Anna O.: A Case of Chemical Dependence," "Hysteria, Psychoanalysis, and Feminism: The Case of Anna O.," "Some More Speculations on Anna O.," "What Was the Matter with 'Anna O.': A Definitive Diagnosis," and Mikkel Borch-Jacobsen's great act of debunking, *Remembering Anna O.: A Century of Mystification*. (In my father's copy of Borch-Jacobsen, there's a note on the flyleaf: "This book fails in 1 way—*no sense of the tragic late adolescence of a gifted woman!*")

There lies Pappenheim like Sleeping Beauty in her coffin of a case study, in the temple Breuer and Freud built for her, the castle Anna O., and around that castle in ever increasing circles grows the thorny field of impenetrable narration, and no one is listening to her, so you can't hear the stories she told. Sorting through this century of contradictory scholarship, I felt my ignorance keenly. I just kept going. It didn't take long for my father's obsession to become my own, and soon I was dodging big ideas about brain and mind, sickness and health. At the 2020 conference of the Functional Neurological Disorder Society, Dr. Mark Hallett—the dean of US neurologists studying brain plasticity and a leader in the field for three decades—gave the keynote address and tried to define the subject at hand. Hallett is square-jawed, bald, and speaks complex thoughts in serious, direct, and unpretentious language. On Zoom (it was early in the pandemic) to the over five hundred medical professionals specializing in the field, he said: "This is my definition as of today, May 20, 2020." Even Hallett, who has spent much of the past several decades devoting his work to the problem, even at the international meeting of the doctors studying the illness, had to put a timestamp on his definition. Everything about FND research is likewise tentative.

I will do my best in these pages to address myself to you, to make clear to you what I learned and what confused me and what I imagined, as I tried to square the new science with the old stories. I will endeavor to be your guide through this knotty, tricky, treacherous territory, but don't be fooled. I'm not addressing myself to you, at least not entirely. This book, at its starting point, was something I set out to do for my dad. Later it became something I did just to hold my world together as my wife got sick. I did some of my research in chemo rooms, and I interviewed some doctors while I was sitting in the waiting rooms of Memorial Sloan Kettering's Urgent Care Unit. This book is an act of compulsion and comfort. I wrote this story so my brain wouldn't fall apart. But then I started to learn something about how minds do fall apart from bodies, how minds are entangled with bodies. In imagining the life of this long-dead woman, I hope, we can learn something about how we see ourselves and each other. Still, I want to caution you, there can be no objective rendering of Pappenheim's breakdown. No matter how rational, theoretical, or fact-based a writer pretends to be, even the most hard-nosed anti-Freudian brief boils down to storytelling.

In his 2017 biography, *Freud: The Making of an Illusion*, Frederick Crews makes the case that everything Pappenheim suffered can be explained by her drug use. His argument begins in facts that are not in dispute: that Pappenheim was given too much chloral hydrate and morphine. "It cannot be a coincidence that every one of Pappenheim's symptoms has been listed as a known effect of one or both of her drugs," he writes. "What then is left unaccounted for?" The most obvious answer is the onset of her illness. For drugs to account for all her symptoms, Crews has to have Pappenheim using chloral before Breuer prescribes it to her. "Could Pappenheim have been self-administering chloral and morphine in the summer and fall of 1880, before Breuer's treatment began?" Crews asks, and then shifts from the interrogative to the conditional. "When Breuer first saw her, she may already have been intoxicated and on a course toward addiction." He doesn't much flesh this story out—the young woman at her dying father's bedside, tiptoeing across the room, finding the white chloral powder, mixing it with water, taking a sip—to do that, he would have to drop his pose of objectivity. Also, his story would be difficult to write convincingly. Leaving aside Pappenheim's character, leaving aside Breuer's competence as a doctor (might he not recognize or suspect a case of drug poisoning, either before or after he prescribed his own doses of chloral?), why would she, who was trying to stay up all night, take a medicine that she knew would put her to sleep? Maybe in the morning, when she was wired from the night, maybe she took it to relax; stole some from the sickroom, secreted it in her pocket, maybe in a brown paper envelope, and then in the privacy of her . . .

No matter how you put this thing together, when you propose a single, all-encompassing explanation, you slide into fiction, and these fictions can vary, even within the work of one storyteller. In 1996, in the *New York Review of Books*, Crews offered this alternative storyline of the Anna O. case, paraphrasing and endorsing the position maintained by Borch-Jacobsen:

> What we know for certain is that Pappenheim had stage-managed the course of treatment, which involved the hypnotic and autohypnotic production of fantasies and hallucinations to which she herself ascribed a purgative effect. The Anna O. case thus resembled, in Henri Ellenberger's words, "the great exemplary cases of magnetic illness in the first half of the nineteenth century. . . . in which the patient dictated to the physician the therapeutic devices he had to use, prophesied the course of the illness, and announced its terminal date." In a word, the founding example of modern psychotherapy was just another instance of Mesmerism in the chatty mode of Puységur and Barberin.

In this 1996 version, Pappenheim isn't a helpless drug addict, she's manipulative, her doctor's puppet master, putting on her sickness and performing its cure. In both versions, Breuer is an incompetent boob.

No doubt, Pappenheim was twisted by the drugs that were prescribed to her. No doubt, she had tendencies toward the histrionic. To paraphrase Adichie, the problem with both of Crews's single stories is not that they're misleading, it's that each is incomplete. What is erased, both times, is any of the stuff Freud might have been interested in—her trauma, her pain, and her yearning. Neither of these accounts take into consideration social and cultural pressures on Pappenheim. Neither begins to explore or speculate about neurology, functional breakdown, the disease that Breuer actually diagnosed—because, for Crews and writers of his era, that kind of suffering, the kind called "hysteria," is illegitimate—a thing we cannot acknowledge as real.

Me? I'm not going to even pretend I know what happened.

3

The Breuer house at Brandstätte 8 has vanished. What's there now is a clothing store with big glass windows, gray stucco walls, and apartments above. Vienna is built in rings, like a tree, or maybe it's more accurate to say that it grew that way, in concentric circles, and Brandstätte is one of the wider streets in the maze of narrow, winding, medieval streets in the center of the old city. In the 1880s, when the Breuers lived there, it was the wealthy aristocratic part of town, and the districts as they went farther out became progressively poorer. Gay, in his psychoanalytic biography, introduces Breuer as warm, paternal, and expert:

> A successful, affluent, highly cultivated physician and eminent physiologist fourteen years [Freud's] senior. The two men were soon on the best of terms; Freud adopted Breuer as one in a succession of fatherly figures, and became a regular in the Breuer household, in some ways as good a friend to Breuer's charming and maternal wife Mathilde as to Breuer himself.

Crews introduces him as a senior hustler in the Viennese medical con game:

> [Breuer] had compiled a distinguished record in physiology but had opted to earn his living as a family doctor. He advised Freud to build his

credentials in neurology while continuing to get trained in general medicine. Then he would be able to accept local patients who presented virtually any complaint, and meanwhile he would be earning a reputation in a
specialty—the one, we may note, that Breuer knew to be lucrative, thanks
to the number of chronically agitated and fabulously wealthy ladies at the
apex of Viennese society.

My Breuer derives mostly from Albrecht Hirschmüller's *The Life and
Work of Josef Breuer* (1978), the most complete and well-researched biography I could find, and also from Louis Breger's lucid retelling of the
Pappenheim-Freud story, *A Dream of Undying Fame* (2009). Both of these
writers see him as a hero, a man whose great capacity for empathy was
both his superpower and his undoing.

We can't know exactly what the Breuer house looked like, but we can
speculate from nearby buildings of similar age and style: four stories tall,
five windows wide, a door in the center with one step down to the street,
a white-washed facade, a line of modest cake-work stucco between the
first and second floor, and another set of decorative moldings toward
the top. The Breuer home was large but crowded. There was his wife,
Mathilde, and their four children, two girls and two boys, the oldest of
whom was twelve. Also servants—a cook, maids, a footman, a governess.
In the winter of 1880, Breuer's scientific research was focused largely on
balance. He was doing experimental work on birds, on their inner ears,
and he must have had some space at home for his microscope and his
dissections. There was a piano in the house (he played), a chess set (he
played), and books everywhere, in all the languages Breuer read, which is
to say most major modern European languages, as well as Latin, Greek,
and Hebrew.

The Breuers were great entertainers, hosted many dinners—his friends
were novelists, philosophers, and musicians—they perhaps had an enormous dining room table, and that's where I will place him at his break-
fast of steak tartare (borrowing Freud's favorite) and black coffee. Vienna
was a city of newspapers. Let's put three of them at the table, *Neue Freie
Presse*, *Neues Wiener Tagblatt*, and *Die Neuzeit*, and let's say that he had
just closed the last, after reading an editorial (which I'm taking from

the next year, 1881) declaring that the Archimedean point for combatting antisemitism was soon to be found. Alongside the papers, I'll place a stack of correspondence—personal, medical, and philosophic—and a stack of cards, mostly from patients, asking him to call.

Among these let's imagine a card from Recha Pappenheim pleading with Breuer to see her husband. I doubt that Breuer was at all personally drawn to Siegmund Pappenheim. ("I was already second-generation Viennese," wrote George Clare in *Last Waltz in Vienna*. "Viennese-born Jews felt resentment toward the less assimilated Jews from the East.") But he made a decision. He would squeeze Pappenheim into his schedule by making him the first patient of the day.

I imagine the footman brushing the shoulders of Breuer's coat (the morning routine), fetching him his hat and stick (the likely accoutrements), and Breuer patting himself down, making sure he had his watch and wallet. The children lined up to be kissed. By 1880, the newer parts of the city had modern plumbing, but there were neither cars nor electricity. Wagons hauled ice to the big houses, and empty milk bottles back to the dairies outside of town. The smells were horse droppings and coal smoke. The lightening sky was visible in the squares but vanished in the side streets, and Breuer was in shadow until he came to the Ringstrasse. The chestnut trees were bare. The trolleys were pulled on iron tracks by teams of staggering horses.

One way to measure the time between Breuer's November 1880 visit to the Pappenheim apartment and the eventual 1895 publication of *Studies* is to think about his children. By 1895, twelve-year-old Robert would be a doctor and Breuer's younger daughter would have given birth to his first grandchild. Another is to consider changes in technology: by 1895, the trolleys would hum along under electric cables. When Breuer wrote "Anna O.," he was recalling another epoch of his life.

There are scholars who hypothesize that Breuer was the Pappenheim family physician. The two men's fathers, Josef Breuer's and Siegmund Pappenheim's, had studied together in the same religious school in Pressburg, what is now Bratislava. However, it's clear from *Studies* that Breuer did not visit the Pappenheim apartment from spring through fall of 1880. Other doctors came to treat Siegmund's tuberculosis, and to operate on his lung, and to examine Bertha—through the fall, she had grown cross-eyed and had developed a pain in her face. Two of Pappenheim's daughters had already died of tuberculosis.

The Pappenheims lived in the Alsergrund district, the neighborhood of newly built apartment buildings that had grown up around the Ringstrasse. Their neighbors were publishers and writers and doctors and lawyers, Jews living next to gentiles as had never before happened in the German-speaking world. The historian Marsha Rozenblit says that we should think of them as *acculturated* and not *assimilated* Jews. The Pappenheims lived among Christians, but not exactly with them. Their apartment was near the university and the bourse. Early morning, and the pedestrians were mostly men, stockbrokers and students. Many of the students had ribbons attached to their hats and walking sticks, identifying fraternities and cultural societies, some of them explicitly pan-Germanic and antisemitic. Some of these students carried swords. As for the adults, in his memoir, *The World of Yesterday*, Stefan Zweig describes the fashions of the time:

> Anyone who wanted to get ahead in life had to try all conceivable methods of looking older than his age. Newspapers advertised methods of encouraging your beard to grow, young doctors of twenty-four or twenty-five who had only just qualified as physicians sported heavy beards and wore gold-rimmed glasses even if they had perfect eyesight, just to impress their patients by looking experienced. They wore long black frock coats and cultivated a measured tread and, if possible, a slight embonpoint in order to achieve that desirably stolid appearance.

Breuer was unfashionably thin but fashionably bearded and stooped, carrying a cane and wearing a top hat, sad-eyed, big-nosed, with flaring ears. In *The Enigma of Anna O.*, Melinda Given Guttmann writes that the Pappenheims rented "a luxurious third-floor apartment," but Carl E. Schorske, a more reliable scholar, describes expensive late nineteenth-century Viennese apartments as sprawling over several floors. The Pappenheims' building was new and had a white stone facade. The first floor was commercial. Breuer turned under an archway and ascended a staircase. At a landing he was greeted by the Pappenheims' butler, to whom he handed his hat and cane. Recha Pappenheim met him in the foyer, a small, gray-haired woman, fifty years old and anxious.

Recha had been born in Frankfurt in 1830, a child of a large extended family of bankers, and a cousin by marriage to the Rothschilds and also to the poet Heinrich Heine. When she had married Siegmund Pappenheim, Recha had married down: the couple had stood under the wedding canopy in 1848, on the border between Austria and Hungary, and ducks had come quacking through the ceremony (that's Bertha's recollection of Recha's story). When they were a young couple, they had lived in the Jewish neighborhood on the other side of the Danube, Leopoldstadt, and then Recha's first baby had died of tuberculosis, and then the segregation laws had changed, and they had moved across the river to their new apartment.

In my imagination I'll map the Pappenheim home as follows—second floor: dining room, ballroom, parlors, kitchen, a central stair dividing the big apartment into halves; third floor: living quarters, with the master bedroom on one side, and the children's rooms on the other, modern flush toilets, big baths, and a smaller stairway up to the fourth floor where there were chambers for the cooks and maids. The rooms on the second floor were taller and wider and lighter than the homey old rooms of the Breuer townhouse. Everything decorative was either ancient and heavy, imported from Germany, or modern and ostentatious. Bertha would inherit some things from this apartment and live with them right up to the time she was dying of cancer and confronting Nazis in the 1930s: a Biedermeier chest, a collection of gold and silver goblets.

Breuer followed Recha up the stairs to the third floor. At the landing I'll put a carved maple clawfoot table, with a vase on top, and above that, an oil portrait of the great rabbi of Pressburg, Moses Sofer. Recha knocked on the bedroom door. From inside, they heard an awful sound. "It's not dry but you can't call it loose, either. There's no word for it." That's how a late-stage tubercular cough is described in *The Magic Mountain*. "It's as if you were looking right down inside and could see it all, the mucus and the slime." The smell hit Breuer as he entered the room. The shades were drawn. The nurse bowed and backed away from the bed in which Siegmund lay. We know for a fact that it was a four-poster, and the headboard was carved with the date 1705, and also with a sun and a cross and the letters IHS for Jesus.[19] (I'm not sure what to make of the old Jewish man sleeping in the obviously Christian bed; it must have been beautiful or comfortable or valuable. Bertha would inherit his bed, and she would sleep in it, and all you psychoanalytically inclined readers can smile knowingly about *that*.) Breuer turned a knob at the base of the sconce by the bedside, and the gas hissed and burned.

Siegmund's eyes were gummy and wet in the bluish light, and it took a moment for him to focus and recognize Breuer. "*Landsman*," he sighed. He tried to make a joke, but a coughing fit interrupted, and Siegmund couldn't make it to the end of his sentence. Breuer took out a stethoscope—the new kind, which fitted both ears, not the long wooden tube from when the two men were children. He asked the nurse to open the window. Pappenheim shivered in his nightshirt. Breuer raised the shirt so that he could see the scar from the summertime operation. Pappenheim's flesh was hot to the touch. The infection had progressed as Breuer had guessed it would. Though it would be a year before Koch isolated and cultured the tuberculosis bacillus, the infectious nature of the disease had been understood since 1865, and Breuer knew the illness with an immediacy that most modern doctors lack. His earliest experimental work had been on fever. In the 1860s, it was generally suspected that fever was regulated by the nerves, but Breuer had proved otherwise, demonstrating that it spread through the bloodstream. Breuer knew about infection: the way bacteria formed colonies, the way that infection could lurk latently under the skin, the way that suddenly an infection could blossom—he had read Lister in English and Pasteur in French. He had spent years, too, experimenting on lungs. His studies on exhalation had gone on for almost a decade, until he identified what is still called the Hering-Breuer reflex, the autonomic response that forces us to exhale. Breuer asked his patient for the names of all the other doctors who had, over the course of the year, treated him.

Pappenheim, sitting on the bed like a punished child, admitted that most of his care came from his faithful daughter, Bertha, his *höhere Töchter*—a bourgeois girl who had finished schooling but who had not yet gotten married. Night after night, Bertha had been attending to him, for at least half a year, since July. Breuer was looking at Siegmund's eyes, pressing down the skin so he could see the pink flesh beneath. He was famous for his calm, for his patience, but he must have been furious. They seemed like civilized people, the Pappenheims. They had the money and the clothes and the apartment, but illness came, and they fell back on atavistic tradition. They might as well have been burning goats to an angry God.

"She has begun to cough," Siegmund told him.

4

In his memoir, *The World of Yesterday*, written in the 1930s when he was living in exile in England, Stefan Zweig described Jewish happiness in late nineteenth-century Vienna:

> Their desire for a homeland, for peace, repose and security, a place where they would not be strangers, impelled [Jews] to form a passionate attachment to the culture around them. And nowhere else, except for Spain in the fifteenth century, were such bonds more happily and productively formed than in Austria.

For Zweig, the last decades of the nineteenth century in Vienna were "The Golden Age of Security," when "people no more believed in the possibility of barbaric relapses, such as wars between the nations of Europe, than they believed in ghosts or witches." Robert Musil, recalling the same period, emphasized not the surface feeling of stability but the chaotic transformation underneath:

> Time was moving faster than a cavalry camel. . . . But in those days no one knew what it was moving toward. Nor . . . could anyone quite distinguish between what was above and what was below, between what was moving forward and what backward.[20]

When Breuer was fifteen, there had been 6,000 Jews in Vienna, in a total population of half a million. By 1880, he was in his late thirties and there were 75,543 Jews living in a city of 726,105. By 1890, there would be more than 100,000 Jews in the city, immigrants from all over the polyglot Hapsburg empire: Hungarian Jews, Galician Jews, Moravian Jews, Bohemian Jews.[21]

Breuer, Freud, and Pappenheim were all children of Jewish immigrants to Vienna, but in 1880 the three occupied distinct social strata. Breuer's father had been a scholar and had married well, and Breuer had been educated in Vienna and raised in the cosmopolitan tradition of Haskalah Judaism, a tradition sometimes called "the Jewish enlightenment." Mathilde, his wife, was the daughter of wealthy wine merchants. Breuer had a lot of money. The Jews who were his neighbors in the center city were Vienna's richest Jews, some of them titled aristocrats. These were the descendants of the court Jews, the so-called tolerated Jews, the Jews who had bankrolled the expansion of the Hapsburg Empire. In the synagogue in their neighborhood, Adolf Jellinek declared from the pulpit, "The freedom of the Jews is at the same time the freedom of Germandom." Jellinek called himself a preacher, not a rabbi, and said that Jews had no specific national characteristics, but "thanks to their universalism they adapt and absorb qualities from the nations in whose midst they are born and educated," and that "the Double-Eagle is for [Austrian Jews] a symbol of redemption and the Austrian colors adorn the banners of their freedom . . . they are the standard-bearers of the Austrian idea of unity."[22]

Siegmund Pappenheim, after he moved to Vienna, did not go to Jellinek's temple. Instead, he helped found and build a synagogue of his own, the Schiffschul, so that he could worship in the tradition of the Pressburg rabbis with whom he'd grown up. According to Elizabeth Loentz, Pappenheim's literary biographer, the Schiffschul's Torah study was carried out in Yiddish[23]—a language scorned by the more acculturated Viennese Jews. The Pappenheims lived in the wealthy, bourgeois part of town, they vacationed in Bad Ischl, the same town where the emperor had his summer residence, but as Loentz imagines it, Siegmund probably spoke some Yiddish at home. In *Studies in Hysteria*, Breuer calls them "a puritanically-minded family." They were old fashioned.

Sigmund Freud in 1880 was twenty-four years old and he lived on the other side of the river with his parents and six siblings in Leopold-stadt, a neighborhood that in certain blocks was still something of a Jewish ghetto. He was born Sigismund Schlomo or maybe Schlomo Si-gismund Freud in Freiberg, in Preborst, a small, rural town that's about five hundred miles west of Vienna. When he was an infant, the family lived above a blacksmith's shop—I take this as a sign of extreme poverty. Imagine the soot, the hammer blows all day, the baby crying all night. His father was a wandering Jew, Jakob Freud, the son of a Has-sidic rabbi in the shtetl of Tsymenitz. Schlomo Sigismund was a child of Jakob's second or maybe third marriage (we don't know). Jakob had succeeded in launching himself out of that medieval world but hadn't exactly landed in the modern. His wife, Amalia, was much younger than he. As Martin Freud, Sigmund's son, would later write, recalling his grandmother:

> A typical Polish Jewess, with all the shortcomings that that implies. She was certainly not what we would call a "lady," had a lively temper and was impatient, self-willed, sharp-witted, and highly intelligent.

The family moved to Vienna when Freud was eight years old, to the neighborhood of the kaftan-wearing, Yiddish-speaking, kosher-keeping immigrant Jews—refugees from violence and poverty and persecution. They lived, as Frederick Crews writes, "in the midst of overcrowding, illness, and penury." There were nine people in a tiny apartment. Money came from the sons of Jakob's first marriage, who lived in Manches-ter. (For Katja Behling, these English Freud brothers were small-time crooks, making "dubious deals" involving "forged money and credit papers."[24]) The bathroom was likely an outhouse in the back. In the autobiographical sections of *The Interpretation of Dreams*, urine and def-ecation repeat themselves obsessively. I can't help but think of the poor country boy forced to share the outdoor toilet with strangers:

> When I was seven or eight years old there was another domestic scene, which I can remember very clearly. One evening before going to sleep I

disregarded the rules which modesty lays down and obeyed the calls of nature in my parents' bedroom while they were present.

Did he piss in a pot, a washbasin, or right there on the floor? His father became enraged and said the boy would never amount to anything—that's what it says in his autobiography, but I imagine it was something more terrible; Freud all his life wrote about how boys were threatened with castration. "I'll cut your dick off!" Or am I imagining some grotesque of my own dad?

———

Adam Phillips says it's impossible to write a biography of Freud, partly for lack of evidence ("there is, for example, very little on record about Freud's mother, a person, we imagine—and he encourages us to imagine—of some importance in his life"), partly because Freud's work is antagonistic to the very idea of biography ("nothing in our life is self-evident, not even the facts of our lives speak for themselves"), and partly because, after Freud, it's hard to take any kind of single-author, single-story of any life altogether seriously ("our knowledge of his, or of anyone else's life—and indeed our wish for knowledge about his life—has to be tempered with a certain irony"). It's also hard to write about him because so many other people have, and so much of that writing is so overwrought. Freud "must not only be considered alongside Darwin or Einstein, but also as a combination of Darwin with Proust, Pasteur with Picasso, or even Weber with H. G. Wells," according to John Forrester. Critics can be equally hyperbolic: Stanley Fish imagines Freud's famous patient the Wolf Man thinking, "This man is a Jewish swindler, he wants to use me from behind and shit on my head," and Fish concludes, "the Wolf Man got it right." For Crews:

> Freud will survive because his essentially medieval (spirit-possession) and romantic (little elves make deeper selves) conceptions, combined with his emphasis on sex, his facile symbolic code, and his courageous-looking but essentially egocentric and prurient encouragement to look for low motives in everyone but oneself, still pack an emotional wallop.[25]

Crews's attack here points out the basic problem of Freud criticism: you can stand over his grave and wallop and wallop, but in the end, the old guy can still reach up and wallop you. Freud's laws remain the shorthand that govern much of our storytelling, the quickest and simplest way we understand other's lives—*he's a narcissist*, we say, or *she's anal*, or *they're repressed*. As W. H. Auden wrote: "to us he is no more a person/now but a whole climate of opinion/under whom we conduct our different lives," and, because *The Interpretation of Dreams* is in significant part a memoir, this "whole climate of opinion" emerged through his own introspection. It's outrageous. "How can an autobiographical writing, in the abyss of an unterminated self-analysis, give birth to a world-wide institution?" asked Jacques Derrida. That's the sum of Freud's accomplishment, to make his life ours, and our lives his.

Freud's mother gave birth to five babies in six years—the place must have been full of vomit and dirty diapers and cheap food and people screaming at each other in Yiddish. ("The adults in Freud's family would have been opportunistically polyglot," writes Adam Phillips, "Yiddish being their shared and exclusive language.") By 1868, the last segregation and discrimination laws were abolished by Emperor Franz Josef. Jakob decorated the apartment with pictures of liberal politicians, Jewish politicians. The poor immigrant family dreamed of success. "Every industrious Jewish schoolboy carried a Cabinet Minister's portfolio in his satchel," Freud later recalled.

He was sent off to the Sperl Gymnasium, where there were only sixty-eight other Jewish students. (By the time he graduated, there would be nearly three hundred.) He dropped the Schlomo and shortened Sigismund to Sigmund. ("Since he never commented on his reasons for shortening his first name, all conjectures about its significance for him must remain purely speculative," wrote Peter Gay, who changed his own last name from the more Jewish-sounding Fröhlich.) In 1930, Freud wrote that his father "allowed me to grow up in complete ignorance of everything that concerned Judaism," but at some point in Freud's childhood, his father did present him with a Bible, the kind with Hebrew on one page and on the facing page German. Jakob rebound the same book and gave it to his son when the boy turned thirty-six (twice eighteen, a Jewish symbol of good luck), and inscribed it, "For my beloved son Solomon." What did he call the boy at home? At the Sperl Gymnasium, Freud was the best student, right from the start. Stefan Zweig, coming from his comfortable bourgeois home, saw his Viennese school building as primitive and stultifying:

> With its cold, poorly white-washed walls, its low-ceilinged classrooms without pictures or any other kind of ornament to please the eye, and the smell of the lavatories that pervaded the whole building, this educational barracks was rather like an old piece of hotel furniture that had been used by countless people before us, and would be used by countless others.

For Freud it must have appeared differently. The toilets at school were certainly fancier and cleaner than the toilet at home. Was it a toilet out back of their building in Leopoldstadt, or just a closet with a hole in the ground, next to the locked shack where the landlord kept the coal? Zweig, a wealthy, cultured boy, recalls his schooling as a burden:

> On the school benches . . . we heard nothing new, or nothing that we felt was worth knowing, while outside there was a city full of a thousand things to stimulate our minds—a city of theaters, museums, bookshops, a university, music, a place where every day there brought new surprises. . . . This enthusiasm for theater, literature and art was perfectly natural in Vienna. . . . Wherever you went, you heard adults discussing the Opera or the Burgtheater. . . . If [our schoolteachers] had paid close attention, they would also have realized that the covers of our Latin grammars in fact concealed the poems of Rilke.

Amalia and Jakob couldn't afford the opera. Sigmund didn't ever have much taste for music, and when he was young he didn't have extra money for bookstores or cafés. Later in life, Freud didn't cite Rilke, he cited Sophocles. Freud "lived far less in Vienna than in his own mind," writes Gay. It was the schoolbooks that impressed him, not the fashionable poets.

Freud was deeply ambivalent toward his father. In *The Interpretation of Dreams*, written not long after Jakob's death, Freud offers a dream image of his father's corpse, laid out on display, literally filled with shit, but with a face that looks like Garibaldi's. At the Sperl Gymnasium, Jews were divided out for religious instruction, and Freud attached himself to Samuel Hammerschlag, his Hebrew teacher, who, in Freud's words, "saw religious instruction as a way of educating toward the love of the humanities." Hammerschlag took Freud on trips to the countryside, took teenaged Sigmund to his home, and perhaps introduced young Sigmund to the eminent neurologist Josef Breuer, who was Hammerschlag's neighbor.

In 1873, the stock market crashed. Antisemites blamed Jewish financiers. Freud was seventeen. He enrolled in the University of Vienna, and, according to an 1875 letter to his friend Eduard Silberstein, Freud suffered some kind of breakdown, involving wild mood swings and insomnia and a feeling as if "his limbs had been glued together and were coming apart again." He was five foot seven inches tall, hairy, and self-conscious about his looks. The university was "a veritable hotbed of nationalistic and anti-Semitic hostility," according to the historian Robert S. Wistrich, "the university students were from the beginning the most aggressively racist and antisemitic of the pan-German supporters." Zweig describes the fraternity boys: "Going on a rampage and goose-stepping through the streets at night." The faculty expressed their antisemitism more delicately. In 1876, Theodor Billroth—the greatest surgeon in continental Europe—argued that "proletariat Jews" did not belong at the medical school, Jews "who are absolutely without resources and have conceived the insane notion that they can earn money in Vienna . . . and simultaneously study medicine."[26]

Medicine wasn't, in many ways, the best fit for Freud's brilliance. "You know," he would later write to Wilhelm Fliess, "that I lack any mathematical talent whatsoever and have no memory for numbers and measurements." He wasn't orderly. "To be tied down to exactitude and precise measurement," Ernest Jones wrote, "was not in his nature." He didn't like the sight of blood. But he had more drive, more energy, than anyone. As he wrote in 1900: "I am actually not a man of science, not an observer, not an experimenter, not a thinker. I am by temperament nothing but a

conquistador—an adventurer if you want it translated—with all the curiosity, daring, and tenacity characteristic of a man of this sort." As a
boy, he liked to think of himself as Hannibal, the dark-skinned invader,
riding the pachyderm of his genius to crush the empire of his oppressors.
Darwin had made the most complex biological problems seem solvable,
and the researchers at the University of Vienna were making enormous
strides in neuroanatomy, and they thought that they were about to reveal
all the secrets of human consciousness through the biology of the brain.
Freud took a class with Carl Claus, who headed the university's Institute
for Comparative Anatomy, and in 1876 Freud was selected to go to the
institute's research station in Trieste. He was eighteen. It wasn't his first
trip out of Vienna—he had gone to London to visit his half-brothers—
but it was his first as a scientist, as an independent young adult. He wrote
funny, charming letters to his friends about his work and his shyness and
his inability to approach beautiful women.

In 1876, no one had yet identified a male eel—no one had discovered
eel testes. The sexing of eels was a problem the greatest scientists in history had worked on—Aristotle, van Leeuwenhoek, and Linnaeus—and
all had failed. Freud spent four weeks in Trieste, over the course of two
trips. He worked eight a.m. to five p.m., dissecting some four hundred
eels. "All the eels I have cut open," he wrote to a friend, "are of the ten-
derer sex." His work was thorough, and from it, his first published paper
emerged. He became close with his professor Franz Brentano, a philosopher who was Breuer's friend, and whom Freud described as "a believer,
a teleologist (!) and a Darwinian and a damned clever fellow, a genius in
fact." Freud sparred with Brentano about the existence of God, but the
sparring must have been good-natured because he got invited to Brentano's house, where they discussed the difficulty in describing the psyche.
How could one use one's mind to describe the mind? Brentano wondered. *How
could one achieve the necessary critical distance to gain an objective view of consciousness?* In 1877, Freud attended a lecture Breuer gave on urology—the
only such lecture Freud ever attended while he was in medical school.
He must have gone not out of any particular interest in the subject but in
hopes of meeting the lecturer. From the start of their relationship, Freud
must have hoped that Breuer would help him move along in his career.

He took a long time to finish his medical degree, and, after a stint in the army, worked in the lab of Ernst Brücke, a leader among the so-called anti-vitalists, those Viennese doctors and scientists who believed that there could be no immeasurable vital substance of the mind—no *psyche*—and that all thought, emotion, and cognition could be reduced to the electro-chemical substance of the brain. Medicine was science, and science was empirical, and the mind could be reduced to the brain. The laboratory and department in which Freud worked was overseen by some of the world's leaders in what we would now call neuroscience. Theodor Meynert, the director of psychiatry at Vienna General Hospital, had a wild black beard and a mass of dark hair and had identified the different layers of brain tissue in the cerebral cortex, and had demonstrated that myelin developed around brain cells over time. For Meynert, psychology based on intro-spection or metaphysics was so much mysticism; "he was a strict deter-minist who dismissed free will as an illusion."[27] Cold, blue-eyed, Teutonic Brücke, director of the lab where Freud worked, had made enormous advances in optics, in the structure and workings of the eye. In this lab, Brücke employed two assistants: Sigmund Exner and Ernst Fleischl von Marxow. Exner did extraordinary work, locating the parts of the brain that governed hearing; Fleischl invented devices for measuring the brain's electricity. It was Fleischl whom Freud worshiped—one of the few Jews on the hospital faculty, and a man who in his spare time, for relaxation, translated Dante into German. Freud fell for Fleischl, hard:

> Rich, skilled in all physical exercises, with the stamp of genius on his en-ergetic features, handsome, sensitive, gifted with all talents and capable of forming an original judgment about most things, he was always my ideal, and I wasn't satisfied until we became friends, and I could take a pure de-light in his ability and worth.

On account of a needlestick during an autopsy, Fleischl had been poi-soned, and for the rest of his life suffered excruciating neuromas and re-quired a series of surgeries to shave back his thumb. He was in constant pain and addicted to morphine, and his tragic nature was perhaps part of his attraction.

"At length, in Ernst Brücke's psychology laboratory," Freud later wrote, "I found rest and full satisfaction, and men, too, whom I could respect and take as models."

He was very good at his job, but he didn't get paid for it. His sisters were thin, and Freud was unable to buy food for them, and this pained and embarrassed him. Freud began to investigate the nervous systems of primitive sea creatures, lampreys and crayfish. The theory at that point had been that different kinds of creatures, vertebrates and invertebrates, had different kinds of nerve cells, but Freud was able to show that the cells were identical and that they differed not in kind but in organization. Some argue that he came close to identifying the neuron—a discovery that was achieved a decade later, by Santiago Ramón y Cajal. Freud slept sometimes in the hospital, and sometimes in his crowded family apartment in Leopoldstadt, where he was the only person who had his own room, which he called his "cabinet." By all accounts, at twenty-four, he was a virgin.

In his *Autobiographical Study*, written in 1925, Freud claims that his first glimpse into the depths of the mind, of what lay beneath consciousness, of something other than pure neurology, came when he went to Burgtheater in 1880 and saw a hypnotist's show.

"While I was still a student I had attended a public exhibition given by Hansen the 'magnetist,'" Freud writes, "and had noticed that one of the persons experimented upon had become deathly pale at the onset of cataleptic rigidity and had remained so as long as that condition lasted."

But it's doubtful—despite his later claims—that Freud actually went and saw the show. In contemporaneous correspondence, his friend Eduard Silberstein invites Sigmund to go with him, but Freud declines. "Keep your mind skeptical," he wrote to Silberstein, "and remember 'wonderful' is an exclamation of ignorance, and not the acknowledgement of a miracle."

Hansen sat volunteers on stage with their backs to the audience, and he handed each a glass ball. The men were told to hold the balls up to their foreheads and stare into them. The magician passed his hands in front of his subjects' faces, one by one, saying that soon they would experience a terrible tensing of their jaws. Sure enough, their jaws began to convulse, and they fell into their trances. Over one man's arm, Hansen made a pass with his palm and the man's arm extended rigidly. Audience members were invited to try to force the paralyzed arm back down. No one could—not until Hansen released the subject from his spell.

Hansen played games with his subjects' memories, made them display strange powers of recall and of suggestibility. He gave one subject a raw potato and told him it was a delicious apple, and the crowd laughed as the man happily ate. He gave another a block of wood, told him it was a baby, and the man rocked the wood block, cooing to it, as if it were his own child. For the finale, Hansen made one man so rigid that the hypnotist could lay his subject's body across two chairs—head on one chair and feet on another, with nothing between to support the torso. Hansen, in eveningwear, stepped on this man's belly and stood, secure as if he were standing on a plank. Public health authorities called in the police and shut down the show.

For a modern reader, the connection between hypnosis and hysteria can seem obscure, but in the late nineteenth century it seemed self-evident: think about the rigidity of the body, the absence of mind. Hypnosis demonstrated a change in consciousness unrelated to any obvious shift in the physiological brain, it implied forces of the psyche that could not be explained by shifts in brain chemistry, and the enemies of the anti-vitalists were delighted. Hansen's show left Franz Brentano "shaken in his conviction that there could be no such thing as unconscious psychic phenomena."[28] Moriz Benedikt, Breuer's colleague, saw Hansen's stage magic as a revelation, explaining and exploring various aspects of the hidden, unfathomable, ineffable depths of the mind. Benedikt lectured on hypnosis and hysteria in March of 1880 (right between Hansen's show and Pappenheim's breakdown). The human brain is like a phonograph, Benedikt argued. The human brain is like a photographic plate. It takes in everything, yet the conscious person is only aware of a fragment of the information the brain takes in.

"Were we not able to suppress countless impressions beneath the threshold of consciousness," Benedikt said, "we could not form any concepts, nor concentrate our attention, nor think or create."[29]

Borch-Jacobsen speculates that both Breuer and Pappenheim may have attended Hansen's performances. For Borch-Jacobsen, Hansen's show plays a central role in the drama of her breakdown—he believes that in her illness she was imitating Hansen's subjects—and Borch-Jacobsen believes that Benedikt's lecture on Hansen shaped Breuer's view of hysteria. Breuer, Borch-Jacobsen writes, "would have maintained only a marginal interest in hypnosis had it not been for the decisive impetus lent to the study of hypnotic phenomena by the demonstrations of the Danish stage hypnotist Carl Hansen."

Were they actually there, at the Burgtheater, at the hypnotist's show? Let's pretend. Breuer is in the lobby, and before curtain he glimpses young, enchanting Bertha Pappenheim standing on the marble stairway, among the glass spheres filled with gaslight.

She turns to her friends and raises her hands. "You are under my power!"

5

Breuer went down the stairs from the old man's sickroom, his doctor's bag in hand, his face grave. He had to see the girl, hear her cough, see if she had tuberculosis. Recha opened the parlor door, and there Bertha Pappenheim sat. Recha called out cheerfully, Dr. Breuer to see her!

Bertha coughed. Her cough was like a bark, like a little dog barking at him.

"No one," writes Breuer in *Studies in Hysteria*, "perhaps not even the patient herself, knew what was going on inside her."

She was cross-eyed. Breuer noticed a muscular spasm beneath her cheek. In *Studies*, Breuer writes, "An eye-doctor explained it (erroneously) as being due to the paresis of one of the abducent muscles." The problem in her cheek is described in Breuer's contemporaneous notes on the Pappenheim case, and her facial neuralgia is also mentioned by doctors who treated her later, when she was in sanitariums, when she was no longer under Breuer's care—a problem of the trigeminal nerve.

The pain seems to have bothered her over a period of five to seven years. It seems that the pain disturbed Pappenheim before her breakdown and that it occurred intermittently through the whole course of her treatments and suffering, persisting long after she stopped working with Breuer. For Borch-Jacobsen, the neuralgia appeared briefly in the spring of 1880 and played, as Breuer wrote, "a quite subordinate role" in her illness. For

Robert Skues, the neuralgia should not be conflated with the more general illness, the hysteria treated by Breuer: "While there was evidently some debate between the doctors as to whether it was of infra-orbital or zygomatic origin, there appears never to have been any question of it being hysterical." For Skues, the pain in her face should be understood as a problem separate from her psychoneurological breakdown.

The ache in her face is something we can't measure—even if we were in the room with her, we could not know its severity—but a trigeminal neuralgia, according to the Mayo Clinic website, causes "extreme shock-like pain that can last anywhere from a few seconds to as long as two minutes per episode." According to the NIH, "the intensity of pain can be physically as well as mentally debilitating." The pain can flare for patients when they eat, drink, smile, or even when a breeze blows across their skin.

Breuer pushed up the sleeves of her dress, to feel her pulse. She had not been sleeping. She had not been eating. In *Anna Karenina*, published just a couple of years before Breuer's visit, a doctor examines young, pretty Kitty Scherbatsky for signs of tuberculosis, and Tolstoy is appalled: "With particular pleasure, it seemed, he insisted that maidenly modesty was merely a relic of barbarism and that nothing was more natural than for a not-yet-old man to palpate a naked young girl." Recha may have felt similar disgust, even as Breuer pressed his stethoscope between Bertha's shoulder blades. He told her to open her mouth. There was no sign of infection. She would not, like her sisters or her father, die of TB.

In *Studies*, Breuer calls her cough a *tussis nervosa*. In his contemporaneous notes he calls it a *tussis hysterica*, and adds, "I classified the patient immediately as mentally ill on account of her strange behavior. Those around her saw nothing of this." Breuer's distinctions between mental and physical illness might have been lost on the Pappenheims. In *Anna Karenina*, the doctor discussing tuberculosis says "there are always moral and spiritual causes." As Susan Sontag has argued, tuberculosis in the nineteenth century was seen as a disease of the will, a metaphor for psychological or moral corruption.

Breuer patted Bertha on the knee, and he stood. Recha showed the doctor downstairs, to the front hall. On the apartment's central stairway, I'm guessing, he made a simple prescription. It was important that she stay out of her father's room. There was the risk of contagion and also of the exacerbation of her anxiety. She must rest, he said. If Bertha could not rest calmly at night, he may have suggested at this point, then she should take chloral, a simple white powder that could be mixed with water and drunk before bedtime. Having made his recommendations, he took up his hat and stick and left, back down to the Ringstrasse.

Early in his treatment of her, Breuer took away Bertha Pappenheim's one real interest and activity, taking care of her father, and prescribed for her one of the two drugs that she would be addicted to for most of her twenties.

"Bertha Pappenheim never spoke about this period of her life," wrote Dora Edinger, who worked with Pappenheim closely in Frankfurt at the JFB.

All the stories we have of her breakdown—the girl watching her father's sickbed, the hallucinations of snakes, the frustrated attempt at prayer, the entire "latent" period of her hysteria, as Borch-Jacobsen points out, all of this comes to us through a series of unreliable narrators. Pappenheim spoke her stories to Breuer when she was sick, drugged, and maybe hypnotized. She went through her memories hundreds of times, says Breuer. He selected from the various accounts to reconstruct her history, wrote notes down in 1882, and then rewrote the story a dozen years later for *Studies*.

She was her parents' third daughter. The second, Flora, died of TB before Bertha was born. The oldest, Henriette, died of the same disease at sixteen in 1865, when Bertha was six. Her brother Wilhelm was a year younger than she. She had attended a Catholic school, where she had learned English, French, and German. She took piano lessons and was taken to the theater. She was passionately fond of Shakespeare and Goethe, but her education ended with her high school, and in 1880 Wilhelm went to university while she stayed home. Historian Marion A. Kaplan writes:

> She may have been jealous of the special treatment accorded [Wilhelm], particularly the education she was denied. . . . Her intellectual gifts were

stifled as she, like her German (and Victorian) middle-class counterparts, trained to become a leisured lady.

Later, in Frankfurt, Bertha Pappenheim complained about the lack of value that Jewish men felt for their daughters:

This can already be seen in the different reception given a new citizen of the world. If the father, or someone else asked what "it" was after a successful birth, the answer might be either the satisfied report of a boy, or—with pronounced sympathy for the disappointment—"Nothing, a girl," or, "Only a girl."

In Frankfurt, Pappenheim kept a picture on her wall of two roosters fighting, and she said it reminded her of the way she used to fight with her brother.

She and Freud were almost exact contemporaries—he was three years older than her and lived three years longer—but while the world opened itself to him, to her it was completely closed. She was trained for Viennese high culture (the romance languages, the piano playing) and then kept apart from it. "The attractive, imaginative, young woman was expected to settle down and await marriage," writes Kaplan. "After completing school, *höhere Töchter* [good daughters] stayed at home and embroidered their dowries until they met suitable husbands." As Zweig puts it, "A girl of good family had to live in an entirely sterilized atmosphere from her birth to the day she went to her bridal bed." Freud, relatively progressive, forbade his sisters (about Bertha's age) from reading Balzac or Dumas, for fear the novels would corrupt their virgin souls. Policing of a daughter's mind and body was the rule. As Zweig writes:

Young girls were not left alone for a moment, for their own protection. Girls had governesses whose duty it was to make sure that they did not— God forbid!—take a step out of the front door unescorted; they were taken to school, taken to dancing classes and music lessons, and then collected again. Every book they read was checked, and above all young girls were kept constantly occupied in case they engaged in any dangerous ideas.

In 1880, Bertha Pappenheim was past twenty and bored. She had essentially two obligations in life: to get married, and to believe in her parents' religion. She did neither. In his contemporaneous notes, but not in *Studies*, Breuer wrote, "In her life religion serves only as an object of silent struggle and silent opposition." And in a letter: "The patient comes from an Orthodox Jewish home though she herself is wholly without faith."

As Kaplan argues in her essay, "For Love or Money," most marriages in both the German and the Jewish bourgeoisies were arranged. Daughters typically had little choice in the matter. Through marriages, families consolidated business alliances. A joke of the time:

Goldberg: Do you hear, the Chinese sell their daughters in the marketplace?
Silverberg: The marketplace! Why don't they do it in private, like us?

From Pressburg to Frankfurt, ambitious Jewish bachelors and their mothers must have yearned for an introduction. Bertha would come with a massive dowry and trousseau. The man who married her would have his fortune made.

Jokes and stories she told later in life suggest that she escaped several planned engagements, but we don't know how many. In her essay on marriage, Kaplan reports that the families of some prospective bridegrooms hired detectives to look into their fiancées' lives. So Pappenheim's illness, even in the fall of 1880—her cross-eyes, her face pain, her lack of sleep and appetite—all these things might have been kept secret from the outside world.

All through the fall she had stayed up, night after night, tending to her father. Self-sacrificing, self-dramatizing, she demonstrated her devotion to her father, even as in silent opposition she refused to play out her obligatory role. She started suffering that pain in her face. She stopped eating. And meanwhile, every day, she had to put on the elaborate costume of her gender and class. Again, I go to Zweig:

Merely dressing to look like a lady—never mind the etiquette of high society—just putting on such gowns and taking them off was a complicated procedure, and impossible without someone's help. First there were the countless little hooks and eyes to be done up behind a lady's back from waist to neck, a maid had to exert all her strength to tie her mistress's corset; her long hair—and let me remind you that thirty years ago all European young women . . . had hair that fell to their waists when they unpinned it—had to be curled, set, brushed and combed and piled by a hairdresser called in daily and using a large quantity of hairpins, combs, and slides, curling tongs and hair curlers, all this before she could put on her petticoats, camisoles, little bodices and jackets, like a set of onion skins, turning and adjusting until the last remnant of her female form had disappeared.

She stayed up every night, and then in the morning was imprisoned in her clothes by her maids. For the rest of the day, she was kept in enforced idleness. Breuer was not blind to her condition. As he writes in *Studies*:

This girl of an overflowing mental vitality led an extremely monotonous life in her puritanically minded family, a life that she embellished for herself in a way that was probably decisive in the development of her illness. She systematically cultivated the art of daydreaming, calling it her "private theater." While everyone else believed her to be present, she was living out fairy tales in her mind, yet was always alert when spoken to so that no one was aware of it. Her domestic duties, which she carried out irreproachably, were almost incessantly accompanied by this mental activity.

The classical Freudian explanation of Bertha Pappenheim's symptoms is that she was acting out the pain in her mind—that's the theory of hysterical conversion, or conversion disorder. "Hysterical symptoms," wrote Freud in 1905, "are the expression of [the patients'] most secret and repressed wishes."

The Freudian conception doesn't include political and social stressors, but Pappenheim's "hysteria," as Marion A. Kaplan wrote in 1984, was "integrally related to the position of women of the day." So many of the great feminists of the late nineteenth and early twentieth centuries suffered breakdowns as they moved from adolescence to adulthood, so many were described as "hysterical." "Her life," writes Kaplan, "can be compared to those of other social reformers, many of whom suffered through crises similar to hers in kind, but not in extent." All over Europe and North America, women were falling victim. Kaplan makes a list—starting with Jane Addams and Josephine Butler—of activists who were afflicted with "nervous depressions and a sense of maladjustment." She quotes the great German suffrage leader Hedwig Dohm:

> When, in place of the knowledge and truth for which I was reaching out, they put into my hand the . . . cooking spoon,—they drove a human soul, which was created perhaps to live splendidly and fruitfully, into a desert of wild fantasies and sterile dreams.[30]

In 1880, Bertha Pappenheim lived in a society that denied her agency, she was under tremendous psychological stress, and she had a terrible pain in her face. FND doctors describe the etiology of the condition as multifactorial, the many stresses of a person's life acting together to disable the brain's capacity to control the body. The pain of the trigeminal neuralgia, the stress of staying up all night with a father who is dying of the same disease that killed her sisters, the gloom of a stifling homelife of boredom through which she persisted in "private theater" and "silent opposition"—I am not here to diagnose Bertha Pappenheim, but if you look at the charts of predisposing, precipitating, and perpetuating factors that can contribute to a functional neurological breakdown, her case ticks off every box. Put enough pressure on any one of us, and we are liable to break.

6

Weeks elapsed between Breuer's November 1880 visit and when he returned to see her in December. If in the first visit she seemed "mentally ill," by the second she was a wreck. In November she sat in a chair and spoke to him. By December, according to both "Anna O." and Breuer's contemporaneous notes, she was unable to get out of bed, suffering weakness, paralysis, and distorted vision. What happened between his first visit and his second? I can only try to assemble a picture here from fragments, the way a paleontologist might assemble a model from fossil scraps. I'll tell you what they suggest to me: that between Breuer's first and second visits, Pappenheim was made drug-sick and she was physically assaulted.

1. In 1880, Hanukkah fell from November 27 to December 4—right between those two visits. According to Breuer's accounts, Bertha suffered a very stressful holiday that year. Something terrible happened to her in Hanukkah of 1880.

2. Breuer's writing about that Hanukkah, in both *Studies in Hysteria* and in his contemporaneous notes, is elliptical and obscure. In his notes, he refers to Hanukkah as "Jewish Christmas," in *Studies*, as just "Christmas." In both, he doesn't give direct description of this harrowing period

71

in Pappenheim's life. He only discusses his patient's memories of the holiday as they were related to him the following year, in December 1881.

In *Studies*, he writes, "Instead of recounting new material, she related phantasms that she had elaborated by day during the Christmas of 1880, when she was subject to powerful feelings of anxiety." In his notes, instead of the word "phantasms," he writes that she recited the same "phantasy stories she had recounted day by day during the 1880 festival, when dominated by extreme anxiety."

3. Borch-Jacobsen makes much of the discrepancy between "phantasy stories" and "phantasms" in *Studies*. He argues that the use of "phantasy stories" in the unpublished account is revealing and shows the truth of the matter: that Pappenheim didn't have any hallucinations, that she just told stories to her doctor.

Contrary to Borch-Jacobsen, Frederick Crews believes that Bertha Pappenheim actually did suffer hallucinations, but for Crews these hallucinations were caused by the drugs she was taking. Crews takes this argument from work done by Sérgio de Paula Ramos, who demonstrated that the chloral hydrate that Breuer prescribed for her likely played a role in Pappenheim's breakdown. Withdrawal from chloral hydrate can cause all manner of distressing symptoms.

4. In Oliver Sacks's *Hallucinations*, there's a great description of chloral hydrate withdrawal, and the hallucinations that can come when one stops taking the drug. As Sacks tells it, when he was in his thirties, he prescribed himself chloral as a sleep aid, and then, when he broke it off, his sanity suddenly dissolved. The symptoms hit Sacks unexpectedly, the day after he stopped taking the drug, while he was at a lunch counter in the Bronx.

As I was stirring the coffee, it suddenly turned green, then purple. I looked up, startled, and saw that a customer paying his bill at the cash register had a huge, proboscidean head, like an elephant seal. Panic seized me; I slammed a five dollar note on the table and ran across the road to a bus on the other side. But all the passengers on the bus seemed to have smooth white heads like giant eggs, with huge glittering eyes like the faceted compound eyes of insects—their eyes seemed to move in sudden jerks, which instead increased the feeling of their fearfulness and alienness.

Chloral is no longer an approved drug in the United States, and the doses described in *Studies* are much, much higher than what any late twentieth-century physician would have recommended. It's reasonable to assume that sudden withdrawal from the drug would cause hallucinations. Sacks was a medical resident in neurology at the time, and very experienced with recreational hallucinogens. Bertha Pappenheim would have no idea what was happening to her.

5. There's a little piece of *Studies*—not from "Fraulein Anna O." but from Breuer's "Theoretical Issues" chapter—that helps me imagine Pappenheim. Breuer writes that:

> Adolescents who later become hysterical are for the most part lively, talented and full of intellectual interests until they fall ill; they often have a remarkably energetic will. This category includes girls who get up during the night to pursue in secret some kind of study that their parents have forbidden them for fear of over-exhaustion.

After Breuer's first visit in November 1880, Bertha Pappenheim was forbidden from getting up at night "for fear of over-exhaustion." We can't know for sure that she ever skipped a dose of her chloral, the way Sacks did before his world turned into a phantasmagoria. However, if she wanted to stay up late, and go to see her father at night, she'd have to skip her sleeping medicine.

6. Sometime later, when she was in Breuer's care, there was a period in which Pappenheim insisted on going to bed with her stockings on, and then she would cry out—at two or three in the morning—asking why she was sleeping in stockings. This little bit of madness is in the notes of 1882, but not in *Studies*, and is something Breuer calls "the stocking caprice," and it's resolved when she makes a confession:

How at nighttime she would creep in to eavesdrop on her father (at that time, night nurses could no longer put up with her), how she slept in her stockings for this reason, then on one occasion was caught by her brother, and so on.

It's never clear what Breuer means when he writes "and so on." It's a tic in his writing, something he resorts to when he wants to avoid saying something unpleasant. We cannot know for certain what happened when Pappenheim "was caught by her brother," but it was upsetting. As Breuer writes, "As soon as she had finished [telling the story] she began to cry out softly, demanding why she was in bed with her stockings on."

There's a very limited period of time in which she could have snuck out of bed in her stockings, against the nurses' orders. It had to have happened after Breuer's first visit because before then Pappenheim was permitted to nurse her father nightly. But it couldn't have happened after the end of December 1880, because by then Pappenheim was sick, paralyzed, and unable to get out of bed. So as I understand it, slipping on her stockings, sneaking down the hallway, and getting caught, "and so on," most likely happened in a very brief window of time—late November to early December—that time period during which Pappenheim was both physically able to get out of bed and to listen at her father's door, and simultaneously forbidden from doing so. The "stocking caprice," in my reading, may well have coincided with the "Jewish Christmas."

7. One of the symptoms that interests Breuer is his patient's periods of temporary deafness. He lists more than two hundred incidents in which she temporarily loses her hearing. One of the ways in which she goes temporarily deaf is "becoming deaf as a result of long periods of listening and eavesdropping, so that she would not hear when spoken to." Another is "becoming deaf through shaking." Pappenheim lost her hearing whenever the world around her trembled, as *Studies* explains, "in the carriage or other such circumstances." In his notes, he writes:

A quarrel in which she suppressed her reply gave her a spasm in the glottis. This recurred on each similar situation. When shaken hard by her brother in such a situation, she became temporarily deaf; each such shaking brought on a repetition.

Apparently, Wilhelm shook Bertha often, and his shaking of Bertha left her unable to speak and to hear. Breuer is clear that her symptoms of deafness started one time when Wilhelm shook her particularly hard: "The origin [of her deafness]: her younger brother shook her angrily when he caught her listening at the door of the sickroom." The "origin" happened, as Breuer specifies, when she was eavesdropping at her father's door—possibly when she was wearing stockings (something awful happened then) and presumably when she wasn't supposed to be there, which, again, would in my reckoning place us in or around Hanukkah 1880.

So here's my story:

One night in the course of the Hanukkah festival, Bertha decided to go see her father. In preparation for slipping down the hall to see him, she didn't take off her stockings, and she avoided taking her chloral. She lay quietly in bed, and when the apartment and the city had stilled, when her mother was asleep, and the lights had all been dimmed, and even the night nurse was resting, she crept down the hall. She listened at her father's door.

Wilhelm, let's suppose, caught her. Maybe he came home late. He didn't want to disturb his mother, or his father, so he stepped quietly through the big rooms downstairs, and up the stairs, past the table with the vase, and the picture of the rabbi—and there was his crazy older sister doing exactly what she had been told *not* to do.

Rapt at the doorway to her father's room—deaf on account of the intensity of her eavesdropping—Bertha didn't notice Wilhelm's coming. He grabbed her, to force her back into her bed. She struggled. He shook her—hard. A spasm closed her throat, and her eyes went wide. In her drug-addled vision, Wilhelm transformed. His face narrowed, his red hair turned into a cock's crest, his mouth became a beak, ready to savage her.

For the next three and a half months, Bertha Pappenheim didn't get out of bed.

The next time Breuer came to the Pappenheim apartment, it was December 1880. How furious Recha must have been. *Tussis nervosa*, he said. Nothing to worry about, he said. Just keep her from excitement. Now the girl can't move her legs.

I place at least seven doors on the third-floor hallway: Bertha's room, Wilhelm's room, Siegmund's room, a room where Recha is sleeping, a bath, a toilet (in Vienna of 1880, there was modern plumbing in the fancy new buildings), and a door to the stairway to the servants' room upstairs. Breuer would rather be thinking about the aural labyrinths of birds, but here he is with the Pappenheims. They passed by Siegmund's room. They could hear the awful coughing inside. They came to Bertha's door. Recha opened it.

Her daughter lay in bed. Her long hair was a mess. Her eyes were crossed. She said she had lost feeling in her legs, but when Breuer approached, she wouldn't let him touch her. She told him that she felt the walls were closing in on her.

He came again and again, through Christmas and New Year's 1881, into January. No matter the weather, he went to the Pappenheims, up the elegant stairs, handing his hat and stick to the footman. He never knew what he would find when he opened her door.

> Pains at the back left of her head; *strabismus convergens* (diplopia or double vision) significantly aggravated by excitement; . . . disturbances of vision that were hard to analyze; . . . contracture and anesthesia of the right upper extremity, and after some time, of the right lower extremity—the latter was also fully extended, adducted and rotated inwards. The same affection subsequently occurred in the lower left extremity and finally in the left arm, although here the fingers retained partial mobility. . . . At its maximum the contracture affected the upper-arm muscles, and later too, when the anesthesia could be tested more precisely, the area around the elbow proved to be the least sensitive.

None of these symptoms would be out of place in a contemporary FND clinic. That her symptoms shifted and intensified is typical of FND. She suffered "absences." Again, typical of FND. Sometimes she didn't recognize Breuer. Sometimes she threw a pillow in his face. "She was 'naughty,' that is to say she was abusive."

> There were two quite separate states of consciousness which alternated very frequently and without warning, and which became increasingly distinct over the course of the illness. In one state she recognized her surroundings, was sad and anxious but relatively normal. In the other she hallucinated . . . would pull off the buttons from the bedclothes and linen with whichever fingers were still mobile, and so on.

Again, that tic of Breuer's writing, that "and so on." At the height of her illness, when contracture had also taken hold of her left side, there were only very short periods during the day when she was to any degree normal. This second state of consciousness is something Breuer categorizes variously as "hysteric," "hypnotic," "absences," and a *condition seconde*." She wrestled with the symptoms' effect on her body, with the drugs' effect on her brain.

> But even these moments of relatively clear consciousness were invaded by the disturbances: the most rapid and extreme changes in mood; fleeting instances of high spirits; but in general severe feelings of anxiety, stubborn opposition to all therapeutic measures, frightening hallucinations in which her hair, laces, and so on would appear as black snakes. And yet at the same time she would always tell herself not to be so stupid, that it was only her hair, etc. In these moments of complete lucidity, she complained of the deep darkness inside her head, of not being able to think, of becoming blind and deaf, of having two selves, her real self and a bad one, that made her do wicked things, etc.

Again that "and so on," that "etc." I'm not proposing FND as a way of explaining all aspects of her crisis—psychological, social, physical—but as a way of thinking about people who break down in similar fashion in similar circumstances, people who are thrown into an abyss where their mind seems to have no agency over their body. She lost all sense of intention.

Toward the end of the case study, Breuer writes, "she brought up various childish fears and self-accusations, including the claim that she had not been ill at all and that everything had merely been simulated." This claim of Anna O.'s, which so many readers use to argue that her illness was just a performance, is dismissed by Breuer as "childish"—and I know what he means, I know that feeling of childlike dissociation, the kid who is throwing a temper tantrum who is simultaneously apart from the temper tantrum, the mourner who is sobbing helplessly but also helplessly observing his own breakdown, thinking, *I don't need to be doing this*, even as the snot runs out of your nose and you scream so loud your throat hurts.

As Breuer tells it, between January and March 1881, Anna O. became increasingly incoherent.

> The first thing that became noticeable was that she could not find words and gradually this became worse. Then her speech lost all grammatical structure, the syntax was missing, as was the conjugation of verbs, so that in the end she was only using infinitives that were incorrectly formed from a weak past participle and no articles. As the disorder developed she could find almost no words at all, and would painfully piece them together out of four or five different languages, which made her almost incomprehensible. Whenever she attempted to write, she used the same jargon (at least initially, until the contracture prevented it completely). For two weeks she was completely mute, and despite continual strenuous attempts to speak, could not utter a sound.

The symptoms of nineteenth-century hysteria do not map precisely onto the symptoms of twenty-first-century FND. For instance, Jon Stone explained to me that nineteenth-century "hysterics" often adopted postures of prayer, postures uncommon in FND clinics in the United States today. Few if any contemporary American FND patients find themselves in this precise breakdown in language—but then again, there aren't a lot of Americans living in polyglot communities like nineteenth-century Vienna. Some FND patients do suffer a "foreign accent syndrome" that can be "highly variable across patients . . . and often cannot be reliably identified as tied to a specific language or dialect."[31] Pappenheim spoke to Breuer in broken German, English, French, Italian, and (I've read speculation) Yiddish, but then she stopped. Sometime in March 1881 something bad happened, something that silenced Bertha Pappenheim completely. Again, Breuer doesn't specify. He only writes that "she had taken great offense at something."

Who could have offended her so? Her relations with Breuer seem to have been unaffected, so I suppose something must have happened in her family. Maybe her mother could have said something intolerable. Maybe her dying father, toward whom she had shown such devotion, said something? She saw him, according to Breuer, only a few times over the first three months of 1881, the last three months of his life.

Here, I'm venturing further into speculation than maybe I ought to, but: Maybe one day Siegmund staggered into her room. Maybe he'd had enough of her jabbering and paralysis and driving her mother crazy. Maybe he came in his slippers and robe and yelled, "ENOUGH!" telling her to behave, to stop talking in all these crazy languages—and his *höhere Töchter* obliged. She didn't say another word. (This theory is perhaps supported by Breuer's original notes, in which he writes about her "not speaking due to anxiety, when her father scolded her without cause.") Or maybe it was her brother, who had been so violent with her, maybe Wilhelm did something worse to her than shaking? We will never know precisely what it was that cast her into silence, and whether this was an unwillingness or an inability to speak.

But it is with this silence that Breuer shifts his diagnosis from a physical hysteria (some lesion in the nervous system or brain?) to a psychological hysteria. "Here the psychical mechanisms of the disturbance came clear to me for the first time," he writes. "I guessed as much and forced her to talk about it." So the first gestures toward talk therapy emerged.

———◦———

There are some interpreters who try to dismiss the psychological aspects of Pappenheim's illness and instead describe her breakdown as biological in nature. Elizabeth Thornton diagnosed Pappenheim as suffering from tubercular meningitis. Lindsay C. Hurst said cerebral sarcoidosis. Pierre Flor-Henry suggested sub-acute limbic encephalitis.

I'm unequipped to evaluate these claims against one another, but all seem premised on an assumption, not so distant from the one held by Borch-Jacobsen (who calls Breuer "gullible"), or by Edward Shorter (who describes Pappenheim as "a woman who simulated some of her symptoms and was suggested into others"), that in one way or another, her doctor was incapable of perceiving what was actually happening, and that from a century away we can see Pappenheim more clearly than Breuer did. This seems wrong. If Bertha Pappenheim's mind was a fireball of invention, Breuer's was capacious, open to everything.

Breuer may not have known all we know about the ways the brain and the mind and body interact (and do we really know that much?), but his erudition was massive, and his perception and patience extraordinary. How we stand erect (his work in the 1880s on balance), how we breathe (his work in the 1870s on lungs), how we get sick (his work in the 1860s on fever), Breuer knew fundamental facts of human life before anyone else. Two of the many things he recognized before everyone else were the brilliance of Bertha Pappenheim and the genius of Sigmund Freud.

He was a great doctor, physician to most of the medical faculty at the University of Vienna (some of the greatest doctors in Europe, including Brücke and Billroth) and to almost all of the wealthy Jewish families in the city (some of the richest people on the continent). He was kept off the medical faculty of the University of Vienna (probably because he was Jewish), but even Billroth read Breuer's work on the labyrinth of the inner ear admiringly: "The pure joy of scientific exploration and thought is manifest in every paragraph." The leading artists and philosophers of Vienna relied on him. Here is his biographer Albrecht Hirschmüller's summary of the subjects discussed in the decades of correspondence between Breuer and Franz Brentano:

> The cosmology of Leplace, Maxwell's electromagnetic theory of light, and Thomson's argument . . . thinkers from Empedocles to Schopenhauer . . . the principal epistemological works of eminent philosophers from Plato and Kant to Mill and Spencer. . . . Brentano stresses the pleasing precision of [Breuer's] argument "in contrast to anything to be found in the German philosophers."

They discussed St. Augustine and Newton, Rousseau, the Talmud and the Bible, Christianity and Buddhism, Voltaire and Goethe, Turgenev and H. G. Wells. Another one of Breuer's patients was the Countess Marie von Ebner-Eschenbach, a novelist who would twice be nominated for the Nobel Prize. She liked to ask Breuer to recommend books to her, and she began her letters to him:

> To Herr Josef Breuer
>
> My dear friend
> The doctor to whom I commend
> My body, spirit, and soul.[32]

Breuer's closest friend was the composer Ignaz Brüll (whose work was part of the standard German repertory until the Nazis banned it), and when Brahms was dying in 1897, Breuer was one of the men who kept vigil. In conversations about consciousness, Breuer moved easily between anti-vitalists like his good friends Ernst Fleischl von Marxow (the polymath Freud so admired, the one with the bad thumb and the morphine addiction, the man who discovered one way to measure the electricity of the brain) and believers in subconsciousness like Moriz Benedikt. As one friend said, "Anyone who had the chance to talk with J. Breuer and to exchange ideas with him would not only be aware of the catholicity and depth of his reading in general; he would be amazed at the extent of Breuer's ability at any time to recall clearly and distinctly details which he has once read or thought over." According to Hirschmüller, "The central theme of Breuer's work is the idea of biological regulation of body functions in the service of capacities which are both meaningful and necessary to the organism as a whole." He "loathed extremes of thought." "By saying only good things about him," Freud once said in a letter to Martha, "one doesn't give a proper picture of his character; one ought to emphasize the absence of anything bad." He was a devoted friend, and throughout the 1880s Freud relied on Breuer for advice and comfort, and Breuer nurtured Freud's intellectual, personal, and professional development.

In the account of his treatment of Anna O., which he published reluctantly, Breuer covered up his own errors, and he did what he could
to hide Pappenheim's identity and to support Freud's emerging theories,
but at bottom I think Breuer was trustworthy, capable, wise, and ad-
mirable, the leading medical practitioner in his city, and in terms of his
treatment of Bertha Pappenheim, he was at least a hundred years ahead
of his time.

Transport the Pappenheims, Bertha and Siegmund, from the nineteenth century to 1995 (the centennial of *Studies*), and the father would
be cured of his TB. Meanwhile, in most hospitals in the Western world,
the daughter's symptoms would be dismissed as play acting, nothing that
was, neurologically speaking, "real." In the world of 1990s post-Freudian
pharmacological psychiatry, a patient like her would get Ambien for
her sleeplessness and Prozac for her depression and Oxycontin for her
face pain, with the real risk of dependence on all three. Breuer's treatment of Pappenheim was, in its use of drugs, similarly flawed. But in
his open-ended observations, his willingness to acknowledge both her
suffering and his own limitations, Breuer did something extraordinary,
something that not many neurologists or emergency room doctors would
have done in 1995: he sat down next to her and listened. He took her
complaint seriously.

At least initially, Breuer's chief technique seems to have been patience.
She had been, before her breakdown, telling herself stories constantly,
and at some point, after her period of silence, perhaps in March of 1882,
she began telling them to him, and he began to listen. Later, Breuer described himself as essentially passive in the interaction:

> The case which I described in the *Studies* as number one, Anna O., passed
> through my hands, and my merit lay essentially in my having recognized
> what an important case chance had brought me for investigation, and in
> my having persevered and observing it attentively and accurately and my
> not having allowed any preconceived opinions to interfere with the simple
> observation of the important data.

Some critics dismiss Breuer's approach. Borch-Jacobsen portrays Breuer as merely obeying his patient's wishes, and he places Pappenheim's storytelling and Breuer's listening in a long list of strange things that nineteenth-century hysterical patients asked of their doctors.

> What real difference is there between the extravagant demands of a Bertha Pappenheim and those of a Joly, the patient whose cataleptic attacks could be made to stop only when his doctor, the Marquis de Puységur, followed the patient's orders and burst into song, accompanying himself on the harp. And what about the demands of Friederike Hauffe, the famous "Seeress of Prevorst," who had Justinus Kerner cure her by building a "nerve tuner" (*Nervenstimmer*)? Or those of Estelle, Despine's little paralytic, who would not walk unless her doctor-magnetist applied gold to her body. It is impossible to escape the feeling that Anna O.'s stories and "reminiscences" also participated in this type of therapeutic bargaining.

With the phrase "therapeutic bargaining," Borch-Jacobsen seems to be accusing Breuer of ceding his authority to his patient, and one can make the argument that all Breuer was doing was providing Pappenheim some kind of placebo, what Oliver Sacks calls "the miracle of attention and care." Sacks uses this phrase in his book *Migraine*, and migraines, like functional neurological symptoms, lie at the intersection of the psyche and the nervous system.

But to answer Borch-Jacobsen's question, the "real differences" between listening to someone's stories and building them a nerve tuner are many. I'll start with two. First, Breuer's therapeutic bargain—his acceptance of Pappenheim's chosen therapeutic technique—had lasting influence. Many people I know have gone to a therapist and talked and been listened to, as I did after my wife's cancer diagnosis; but I don't know anyone whose therapist paints them with gold or sings to them with a harp. Second, unlike the other doctors, Breuer didn't *do* anything (no singing, no building, no gold) while Pappenheim performed.

If she was the one who proposed the bargain—who invented the talking cure—he was the one who approved the deal. Breuer didn't attend to her as Freud would later attend to his patients, with a theoretical agenda or a psychoanalytic dogma. Breuer certainly didn't listen to her as neurologists do now, hoping to collaborate on a "narrative with healing power." As far as we can tell, he simply gave her his time and attention. He gave her the floor. Elsewhere in her life, she had no control of anything, but while Breuer sat with her, she exercised power over her mouth, and her mind, and she got something she perhaps wanted—the attention of one of the most eminent medical men in the city. In this one delimited space, she was in command. Or partly so. The story goes that her hysteria robbed her of her German. She could talk to him only in English.

Here is one of these places where it's so hard to draw any line between abilities and intention, between agency and incompetence, between performance and helplessness. In Moriz Benedikt's theory circa 1880, Pappenheim's mind is a phonograph that has recorded the English language, and in her hypnotic state, the subconscious language gets played back, despite her will, and this is an expression of what lurks in the fathomless depths of her mind. But that's not the way contemporary psychology describes memory or language.

It's unlikely that anyone else in the apartment spoke English as well as she and Breuer did. The maids didn't, and her parents didn't, and Wilhelm at the gymnasium learned classical and not English or Romance languages. So, she and Breuer stumbled—whether through her intention or the happenstance of her condition—into a secret code, a private language. And so the pattern emerged; she told stories, and he listened. There are still doctors, all over the world, who will not listen to their patients as Breuer listened to Pappenheim.

The charming, urbane, middle-aged man called on her, day after day, sitting alone in a room with one of Jewish Vienna's most marriageable daughters, listening to her stories, speaking to her in their private language. Pappenheim ate only oranges, according to Breuer, which he alone fed her—did he slip the segments one by one into her waiting mouth?

Freud spent a lot of time in the Breuer apartment in the early 1880s, and he always thought that Breuer was sweet on Pappenheim. Maybe Breuer spent all that time in her bedroom because she was brilliant and beautiful and funny and her stories were charming. Whatever pleasure he took in it, his treatment seemed to have some beneficial effect. She told her stories and her paralysis relaxed. She could move her arms and legs. "The squint now also improved, eventually recurring only in moments of intense excitement." Her agency expanded, from control of her stories to control of her body. On April 1, 1881, she got out of bed for the first time since December.

But then, on April 5, her father died, and she fell apart.

7

After her father's death, "people told her nothing but lies." That's according to Breuer's notes of 1882, but it is omitted from *Studies*.

Maybe the Pappenheims were only following doctor's orders, keeping their daughter from stimulation, excitement, and knowledge. They hid her father's death from her so as not to upset her. But their deceit didn't calm her; it drove her nuts. "At the very moment her father died," Breuer writes in his notes, "she cried out to her mother in terror, beseeching her to tell the truth." Bertha later said she felt she had been "cheated" out of a final glimpse of her father.

She collapsed. "Violent excitement was followed by a deep stupor lasting about two days." Men from the burial society of the Schiffschul must have come to perform the ritual washing of the corpse. An older member of the congregation, who maybe made his living this way, sat by the coffin all night. Siegmund was buried in Pressburg, near his father. Modern trains make the trip in an hour, following the Danube through the little Carpathians. The Orthodox cemetery is near the river, not far from the tomb of Rabbi Moses Sofer. What is now Slovakia was then Hungary. Recha and Wilhelm made the trip without Bertha. They were surrounded by Jews from Siegmund's Pressburg childhood. Wilhelm threw a shovelful of earth on his father's coffin. Then they got back on the train, back home to Vienna. Breuer arrived at the apartment that night. In his notes (but again, not in *Studies*) he writes:

> I found her calling for me and wrestling with the others in profound agitation. When I entered she allowed herself to be put to bed quietly, saying over and over again: Don't tell me any more lies, I know my father is dead.

In the days after, the Pappenheims sat shiva. On the second floor, I imagine the ceremony of grieving, the mirrors covered, visitors paying respects. Upstairs, Bertha was in bed. Breuer paid his next call on April 7. She surprised him by saying, "'Buona sera, dottore!'—then suddenly leaping up—'E' vero il mio padre é morto?'" In Italian: *Is it true my father is dead?*

> When I replied that she had already known for a long time, she replied at last, yes, that must be true, she had a feeling that she must have known already, it did not feel inside her as though she had only just come to know it.

She told Breuer that she would "have nothing more to do" with her family. She was furious at being excluded from their grief. As Breuer notes dryly, "This was the origin of her disturbed relationship with her mother."

Members of the congregation were visiting downstairs. Martha Bernays (not yet Martha Freud) must have come to town by train to pay her respects to the family of her deceased guardian. Maybe she left the gathering to go up to the third floor and see Bertha.

In the aftermath of her father's death, Pappenheim's vision problems became acute. "Looking—with delight—at a bunch of flowers she could only ever see one flower at a time." Faces baffled her. She had to perform what she called in English "recognizing work," saying "the nose is like this, and the hair is like that, so it has to be so-and-so." The contractures of her right leg and right arm reappeared, but according to Breuer, these "were not deep." She was still speaking only English. She could not, or would not, understand German. "She clearly felt the presence of her mother and brother painful."

On April 14, 1881, just after the mourning period ended, and after the first two nights of Passover had passed, Breuer brought a consultant to the apartment. He is unnamed in *Studies*, but in the notes is identified as Richard von Krafft-Ebing, whose masterwork, *Sexual Psychopathy: A Clinical Forensic Study*, would appear the year after he visited the Pappenheim apartment. Krafft-Ebing was square-headed, powerful, with a mustache and clean-shaven chin. They met not in Bertha Pappenheim's bedroom but in a parlor. She was sitting up, reading what Breuer calls "the clown scene in *Hamlet*." She "ignored [Krafft-Ebing] completely, as she did all strangers," Breuer writes in *Studies*. He calls this phenomenon "a negative hallucination."

Breuer showed off more of her symptoms to his colleague. "I demonstrated all her peculiar characteristics." He brought with him some writing in French and showed it to Pappenheim. "'That's like an examination,' she said, laughing." She teased Breuer gently, and then she read the words aloud but in English, translating as if automatically. Krafft-Ebing "tried to intervene in the conversation, to make her notice him, but in vain." The great sexologist must have been unaccustomed to being snubbed by an attractive young woman. He stabbed her leg with a needle. This is in the notes, but not in *Studies*, and she cried out, but kept ignoring him. He lit a piece of paper on fire and he blew the smoke in her face. This "final test," Breuer writes in his notes, "turned out successfully but was rather unpleasant."

"She saw a stranger," and she tried to run away. She "rushed to the door to take out the key." But she didn't make it out of the door. My guess is the key was gone and the door was locked. She "fell to the ground, unconscious; there followed a short burst of anger, then a bad attack of anxiety which I had great difficulty calming down."

After this, Breuer was gone for several days, traveling. During his absence, Breuer writes, Pappenheim "maintained total abstinence." She ate nothing. She drank nothing. She didn't sleep, and I suppose she didn't take her medicine. By the time her doctor returned from his holiday trip, her condition had changed. "She had gone without food the whole time, was full of anxiety, and her hallucinatory absences were filled with terrifying figures, death's heads and skeletons." Crews's argument, that she's drug sick, is compelling: she had been taking large doses of chloral for weeks, and then she seems to have abruptly stopped.

The days took on a new shape from April to June. She was drowsy all afternoon and toward evening fell into "deep hypnosis," and that's when Breuer sat with her, and more stories emerged. Alison Orr-Andrawes suspects that Breuer's bedside presence calmed her, that he gave her a small dose of chloral to counteract her DTs, and that dosed with drugs she recounted her terrors. Breuer writes: "Her mind was relieved when, shaking with fear and horror, she had reproduced these frightful images and given utterance to them."

After her storytelling session, according to Breuer, "she would wake up lucid, calm and cheerful." And then she "would sit down to work and write or draw far into the night, and was quite reasonable." She was over-flowing with fiction. Her mind was falling apart.

By May, Breuer writes, "the evening presentations ceased to resemble more or less spontaneous poetic compositions and turned instead into a series of dreadful and terrifying hallucinations." If each evening she was calmed by Breuer, all day she was a terror to her family. She threatened to kill herself, saying she would jump out the window. Recha and Wilhelm, still mourning Siegmund, must have been desperate. Finally, on June 2, two months after her father's death, she was taken from the apartment "without deception but not without force."

I imagine the orderlies, large, polite, intimidating men. I imagine the girl screaming and kicking, the flurry of her skirts as at dawn she's carried down the stairs and forced into the carriage, the hoofbeats on the cobblestone as they move her out of town. In the shaking carriage, she went deaf and she lost her ability to scream.

———————

Inzersdorf is now an industrial neighborhood within the city limits of Vienna, about five miles from the center of town. In 1882, it was bucolic. The sanitarium was the former summer palace of the Prince Ferdinand von Lobkowicz, one of Mozart's patrons, and it has since been destroyed. Pictures show a long, low, white building with a large lawn and neat hedges cut into topiary domes. There were some twenty-five patients in the building proper. Pappenheim wasn't kept there, but in a cottage on the grounds. She arrived in a weirdly calm state, not unlike the one immediately after her father's death. She experienced wild mood swings.

> The move was immediately followed by three days and nights completely without sleep or nourishment, by numerous attempts at suicide (though, so long as she was in the garden, these were not dangerous), by smashing windows and so on, and by hallucinations unaccompanied by *absences*—which she was able to distinguish fairly easily from her other hallucinations.

That's the Strachey translation, but Nicola Luckhurst renders it differently, as "hallucinations without absence, which she was well able to distinguish from the others." At this point, it seems, she was no longer falling in and out of dissociative states, but she was seeing things constantly—snakes, skulls, skeletons—and she knew that her visions were not necessarily real. Breuer's "and so on" might cover other messier, abdominal symptoms of withdrawal from chloral, like nausea, tarry stools, and vomit with the consistency of coffee grounds.

Melinda Given Guttmann writes that Pappenheim was "tortured" at Inzersdorf, that she was dosed with arsenic, and that electric eels were applied to her face. Those were the treatments for the kinds of face pain she suffered, as were doses of quinine, and likely it was at Inzersdorf that she was given morphine, the other drug on which she became dependent. But if Pappenheim was fearing the horrors of the early nineteenth-century madhouse—chains and whips and being hung from the ceiling in an iron cage—she didn't find any of it. Breuer had put her in the most comfortable, private spot he could. The director, Hermann Breslauer, subscribed to a fairly liberal, undogmatic version of S. Weir Mitchell's "rest cure." She was not confined to bed. She was allowed to read and write and walk the grounds. They tried to give her hot baths, but gave up because the baths "had a harmful effect on her by provoking hallucinatory absences." Cold showers worked better, as did rubdowns. Her initial panic subsided after a few days. Usually, she woke in the afternoon after a drug-induced sleep, and then fell into that strange state that Breuer describes as her *"condition seconde"* or "her evening hypnosis." He found her in the garden in the long June dusk. When he appeared, she didn't trust her eyes. She took his hands in hers to assure herself that he was actually there. She wasn't drinking water, she wasn't eating bread. Just oranges and melons, which he fed her. He sat there "like a sultan with Scheherazade," and she told stories.

"The talking cure," which she spoke originally in English, seems like a play on the American phrase "rest cure." Breuer says that Pappenheim's other name for their invention, "chimney sweeping," was "humorous," and these are the only words we have that suggest her conception of the process—of the way talking to Breuer provided relief from her symptoms and her stress. Rachel Bowlby, in the introduction to the Penguin edition of *Studies*, points out that when a chimney is swept, "what is removed is only the unmourned ashes and dust of daily life. And the blackness of the chimney is not itself threatening or ominous; it is the remains of a warm hearth." Pappenheim's was a very humble everyday catharsis, and as Bowlby points out, the source of the word *catharsis* is the most humble of all everyday events. "In Aristotle's theory of tragedy, the *Poetics*, this word, also associated with bowel movements, is used to describe the freeing effect of watching a tragedy, vicariously letting out emotions that would otherwise accumulate and cause pressure." In Bowlby's footnote on catharsis, she refers to a classic essay on Aristotle by Jacob Bernays.

Jacob Bernays! I thought. My father's *chochum!*

In my mind's eye I saw the manila envelope again, his handwriting in English and in Hebrew, and inside the big plump photocopy he had given me that I had not yet read. There he was, my ancient dad in his underpants, standing in front of me, teary-eyed and urgent. "She loved the theater!"

So this is what I had learned at last, that my dad's idea is more or less the same as Rachel Bowlby's canonical version: Jacob Bernays was Martha's uncle, and Bernays died just a few days before Pappenheim was bundled off to Inzersdorf. It's a small step to think that a young Jewish woman who carried around a copy of *Hamlet* would have been interested in a famous rabbi's ideas about tragedy, especially if that rabbi was her good friend's uncle. Pappenheim need not have read the essay, or even the obituaries of Bernays that were in the papers at the time.

Bernays's ideas about catharsis were alive in the culture; Peter Swales, citing Hirschmüller among others, argues that, in 1881, these ideas had "become a very fashionable topic of discussion among the fin-de-siècle Viennese *haute bourgeoisie*." Maybe when Pappenheim said "chimney sweeping," she was making what Breuer would have understood as a reference to Bernays and Aristotle, an erudite joke about poop and neurology and tragedy—showing her erudite doctor that she could be pretty sharp, too. She was funny and trenchant, and in this version of intellectual history—which accords with Ernest Jones's vision (i.e., about as close as you can come to the official history of Freudian thought)—the line of theoretical descent goes: Aristotle, Bernays, Pappenheim, Breuer, Freud, your mother, your kindergarten teacher, and your therapist, all of them telling you that if you talk out your problems you'll feel better.

The talking cure, the chimney sweeping, calmed her. But she didn't do it on the nights when Breuer was not there. On those nights, the doctors at Inzersdorf tranquilized her with huge amounts of chloral. She got five grams a night. There are currently no FDA-approved products that include chloral hydrate. In 2012, chloral hydrate went off the market in the United States. Before then, the maximum recommended dose was one gram, not to exceed two grams in a twenty-four-hour period. The recommendation, furthermore, was to wean patients slowly from the drug, so as to prevent delirium. But for Pappenheim, these heavy doses were alternated with days when she got no chloral at all. They drove her mad. Her behavior became bizarre. In the middle of a conversation, she'd run off and climb a tree. She got increasingly upset, and sometimes in those sunset somnolent states, she didn't want to play along, didn't want to talk. "I had to work hard, pleading, chatting, and especially repeating the stereotype formula: 'And there was a boy' [in English] until she suddenly 'caught on' and began to speak." He said "*sandwüste*"—German for sandy desert—and she told a story about the desert "and so on." Sometimes her storytelling didn't relieve her tension, and then Breuer was "obliged" to drug her.

When he was there, the chloral led her to a state of "euphoria"; when he was not, she felt despair and anxiety. Pappenheim was a person of enormous will and determination, and despite the drugs, despite her unhappiness at Inzersdorf, she habituated herself to life in the sanitarium. She began to assist the doctors, volunteering to help some "poor, sick" patients. There was a large Newfoundland dog on the premises, and she befriended and took charge of it: "And it was splendid to see how when once her darling attacked a cat, this frail girl took a whip in her left hand and beat off the huge animal to rescue its victim." For six weeks, during the hottest time of the summer, she refused to drink.

Through all July, she lived on fruit. But one evening, during her storytelling session, she recalled an upsetting vision: she remembered seeing her maid's dog, "the revolting animal," drinking out of someone's water glass. Immediately after giving voice to this memory, she lifted the glass of water beside her and drank. After that story was told, Pappenheim's inhibition against drinking water vanished.

This is the breakthrough moment, the proof of the talking cure's efficacy. "Hysterics suffer from reminiscences." Breuer's explanation is that the memory of the dog drinking was repressed and lurking under the surface of her consciousness. Once it was spoken, the anxiety around the memory dissolved, it no longer needed to be enacted physically, and it vanished—the infectious material was removed, the chimney was unblocked, and she could act and speak freely. It's *the* moment when Pappenheim's invention, the "talking cure," is moved into a theory of the mind: That the repressed information lurking below can be brought up, and once brought up, can be faced and resolved.

There are other potential explanations for her sudden ability to drink. Maybe the storytelling just distracted her from her fears, and in the momentary distraction she lifted the glass? But Breuer's interpretation has held ground since the 1880s. She dredged up the memory, and through telling the story, she unburdened herself of the symptom. It must have been thrilling for him to witness, and feel he'd grasped it, the way horror lurks under the surface of the mind and can breach, like a deep-sea monster, and dissolve in the sunlight of awareness.

Back and forth, Breuer went, night after night, week after week, from Vienna to Inzersdorf. If he was at the sanitarium at sunset in June—nine p.m., more or less—what time of night did he get back home? He must have missed dinner parties, theater performances, operas, and concerts.

Current scholarship suggests that it's doubtful that Mathilde Breuer threatened to kill herself over his trips out to Inzersdorf—but I bet his wife didn't like his spending so much time with a pretty young woman.

It's hard to tell the precise sequence of events from *Studies*—in my cluttered account above, I've smoothed out timelines and speculated motives and done so for narrative clarity—but sometime after the breakthrough with the glass of water, Breuer stopped visiting Pappenheim. He went on vacation with his family, for a few weeks, to the country. Breslauer attempted to employ Breuer's techniques, sitting by Pappenheim in the evening, saying, "There was a boy," but now she wouldn't play the game. He gave her chloral. When Breuer returned, Pappenheim was "wretched," "ill-tempered," and "malicious." Her stories were just "her hallucinations and . . . what had irritated her over the previous days." These hallucinations were, according to Breuer, "formulae of phantasy rather than being elaborated into poetic creations." She was eventually released from Inzersdorf in August and allowed to return to Vienna.

In her absence, Recha had moved to a new apartment in the center city. It's not clear precisely when Recha moved—in *Studies*, Breuer writes the spring of 1881, and I wonder if they put away Bertha in part to facilitate this move. The building to which Recha moved at Neuer Markt 7 is gone, but Neuer Markt 6, across the street, is still there, a big white apartment building, a much bigger building than the old one, with (I imagine) a much smaller apartment than the one they'd rented in the Alsergrund. It's unclear whether or not Wilhelm lived with Recha in the new place. Bertha was miserable there. After a week, she went back to Inzersdorf. But that didn't work, either, and in October she was in Vienna again.

Breuer looked for a good place for her. He wrote to Robert Binswanger, the director of the Bellevue Sanitarium in Kreuzlingen, Switzerland, one of the fanciest sanitariums in Europe, asking if he could move Pappenheim there. But there was no room. In November, Breuer wrote Binswanger again, saying that the need to move her was urgent: "An attempt is being made at this very moment to acclimatize the patient to her family; she is—or at least was—undergoing crucial convalescence. The attempt will probably fail."[33] By December, according to Breuer's notes, Pappenheim "was agitated, excitable, depressed and out of humor." Hanukkah came, and she took another turn for the worse—she was plagued by horrible memories and was "dominated by extreme anxiety." The talking cure helped her through the holiday; after telling Breuer her stories, Pappenheim felt "considerable relief at the end of this series," and that's it, nothing more of Breuer's original record.

The contemporaneous notes break off in the middle of a page, and what comes next in *Studies* is the miracle cure, the part of Breuer's story that is most unbelievable, and the part for which there are no supporting documents whatsoever.

PART TWO

Imagining Hysteria

8

For most of the last seventy years, the dominant notion in medicine and in academia has been that the disease that afflicted Bertha Pappenheim did not exist, that Josef Breuer was treating a medical mirage.

"Where have they gone, the hysterics of yesteryear," asked the psychologist and philosopher Jacques Lacan, referring to the characters in *Studies in Hysteria*. "Those marvelous women, the Anna Os, the Emmy von Ns?"

The most current medical answer to Lacan's question seems to be: neurologists' offices, FND clinics, and please, please don't call them "hysterical."

———•———

Since ancient times, physicians have been able to describe the difference between seizures caused by epilepsy and seizures of the kind Lacan's "marvelous women" suffered. The former kind of seizures are caused by identifiable electrical storms in the brain; the latter kind have no immediately discernible somatic neuropathology. The ones without a clear biological correlate are sometimes called functional seizures, and sometimes psychogenic non-epileptic seizures, or PNES, and they present differently from epileptic events.

Functional seizures tend to involve the thrusting of the pelvis (in the old scientific literature, you see illustrations of women forming themselves into hoops), they last longer than epileptic seizures do, and patients having these kind of seizures (unlike those with epilepsy) tend to weep. For decades, in hospitals and medical schools, physicians—both neurologists and psychiatrists—have behaved as if patients suffering from functional seizures are not actually sick. The following capsule narrative comes from a 2021 article in the journal *Epilepsy and Behavioral Reports*:

> A grand rounds speaker showed videos of patients with epilepsy and contrasted them with patients with functional seizures. One of the patients with functional seizures fell out of bed—and the room roared with laughter. A physician seated behind me muttered, "These patients will do anything to sell their episodes."

This kind of contempt has been around for centuries.

In the eighteenth century, Alexander Pope wrote mockingly about women "who give th' hysteric, or poetic fit." While epilepsy is near universally understood as something that is observably *happening* to patients, functional seizures are too often thought of as something patients are *doing*. People with functional seizures are often told that nothing is "really" wrong with them. In a modern hospital, you can chart an epileptic seizure on an electroencephalogram, but a functional seizure will show a normal EEG. Interestingly, about 10 to 15 percent of patients with functional seizures also suffer from epilepsy.[34]

Functional seizures are one of the many kinds of symptoms that are categorized under the umbrella term of FND. Modern medical researchers describe different categories of FND, including functional seizures, movement FND (sometimes "functional movement disorder," or FMD; for instance, patients who suffer involuntary muscle contractions called dystonia, or who suffer tremors, limb weakness, or have trouble walking, swallowing, or speaking), and sensory FND (for instance, patients who go blind or lose sensation down one side of their body). There is a spectrum of related brain-mind-body disorders that are classified as functional—symptoms related to pain, fatigue, or intestinal distress—but many of those are, medically speaking, categorized separately from functional neurological symptoms; they're not symptoms neurologists treat.

Whatever the name for these conditions, they remain a problem that crosses cultures and history, and the study of these conditions is as old as medicine itself. Aretaeus of Cappadocia, a Greek physician of the second century AD, described the condition the way I was taught to think of it as an undergraduate, when I was told that "hysteria" was a silly old myth, an imaginary disease of women, believed to be caused by a wandering womb:

> In the middle of the flanks of women lies the womb, a female viscous, closely resembling an animal; for it is moved of itself hither and thither in the flanks, also upwards in a direct line to below the cartilage of the thorax, and also obliquely to the right or to the left, either to the liver or the spleen; and it likewise is subject to prolapsus downwards, and, in a word, it is altogether erratic. It delights, also, in fragrant smells, and advances towards them; and it has an aversion to fetid smells and flees from them; and, on the whole the womb is like an animal within an animal.

If the womb wandered into the eyes, so the classical theory went, the patient went blind. If it went to the legs, the legs spun out of control. Paralysis. Paresis. Unusual walking patterns. If the womb sidled up toward the mouth, it caused *globus hystericus*, the feeling of a lump in the throat, a common functional symptom that at its most severe can interfere with speaking and swallowing.

The term "hysteria" comes from the Greek word *hystera*, meaning "uterus," and medical conversation around hysteria has for centuries been tied up with hatred of women and fear of their sex and their sexual desires and their longing for independence. To this day, according to the higher estimates, as many as 70 percent of diagnosed FND patients are women.[35] The condition in the Middle Ages was sometimes seen as divine possession: St. Teresa of Ávila is the patron saint of hysterics. (In *Studies*, Freud and Breuer still refer to the symptoms of hysteria as "stigmata.") It was also seen as demonic possession. In 1602, Mary Glover, a fourteen-year-old girl in London, became "speechles and blynde." Her hand became paralyzed, then her arm, then the left side of her body. She suffered "fittes" in which "she was turned rounde as a whoop." She seemed "dumbe, blynde, and senseless," yet her hands performed strange pantomimes, like she was shooting a bow or an arrow.[36]

Two flags that contemporary neurologists use for describing symptoms of FND are "incongruence" and "inconsistency"—that is, the symptoms don't correspond to any obvious patterns seen in other neurological conditions, and they don't always correspond to each other. A case of functional paralysis can move from one side of the face to the other. A patient who is unable to walk can break into a run. And yet over time, the patients—whether Mary Glover in Elizabethan England, or Bertha Pappenheim in Freud's Vienna, or patients in the Mayo Clinic's FND treatment center today—all seem to experience the same variants of incongruent and inconsistent problems.

One of the first appearances of the term "hysteria" in English literature is spoken not by a woman but by King Lear, who upon being betrayed by his daughter Regan cries out: "Oh, how this mother swells up toward my heart! / *Hysterica passio*, down, thou climbing sorrow!" It's as if the King has a wandering womb, and he seeks to command it to stay down below. So many FND patients still describe it this same way that King Lear did: a force emerging from within the body, occupying their body, overpowering their body.

Recent scholarship argues that the Greeks didn't really have a fully formed concept of "hysteria" as an illness—it only became so by Shakespeare's day, and by then the idea of a wandering womb was on its way out. "Their misfortune does not only proceed from a great indisposition of the body, for the *mind* is still more disordered," wrote the seventeenth-century physician Thomas Sydenham. Jean-Martin Charcot, the great nineteenth-century French neurologist, wanted to set a more specific, modern, physiological definition. Charcot, the "Napoleon of the neuroses," kept a pet monkey and put on strange, dramatic, public exhibitions of his female patients' conditions, performances that many historians have dismissed as histrionic and sadistic, but that many neurologists still regard as the foundational work of their discipline. In the early 1880s, Charcot characterized hysteria by its stages and symptoms and hypothesized that it was caused by dynamic lesions in the brain and nervous system. But he never found those dynamic lesions.

Doctors are now looking for the kinds of neurological, biological correlates that Charcot was looking for—and among the leaders in this neuroscientific investigation is Dr. David L. Perez, of Harvard and Massachusetts General Hospital.

Perez, today in his forties, is qualified as both a neurologist and psychiatrist. He started his FND clinic at Mass General in 2014, under the auspices of the neurology and psychiatry departments, but soon his clinic was upgraded to its own FND unit. Perez has many more patients referred to him than he can comfortably manage (the waits for an appointment can be long), and his research is generously underwritten by the US government. He is bespectacled and bearded, and pink-skinned and youthful, and has all the drive, energy, and intensity he must have had as a straight-A undergraduate.

"What kind of doctor am I?" he says. "I'm a brain doctor."

He is a man on a mission: through his work on FND, he seeks to "bridge the great divide" between neurology and psychiatry, to link, in Oliver Sacks's words, "the universe of human meaning and of natural science." Patients who come to Perez's clinic generally arrive via referrals from neurologists: they've already been diagnosed with FND (or are suspected by other neurologists of having the condition). At their first meeting, Perez engages each patient in a ninety-minute interview, and for each patient, he aims to confirm the diagnosis and to work collaboratively with the patient to develop a treatment plan.

"The patient-centered treatment plan is essentially developed through the neuro-psychiatric perspective," he told me.

All kinds of people develop FND, busy professionals, the chronically ill, the young, the old, men and women, and each of Dr. Perez's patients requires a specific combination of treatments—some need talk therapy, some need speech therapy, some need physical therapy, some need pharmaceuticals for their concurrent neurological and psychiatric conditions. And each individualized program has a particular emphasis and set of goals. The first step is validation and empathic listening—Perez paying careful attention to the patient's story—and the second step is the patient's acceptance of the diagnosis and plan.

"It matters," Perez told me, "if the patient has never seen a psychiatrist and has been suffering subthreshold anxiety for decades, but is working 75 hours a week and is a lawyer and also has three children at home; versus a patient who has chronic suicidality, poor impulse control, active emotion dysregulation, and has been hospitalized over ten to fifteen times with a range of active mood, anxiety, and trauma-related symptoms." Two patients with nearly identical disabilities can, depending on their circumstances and experiences, have widely divergent needs. "Both of those kinds of individuals can have FND, and the symptoms can be the same, but the treatment plan has to be different."

———————

Kyla Kenney is in her middle forties and married, a mother of two, dark-haired, with a high forehead and strong jaw and intense brown eyes, a woman who has lived a life of trauma and psychological distress. She's a professional singer, a mezzo-soprano with a melancholic range and resonance, and she sings often at funerals, weddings, and masses in the Providence, Rhode Island, metropolitan area.

"I've been sick most of my life, with no answers," Kenney told me. She told her story to me with ease and humor, comfortably navigating the worst of it with disarming charm. Her childhood, as she recalls, was full of anxiety and fear. There was chronic illness in her family. Her first memory of terror is medical and nightmarish: doctors pushing tubes into her, and Kyla screaming out for her father.

In high school, a music teacher groomed her in a sexually predatory way, from the time she was fourteen until adulthood. ("My baby's legal!" he sang out on her eighteenth birthday.) She was first prescribed anti-anxiety medication and antidepressants when she was nineteen, and all through early adulthood she was plagued by mysterious complaints. For Kyla, her physical symptoms and her anxiety and depression run together in a vicious circle, feeding off one another. Her FND symptoms make her anxious and depressed, her anxiety and depression intensify her focus on her symptoms, and the symptoms are aggravated. She was a flautist in college, despite the tremors in her hands. "Playing the flute when you've got the shakes is not that easy," she told me. When she'd make mistakes, she'd laugh them off. The loss of control of her hands was anxiety provoking, and the anxiety led to difficulty breathing. She was given a host of diagnoses—from hypoglycemia to asthma—and referred to rheumatologists and endocrinologists, none of whom could resolve her persistent tremors and attacks.

"I wanted to die," Kenney told me frankly. "My prayer every night was please don't let me wake up." She remembers being twenty years old, lying on the floor, with her mother holding her, and Kyla crying out to God, "Why won't he take me now? I don't know why he makes me wake up. Why won't he just take me?"

"No one believed I was sick," she told me. "I wanted the pain to stop. I wanted the pain to die."

She was prescribed Ativan: one milligram in the morning, one milligram at noon, and one milligram at night, and then more as needed. "I followed doctors' instructions to a T," she told me. "I tried several times to stop the medication, but kept going back. My doctors continued prescribing it with no conversation." Over a twenty-five-year period, she became dependent on the drug. Kyla is exactly the kind of patient with whom physicians become impatient, and she knows it, and she told me stories of the way she was hustled in and out of their offices.

"I can't take your vitals," she remembers one doctor telling her. "You need to stop crying."

"Your tests came back fine," another said, "but because of your symptoms we will treat you."

"I can't help you," another doctor said, "you need to see a psychiatrist."

Once, with her heart racing above 150 beats per minute, she was dismissed from a physician's office and told to drive home on her own.

Through it all, she remained active, married, raising her kids, and working as a pianist, singer, and music teacher. The year 2016 was difficult for her. Several friends died. There was a flood in her house, and she lost her kitchen. She woke up on the morning of October 8, 2016, in pure, dark terror.

The room was spinning. She had no sense of balance. Her heart was racing, pounding like it wanted to escape her chest. She had what she describes as "internal shaking," like everything inside her was trembling, and the right side of her body was in a tremor. She had pain in her head—"I didn't even know that kind of migraine existed"—a pain that affected her entire face. She had tunnel vision. She had to get to work, to the church, to sing at a wedding, but she was incapacitated.

"The shaking became unreal," she told me, "like someone was just literally shaking my insides"—her description reminds me of classical and Shakespearean language about hysteria, an animal within the animal, a force rising up from within.

She drove to the wedding, with her eyes struggling to focus on the road. She sang, though even as she was singing, she could hear her heart pound. She had a terrible pain in her face, pressure all around her eyes and nose. Everyone around her dismissed her physical symptoms, she said, no one believed she was suffering anything more than her "typical anxiety."

Her primary care provider upped her anxiety and depression medications, to no effect. She saw a dentist, an eye doctor. One prescribed a series of antibiotics, on the theory that she had a sinus infection. Another prescribed guaifenesin, an expectorant usually not to be taken for more than nine days—he kept her on it for five months. At one point, a year into her suffering, a psychiatrist suggested she undergo shock therapy.

She decided—through much research, she told me, and with a strength she credits to her faith in God—that her problem was neurological, and she began calling every neurology department at every hospital in the Boston area, and that's how she ended up at Massachusetts General, in the office of Dr. Haatem Reda, a young neurologist, an intellectually curious and sympathetic man. It was December 2018.

She held out her right hand to Dr. Reda, and he examined her tremor. He asked her to lift her left hand beside her right, and to gently and systematically touch her left thumb to each finger of her left—her good—hand. As she pressed together the digits of her left hand, the tremor of her right hand vanished. In the language of neurology, the tremor showed variability and distractibility.

"What the heck, why is it stopping?" she asked.

"Don't be upset," Dr. Reda told her.

"No one believes me," Kenney complained.

"I believe you," he said. "There's a functional problem." The tremor's distractibility demonstrated that the nervous system of her right hand was intact. This was a rule-in diagnosis, a demonstration of the cause of her tremor. "This is a software issue, not a hardware issue," said Dr. Reda.

Unlike every physician she had seen up to that point, he diagnosed her tremor positively, not negatively, and not with guesswork, but with a clear and convincing test—he didn't tell her what she didn't have, he didn't tell her that her problem was psychological; instead he embarked on forging a story with her, forming a narrative with healing power.

"We have to retrain your brain." He told her to make an appointment with Dr. David Perez at the FND Unit.

Unfortunately, Perez had no openings until May. In the meantime, Dr. Reda directed Kyla to the book used in Perez's clinic, *Overcoming Functional Neurological Symptoms: A Five Areas Approach*. Reda recommended she take up an engrossing activity to distract her brain from its obsessions—Kyla decided to learn Italian. "Try to change the direction of your thoughts," was his advice, and then in May, finally, she had her first appointment at the FND clinic.

"I've never ever met a doctor like Dr. Perez," Kyla told me.

"Tell me," he said, as Kyla remembers it. "What's going on?"

At first, she couldn't answer. She was crying. She was shaking. Instead of describing her symptoms for Dr. Perez, she began to list all the things she once could do that she could do no longer.

Perez confirmed her diagnosis, and as he did so he helped her construct a narrative of her own illness. "He explained how the brain worked, the amygdala, the insula, all the anatomy of my brain," Kenney told me. "I was crying hysterically pretty much the whole time." But the anatomical descriptions helped her. "If I understood, if I was able to visualize what's going on, I was more able to work with the problem." She began to describe her fears. "One of the biggest symptoms I had was sheer fear," she told me. When she complained to Perez about the way her symptoms assailed her, he said, in Kenney's words, "Of course that's going to happen. Your nervous system is revved up, so you're not getting the right signals. It's not functioning properly, but we're going to work with you."

"Never have I had any doctor that compassionate," Kenney told me. "All you need is someone to say, 'I get it,'" Kenney told me. "'It must be scary,' 'you must feel alone,' 'I've got you,' 'we'll figure this out,' 'there's hope.'"

They discussed a treatment plan together: cognitive behavioral therapy, occupational therapy, and simple, calm diaphragmatic breathing. "I had tried to meditate before," Kenney told me. "But I came to the conclusion that it was something my brain just couldn't do." Perez had her begin very simply, just one minute at a time. Over the weeks, months, and years, she developed a meditation practice, one that helps her enormously. "It started calming me down enough in order to focus. And it taught me that it's okay to take ten minutes of the day to focus on myself."

She was assigned to Julie MacLean for an eleven-week course of occupational therapy. "What does your day look like?" MacLean asked Kenney on their first meeting. They began to work on pragmatics. Making sure she got out of bed, that she showered by noon. That she ate. They built Kenney a schedule. Instead of dwelling on negative thoughts, Kenney could practice Italian. She could try to work out a new piece on the piano. She could bake something—Kenney likes to bake.

"When I have a physical symptom," Kenney told me, "that is what my brain is doing: thinking about that specific physical symptom. Thinking about how bad it is makes it worse. When I was doing things, at least, my focus was on some other activity."

MacLean worked to help Kenney find concrete ways to distract herself out of the grips of anxious, ruminative thought patterns. At one point, she gave her patient a bunch of different candies and asked her to pick out the one that tasted worst to her—Super Sour Warheads, it turned out—and now Kenney carries them with her, and when she begins to find herself in obsessively bleak thoughts, she puts one in her mouth, and it shocks her out of her old thought patterns. Simultaneously, she was working with Ellen Godena, a social worker expert in treating FND with cognitive behavioral therapy. She met Dr. Perez on May 15 and started working with Godena on May 17.

"I started telling her all about how horrible my week was, and all the awful things I'd experienced, and she just cut me off. She said, 'Okay, rough week. What are we going to do about it?'"

One day, Kenney came in sobbing.

"I couldn't stop crying because things were so terrible, and she just looked at me. No therapist has ever done this with me before. She just looked at me, and said, 'I can't help you until you stop and realize what we need to do here.'"

Godena worked with Kenney on concrete ways of coping with her symptoms and her unhappiness. Together, they filled out a form to better understand Kenney's vomiting and nausea. Kenney shared this with me. Under PHYSICAL SYMPTOMS, she wrote: *shaking, hands and feet, feeling hot and cold, feeling like I'm blacking out.* Under EMOTIONS, Kenney wrote: *fear, anger/frustration, lonely, tired, defeated.* Under AUTOMATIC THOUGHTS, she wrote *life ends and there's no stopping that,* and *here we go again.* Under COGNITIVE DISTORTIONS, Kenney wrote: *Magnifications.* The chart helped her see how her thoughts intensified her symptoms.

Still, sitting at a funeral, getting ready to sing, Kenney can find herself in old bad habits—gripped by depressed, anxious ruminations, imagining someone she loves in the coffin, imagining the end of everything she loves. But before her tremors begin, before she becomes incapacitated, she'll take a Super Sour Warhead, and she'll try to find a new set of thoughts.

"My brain is like a big field," Kenney told me, "and all my negative thoughts have been walking down this one area. So there's a beautiful path to all the negativity, because my brain knows that path so well." The path is marked as if with billboards. "WE'RE GOING TO DIE, or THIS WON'T WORK OUT WELL. That path is worn and clear. Now, I'm trying to create a new path in a different part of my brain. A path that's saying, 'everything is OK,' or 'life doesn't have to be this way.'"

The work is not easy. I spoke with Kenney in the summer of 2022, four years after she had begun treatment at Mass General.

"It's only in the last six months that I feel like I've really come out of it," she told me. "I'll hear myself laughing and it'll shock me—I can't believe it! Is that me, *laughing*? Holy crap! My family makes fun of me because I'm super sensitive. Before when they made fun, I'd get really upset. I'd say, 'You don't understand.' I would turn it into a big emotional argument. But now I sit there and laugh."

This, for Kenney, is the opposite of FND: laughing together with the people who love her. Her symptoms afflict her less violently, her life is happier, and Kenney is the protagonist of a story in which she has taken control.

"It's a bit peculiar," Dr. Perez told me, "that there are two medical specialties for the same organ."

The organ he has in mind is the brain, and the specialties are psychiatry and neurology. His treatment and research into FND operates in both specialties simultaneously, and he sees the mind, brain, and body holistically (the phrase he finds himself using, he told me, is "brain-mind-body").

"We think of functional neurological disorder as a network-based disturbance," Perez explained.

Contemporary neuropsychiatry conceives of the brain as operating through several interrelated networks, different sets of different parts of the brain working together to bring about different cognitive tasks. In the brain there is a motor planning network, and a network to figure out what's important in the world (called the "salience network"), and a network for our internal mind-wondering and self-reflections (called the "default mode network"). FND patients don't suffer any overt structural damage to any particular brain part—neither to the amygdala, the little node deep in the brain central to much of our threat and salience processing, nor to the right temporoparietal junction, which is associated with the reorienting of attention and performing calculations that contribute to the sense of self agency (that when a person moves, that person perceives themselves as the author of those movements). But in images of FND patients' brains of the kind produced in Perez's lab, researchers can observe irregularities that suggest unusual network connectivity.

For Perez, FND is "a multi-network brain disorder." Scans of his patients show abnormalities both "within a given network and across different networks." The working hypothesis is that in a patient like Kyla, threat/emotional processing, other bodily information processing, and motor control get somehow scrambled, causing breakdowns in movement and in perception. Altered feedback cycles and feed-forward cycles within the brain—information reinforcing itself in unhealthy patterns—can cause problems like Kyla's limb shaking. The goal in treatment is to retrain the patient's brain so it can relearn the proper pathways. In this way, FND doctors are reconceiving thought, emotion, and even human agency—the ability of a person's mind to control their own body—as biological, physiological, and psychological. As Perez explained it to me: the brain shapes our life experiences, and our life experiences shape our brains. Bridging the gap between psychiatry and neurology means challenging our basic preconceptions about mind, brain, and body, and about health and disease.

"I think what's most exciting about FND," says Dr. Perez, "is that because it sits right in between neurology and psychiatry it very clearly challenges these artificial distinctions between physical health and mental health that are pervasive in society and are very problematic. Ultimately mental health is physical health. I see patients who can't walk, who can't speak, who drag a leg, who have convulsions. Yes, there are cognitive, affective, and perceptual disturbances in this population, and these disturbances are important, but my patients' symptoms are every bit as real as patients with stroke, Parkinson's disease, and multiple sclerosis. Every bit as real, and every bit as brain-based."

Doubters may still want to call FND a "waste-basket" diagnosis, but that's inaccurate. There's variation within Perez's patients' suffering (seizures, tremors, gait disorders), and his patients struggle with a variety of comorbidities (anxiety, disease, depression, and trauma), but similar variations can occur in other neuropsychiatric diagnoses, like autism or migraine. FND is a rule-in diagnosis. A physician can see if a tremor is distractable, if a patient who can't walk can run, and—with a test called "Hoover's sign"—if an apparently limp leg can apply force. FND is demonstrable within a clinical setting. Contemporary physicians who doubt the actuality of the condition are expressing more clearly than anything else their prejudices. They are stuck in old ideas, dualistic notions, the belief that the mind is separate from the body, that "hysteria doesn't exist," or that "conversion disorder" is just a psychosomatic expression of repressed desire.

In the interpretations and reinterpretations of Bertha Pappenheim's illness, we see a compendium of such prejudices, a 150-year history of very smart people unwilling to accept a basic fact: that mind, brain, and body are of a complicated piece, and that, given such complexity, there will be breakdowns. Our struggle to understand Pappenheim is our struggle to understand ourselves.

9

Hailey Hooper-Gray's story begins with pain, an obliterating pain. Her teenaged years were interrupted by surgeries. In 2016, when she was fifteen, a mass was discovered in her knee—initially the doctors wondered if it was cancerous, but it turned out to be a cyst, and she required two surgeries, one to remove the cyst, and another to repair the cartilage underneath. By the time I first spoke with her, five years later, she would be looking forward to her sixteenth surgery.

Hailey lives with her mother in southwest Colorado, in Lake City, a small paradisal town whose school's sports teams are called the Fourteeners, for the fourteen-thousand-foot mountains that surround the village. Her parents are divorced but still friendly, her mother a school aide, working with learning-disabled kids, her father works construction in the nearby town of Crested Butte. Hailey at seventeen was an ambitious kid.

"I was kind of a badass," she told me. She was taking extra classes in school and AP classes, and driven to attend college, dreaming of becoming a writer.

She has a round, cheerful, pretty face, glasses, pale skin, rosy cheeks, and a matter-of-fact manner, and she's smart and enormously expressive, and she told me her horror story with the urgency and seriousness of a born storyteller, and without a trace of self-pity.

Hailey was born with a deformity to her sternum, a mild deformity, as she understood most of her life. "My chest looked weird," she told me, but it didn't cause any serious problems. But in 2017, not long after the surgery on her knee, a CT scan revealed that the deformity would become dangerous if it were not attended to. Soon she was visiting pulmonologists and cardiologists and surgeons. She was prescribed a Nuss bar procedure—a metal bar to be inserted into her torso, to correct the shape of her ribcage.

"Sort of like braces for your chest," she said to me. A Nuss bar is the largest piece of metal that doctors put into a human being.

Hailey was told that the Nuss bar procedure was the most painful surgery performed at Children's Hospital Colorado in Aurora, and one of the most difficult from which to recover, and for her the surgery turned out to be a disaster, and its consequences and sequelae were Hailey's entry into a new state of existence. From the straight-A student, playing sports and running for student government, she would become a cripple, unable to talk, unable to walk, unable to eat, suffering strange seizures, with a condition that seemed inconsistent and incongruent with her injuries, a condition that, for a year of her life, no doctor would treat, and most would not accept as real.

After the Nuss bar was implanted, Hailey was given an epidural to manage her pain. The epidural was prescribed for the first three days of her recovery, but its needle was poorly placed.

"The entire left side of my body stopped functioning, basically, and the left side of my face drooped like I was having a stroke," she told me. "The medication was traveling up my spine and they caught it within minutes of it reaching my respiratory system and shutting down my respiratory system and killing me."

The needle was detached, and Hailey's body returned to ordinary function, but she had insufficient medication to dull her overwhelming pain. She soldiered through it. On July 30, only three weeks after the surgery, Hailey went off to summer camp, ready to resume her ordinary life. But she could not return to normal. By early August, she was back in the ICU in Children's Hospital Colorado, suffering sepsis. Her body had rejected the Nuss bar. In the course of two weeks, she underwent five surgical procedures. She was attached to a wound vac machine: two holes on either side of her chest, with what Hailey described to me as a "power washer hose" cleaning out her insides.

"Instead of stitching me back up, they basically took this piece of foam, they shoved it into the wound, and put a suction cup on that, and then sealed it all up with medical grade Saran wrap."

Her wounds were so deep that when the dressings were changed, she could see down into her ribs. She was on blood thinners, and one night suffered a grotesquely bloody nose. "Have you ever seen like a really, really bad horror film where someone's arm gets chopped off?" It was like that, she told me.

She went home in a wheelchair, attached to her wound vac machine, dependent on an oxygen tank—but come the change in seasons, Hailey insisted on going back to school, wheelchair, wound vac, and all. "We'd be writing in English class and the machine would be making its sucking noises and everyone would just look up at me." This was the beginning of her junior year of high school. She planned to take a 0-hour AP biology class, before the rest of the school day began. She ran for class president. "When I gave my class president candidate speech," she wrote me in an email, "I got up out of my wheelchair, let my wound vac tubes and oxygen tubes fall down by my side and held myself up by resting on the podium. I then proceeded to list off some of the most influential people and thinkers of the last century that all had some form of disorder or disability. Stevie Wonder, Stephen Hawking, Franklin D. Roosevelt, Helen Keller." She did not win the election.

At the same time as she was recovering from the Nuss bar trauma, Hailey was afflicted, coincidentally, by a scourge of ovarian cysts. Whether these were related to the earlier cysts in her knee, no one knows. But they were horribly painful and persistent, cysts popping inside of her from August all through fall into the winter, and then in January she had to return to Aurora to have another procedure on her chest. The Nuss bar had to be stabilized.

She was recovering from that chest surgery when, on February 17, she suffered yet another hemorrhagic ovarian cyst—and that was when Hailey broke down, when something inside her shifted. In an emergency

room in Gunnison, Colorado, the FND began to present itself. Like
Mary Glover in sixteenth-century England, like Bertha Pappenheim in
nineteenth-century Vienna, like Kyla Kenney across the country from
her, Hailey had a strange force inside her: an illness that began to move
within her, like an animal within an animal.

Her symptoms were inconsistent and incongruent with any physiological ailment, and the physicians who saw her, both neurologists and
psychiatrists, didn't know what to do. For the doctors in the ER in Gunnison, her symptoms were all in her head. They were not real. In the ER,
Hailey was vomiting from the pain, then dry heaving, then passing out.
She kept on reviving, dry heaving, and passing out again. As Hailey tells
it, her doctors insisted there was no actual problem.

Her mother, Karen Hooper, told me that an ER doctor "called me into
his office and said your daughter's not even passing out—she's faking. He
told me that I was enabling her."

Again, this is Hailey's telling, but this kind of treatment of FND patients, particularly teenagers, is not unusual within most contemporary
medical settings. Here's another one of those capsule narratives from the
same article in the journal *Epilepsy and Behavior Reports*:

> A teenage girl was brought to our emergency room experiencing events
> that were suspicious for functional seizures. After watching her for 30 sec-
> onds, the attending lifted the girl's arm above her face and dropped it.
> Seeing that she diverted her arm, thus not hitting her face, the attending
> announced to the room, "Ok, honey you can stop now," and walked out of
> the room.

In all the epistemologies of all the hospitals and clinics and emergency
rooms that Hailey Hooper-Gray visited in the first years of her suffering,
her illness was seen as an act.

The doctors needed a physical, biological explanation for Hailey's
symptoms, but there wasn't one. One physician began to suspect that
Hailey was in fact pregnant and would not believe her when she said

she had never yet had sex. Despite her fainting, despite her dry heaving, she was discharged. Her symptoms made the drive home to Lake City impossible.

Her fainting continued all the way home, along winding mountain roads—fainting sometimes every minute, and then reviving. From a friend's house in Gunnison, Karen Hooper called the doctors at Children's Hospital, who wanted to check on the status of her Nuss bar. But it was in the middle of a snowstorm, Aurora was five hours away, and there was no way Karen was going to drive that distance in that weather with a child whose body seemed completely out of control, a child who when she fainted sometimes fell backward and began choking on her tongue. So it was back to the emergency room in Gunnison, and then, once the snowstorm had passed, a four-hour ambulance ride to Aurora. It was awaiting this ambulance ride that Hailey had her first full-on seizure, the lengthy, crying, body-wracking seizure so typical of people with her condition.

"The most terrifying thing I've ever experienced," said Hailey. "It felt like someone who is a lot stronger than me like physically grabbed me, and was like taking me away, and trying to like kidnap me or something. I was trying to fight back against that, but they are so much stronger than me. I'm not able to make any difference, and so then there's this place where you're going, 'Oh my gosh what's happening to my body?' And you try and you try, and my legs and my arms and everything is shaking, and you're telling yourself to be still—and still it's not happening, and then you realize that there's nothing you can do."

This is when the doctors began to describe her symptoms as psychosomatic, as manifestations of PTSD and anxiety. Both Karen and Hailey were confused. "It was like they were saying she was crazy," Karen said.

Or as Hailey put it, the doctors believed "that it wasn't something that was happening to my body, but that it was something that was happening to my mind, separate from my brain. That it was not a neurological symptom, that it was a psychiatric symptom."

She spent some time on the medical wards of Children's Hospital Colorado. She lost her ability to speak, and then her ability to swallow. These losses were transient. She could talk, and then she couldn't, then she could again. She could swallow, and then she couldn't, then she could. They tried to transfer her to the psychiatric wards, but the psychiatrists didn't know what to do with her. The attending physician said, in Hailey's words, "This program is for patients who are going to hurt themselves or hurt someone else. That is not you. I'm not saying you don't have anxiety and PTSD, but you don't need to be in a psych ward."

Just as most neurologists are not happy treating psychiatric disorders, so most psychiatrists are not happy trying to get people out of wheel-chairs, or helping them relearn how to swallow and speak. Patients struggle with the stigma of a psychiatric diagnosis—a diagnosis that does not match their experience of their symptoms—and mental health professionals struggle with the mystery of FND. She was discharged, according to Hailey, still symptomatic and without being offered any treatment options. "The diagnosis I got from neurology wasn't even clear," she told me. "It used the terms somatoform disorder and conversion disorder interchangeably and then way down in the fine print mentioned FND." Back in Lake City, Hailey was already seeing a psychotherapist and a physical therapist for the anxiety and trauma surrounding her surgeries. Those doctors didn't know what to do with her new symptoms. There was nothing left to prescribe for her.

For her part, Hailey didn't believe her symptoms were purely psychological. "I knew what intense anxiety felt like, and this felt very different." For Hailey, there was no problem with her mind, no problem with her loss of rationality—no deep dark hidden trauma she was failing to express. It was purely, in her experience, a physical problem. Her body was out of her control.

In March, she met with her teachers, hoping to reenroll in school. She was as ambitious as ever. But her AP biology teacher tried to dissuade her, and soon, all the teachers in the room tried to dissuade her. "They thought the work-load was too much, and my symptoms were so unmanageable that they suggested I drop out." By mid-March, she was at home without schooling and her inexplicable, seemingly incurable symptoms only got worse. Paralysis set in, from the neck down. Hailey, always so verbal, always so active, could communicate only by blinking, once for yes, and twice for no, three times for "I love you," four times for "fuck this," and five for "help." But that, too, would come and go over time, and there were some days when she was bedridden with pain, and some days where she could go to the kitchen and bake cupcakes and pies.

10

If you look in the *DSM-5*, the bible of psychiatry, you'll see two alternate names for the same condition, the twin diagnoses that Hailey Hooper-Gray received: "conversion disorder" and "FNSD." (Though psychiatry puts that "S" for "symptom" between "neurological" and "disorder," most neurologists prefer not to, and so the common neurological term is FND.) These are all designations for the same illness, but they imply different understandings. "Conversion disorder" goes back to Freud and psychoanalysis, implying a psychic struggle around the mental repression and physical expression of a traumatic memory. FND, or FNSD, emerges from neurology and attempts to place the same symptoms in a neuropsychiatric context.

In the psychoanalytic understanding, the talking cure is an attempt to purge the patient of the hidden traumatic memory, a memory the patient is not even aware of. In the neuropsychiatric understanding, the treatment involves the development of a narrative, not psychoanalytic but based in emerging brain science, an understanding between patient and doctor that moves toward retraining the body.

"Conversion disorder" and "hysteria" are virtually synonymous, and this can make patients tremendously uneasy with the terms. Siri Hustvedt, in her memoir *The Shaking Woman, or a History of My Nerves*, remembers receiving the diagnosis of "conversion disorder" and thinking:

My fit had been *hysterical.* This ancient word had been mostly dropped from the current medical discourse and replaced by *conversion disorder,* but lying beneath the newer term is the old one, haunting it like a ghost.

Hustvedt's language seems poetic, but it's precise. Here's Oliver Sacks, in his book *Hallucinations,* discussing "hysteria" and "conversion disorder" in regard to the Pappenheim case:

Severe stress accompanied by inner conflict can readily induce in some people a splitting of consciousness, with varied sensory and motor symptoms, including hallucinations. (The old name for this condition was hysteria; it is now called conversion disorder.) This seemed to be the case with Anna O., the remarkable patient described by Freud and Breuer in *Studies on Hysteria.*

Here's a list of symptoms of "conversion disorder" from a 2010 paper on dizziness coauthored by the Mayo Clinic psychiatrist Jeffrey P. Staab (he now is the chair of the Department of Psychiatry at Mayo and prefers the term FND), and this list is almost identical to the list of symptoms in the preface of *Studies*:

Paralysis/paresis, behavioral (non-epileptic) seizures, unusual walking patterns, unusual motor activities, and sensory disturbances, including hearing or vision (i.e., sudden blindness, deafness, or muteness).[37]

The shifting names reveal our shifting attitudes and assumptions about the illness, our evolving understanding and misunderstanding of something we don't quite grasp. If you look backward through successive editions of the *DSM,* you can unearth the genealogy of diagnostic terms, and see the separations. In 1992 and 1994, the condition was called "conversion disorder"; in 1968, it was "hysterical neurosis, conversion type"; in 1952, it was "conversion reaction." If you go half a century further back than that, you start to see the word "functional"; in 1913, Freud's disciple Ernest Jones declared that psychoanalytic understanding of hysterical conversion had erased "the now antiquated expression of 'functional nervous disorder.'" Today, the word "functional" has returned, meaning the same thing it used to mean. A 2022 *Nature Reviews Neurology* article describes Thomas Sydenham's seventeenth-century diagnosis of "hysteria" as "a historical term for FND." For centuries, we've been running around in circles.

For almost as long as there have been doctors interested in this condition, there have been others who doubted whether it existed at all. In 1878, Charles Lasègue, a French physician, called hysteria "a wastepaper basket of medicine where one throws otherwise unemployed symptoms." Lasègue argued that "the definition of hysteria never has been given and never will be." Soon after Lasègue wrote those words, Charcot began his attempts at a clinical, neurological definition of hysteria, but even as he was searching fruitlessly for those dynamic lesions in the brain, his rival Hippolyte Bernheim argued that Charcot's patients were only performing symptoms that had been suggested to them under hypnosis, and that Charcot's hospital at Salpêtrière was "a culture of hysteria."

Charcot and Bernheim represent the poles of an age-old argument: for one, this is a biological phenomenon; for the other, a cultural and psychological one—on the one hand, real, on the other, imaginary. Freud stepped into the middle of this divide with his psychoanalytic vision: that the problems were psychosomatic, the mind operating on the body, the unexpressed trauma converting symbolically to physical symptoms.

In 1907, hysteria was the central preoccupation of brain doctors. Lecturing at Harvard, Pierre Janet said: "I am convinced that in our times, every well-educated man wishing to have an opinion on philosophical problems ought to know something of this singular mental disease." The next year, 1908, the Harvard neurologist Bernard Sachs—a man who had studied with many of Janet's same teachers—declared in the *Journal of Nervous and Mental Diseases* that it was a psychiatric problem and advised that neurologists should give up the disease altogether and leave it to the analysts:

> While hysterical and neurasthenic patients, and others of the same order, are numerous enough, their ailments and sufferings are, after all, less important than the sufferings of those who are affected with various forms

of organic spinal disease, say tabes, lateral sclerosis, and the like. Let us [neurologists] try to do more for these patients . . . and not let us waste too much energy on what people call psychotherapy.

In the years after World War II, psychiatry like neurology turned its back on these patients. Psychiatrists began to question the disease's prevalence. Paul Chodoff in 1954 wrote that "hysterical phenomena undoubtedly occur less frequently than formerly." In the mid-1960s, the psychiatrist Ilza Veith announced "the near total disappearance" of the illness.

In 1965 in the *British Medical Journal*, the neurologist Eliot Slater published an influential paper insisting that as a disease, "hysteria" did not exist at all: either the symptoms could be explained by other psychological terms (Slater proposed "schizophrenia and malingering") or the symptoms would soon be explicable and definable neurological phenomena, that soon neurology would disclose the somatic source of every given patient's particular problem, be it paralysis or seizures or blindness. For Slater, the patients were either crazy, faking, or they had some nameable physical abnormality, as yet undetected.

No evidence has yet been offered that the patients diagnosed as suffering from "hysteria" are in medically significant terms anything more than a random selection. Attempts at rehabilitation of the syndrome . . . lead to mutually irreconcilable formulations, each of them determined by their terms of reference. The only thing that hysterical patients can be shown to have in common is that they are all patients. The malady of the wandering womb began as a myth, and a myth it yet survives. But, like all unwarranted beliefs which still attract credence, it is dangerous. The diagnosis of "hysteria" is a disguise for ignorance and a fertile source of clinical error. It is in fact not only a delusion but also a snare.

After Freud, Slater's essay is probably the single most influential piece of writing on the subject. "Hysteria" was erased—nonexistent, neither psychiatric nor neurological. A gulf in medicine appeared, between psychiatry and neurology, and the gulf was the unspeakable word, an epithet.

What was once the central obsession of brain and mind medicine became an absence.

Where had hysteria gone?

In 1992, in their landmark book *Freud's Women*, Lisa Appignanesi and John Forrester speculated that "psychoanalysis killed off hysteria in a process of 'psychological gentrification' . . . that the introduction of psychological terms to the patient culture made the path of conversion, of speaking through the body, unavailable." Appignanesi and Forrester point to a study from the 1970s of the wards of the University of Vienna General Hospital, which suggested that "southern European immigrants displayed numerous old-fashioned hysterical symptoms, whereas indigenous Austrians were no longer capable of displaying such symptoms." For Appignanesi and Forrester and psychoanalytic writers of their era, to suffer these symptoms was to be somehow of a different culture, unsophisticated or backward. As Andrew Scull put it in his 2009 *Hysteria: The Biography*: "The old-fashioned somatic symptoms have become increasingly suspect among the more sophisticated classes, and hence most physicians observe that obvious conversion symptoms are rarely encountered, and, if at all, only among the uneducated and the lower strata."[38] Whether it's called "hysteria" or "conversion disorder," this condition has always been associated with the voiceless and the despised—women, immigrants, the poor. Scull wrote:

> Hysterical patients still present themselves in neurological waiting rooms, only to be turned away by doctors who have little interest in seeing or treating them. In the process, an age-old disorder becomes almost literally invisible. Shunned by the doctors they seek to consult to validate their symptoms, and defined out of existence by a pharmaceutically oriented psychiatry, . . . hysterics find themselves modern medicine's untouchables.

But even as Scull was writing, the ground was shifting.

Neurologists in the United States and the United Kingdom—groups centered around Mark Hallett at the NIH and Jon Stone in Edinburgh—were developing research interests in these patients who had been so long ignored. New technology allowed doctors who were taking a serious look at this ancient condition to offer evidence of its existence.

In 2000, the British neurologist Sean Spence published a breakthrough study in *The Lancet*, "Discrete Neurophysiological Correlates in Prefrontal Cortex During Hysterical and Feigned Disorder of Movement." Spence's study compared three sets of people: (1) patients with arms paralyzed with what Spence called a "hysteric" disorder; (2) people mimicking that condition, faking the disorder; and (3) people who could move their arms freely. Positron emission tomography (PET) scans demonstrated that the brains of the subjects with the "hysteric" disorder looked different than the brains of people in the other two groups. It wasn't that there were any lesions or breakdowns in the patients' brains—it was that there were intense connections between parts of the patients' brains, connections that the other two groups lacked.

In 2005, in the *Journal of Neurology, Neurosurgery, and Psychiatry*, Alan Carson and Jon Stone and several colleagues published an article affirming Spence's results. Carson and Stone used fMRI brain scanning to compare two groups: in one group, patients with FND, and in the other, actors who were imitating the same disorders. The patients' brains and the actors' brains showed notable differences, different patterns in network connections. Again, Carson and Stone didn't see breaks or lesions in the FND patients' brains—nothing in the hardware—but the patients' brains seemed to be somehow programmed wrong; they were making connections that didn't exist in the control group. "Is Hysteria Real? Brain Images Say Yes," ran a 2006 headline in the *New York Times*. As a 2020 *Scientific American* article put it: "Researchers have begun to understand what happens in the brains of patients with this enigmatic illness."

The biomechanics can be hard to grasp. Gone is the kind of old-fashioned mental map that sections off areas of the brain the way a butcher's chart describes cuts of beef: one place for fear, one place for thought, one place for movement. Instead, neurologists describe networks, complex, interweaving skeins of neural activity. Though there are sections of the somatosensory cortex that correspond with sensation in the fingers, there is no single brain region that has control for a given operation of the hand. Rather, there are patterns of connectivity, sensorimotor networks in the brain such that different brain regions work in concert to achieve different kinds of consciousness and control, prediction, reaction, and response. The default mode network, composed of the amygdala, the hippocampus, and the cingulate gyrus, comprises those parts of the brain that work together to govern emotion. The salience network—the amygdala, the anterior insula, and the dorsal anterior cingulate cortex—work together to identify what's important. When the salience network helps you determine the importance of the yellowjacket perched on the rim of your Coca-Cola can, the fear response helps you jump back, and the release of your fingers as you put down the can corresponds to excitement in the somatosensory cortex. The whole brain is active in a bogglingly complex cross- and inter-network dance. Carson and Stone's scans of FND patients' brains showed unusual interconnections between networks, including connections between the emotional and salience networks. But Stone is somewhat skeptical that brain scanning has yet achieved any kind of real authoritative explanation of FND.

"What do the brain scans tell us?" he told me. "Probably that the brains of people with FND are not working properly. That they are probably not functioning in areas that relate to your sense of body ownership, that those bits of the brain are probably abnormally connected to other bits that relate to emotions." Maybe the scans correlate with the causes of the patients' disabilities, he said, but maybe their having sat in a wheelchair for a decade affects the way a patient's brain looks on a scan.

"I think it's been useful for the field to show that there's something going on in the brain," Stone told me. "But as I say to people, in what other organ would it be, this disorder? Where else would it be?" The brain scans show what to Stone was already obvious: that people were actually suffering, that FND was not a sham, what doctors often call "malingering."

Those fMRI studies of the early 2000s do not mark an end point for interest and research. They mark the beginning, and researchers around the world are now conducting complex experiments involving brain scans and FND—some leaders in the field, in addition to David Perez at Harvard, include Valerie Voon at Cambridge in the United Kingdom, and Indrit Bègue in Geneva. These are pioneering efforts, using new technology to attack a long-ignored field, in an attempt to achieve an ancient dream of neurologists, the dream of explaining human thought and consciousness through the understanding of neuroanatomy.

The first International FND Neuroimaging Workshop met virtually on June 17, 2020. The thirty participants included Alan Carson, Mark Hallett, Kathrin LaFaver, David Perez, Jeffrey Staab, Jon Stone, as well as researchers from Austria, Australia, Canada, Iran, the Netherlands, and Switzerland. The results of the meeting, published in 2021 in *Neuro-Image: Clinical* with Perez as the lead author, argued that while the brain imaging–based study of FND "remains in the early stages" and the malfunction in brain matter "remains incompletely understood," certain conclusions could be drawn.

First among these conclusions is that "brain dysfunctions in FND are distinct from feigning." These doctors are certain that their patients are genuinely suffering, that they are experiencing something that is demonstrably different from acting, pretending, or malingering—and that the differences are evident in neuroimaging. Second, "that the pathophysiology of FND implicates multiple brain networks across functional and structural neuroimaging studies"; that this is not one single breakdown, but a complicated, dynamic problem among and between different networks of the brain. Third, the authors declare, "linking neural mechanisms to etiological factors is still in its early stages": they know that something is happening, they can begin to see *how* it is happening, but they do not know *why*. Furthermore, these researchers—at the NIH, at Mayo, at Harvard, at Brown, at the University of Toronto, at Kings College, London, and at peer institutions all over the world—see historical continuity between their work and the work of doctors studying hysteria in nineteenth-century France. They use the term "FND" where once their forebears used the term "hysteria":

FND was of great interest to early clinical neuroscience leaders, with Jean-Martin Charcot stating "the neurological tree has its branches, neurasthenia, hysteria, epilepsy, all the types of mental conditions, progressive paralysis, (and) gait ataxia." Despite Charcot's integrated perspective and forward-thinking "dynamic or functional lesion theory" for FND, limitations in available neuroscientific tools at the time contributed to a singular focus on psychological conceptualizations as originally posited by Sigmund Freud.

In certain ways, contemporary neuropsychiatric researchers are more modest than twentieth-century psychoanalysts. Freudians claimed that they knew where hysterical conversion came from, and that they knew how to cure it. Current researchers are only saying that FND happens, that it exists, and that it has always existed. The neuroscientists' evidence-based descriptions are more restrained, too, than the claims made by academic theorists of the late twentieth century, who, without looking at the brains of any patients, claimed that "hysteria" was not a neurological, biological condition. There's no claim being made to a final, total description of the disorder. What all this brain imagining ultimately achieves is to put the focus back on the patients, back on the actuality of their suffering.

"In order to understand FNDs completely," Mark Hallett has written, "it is really necessary to understand the physiology of consciousness."[39] I wonder if that kind of understanding of mind and brain will be achieved in my lifetime. Neurology has been hoping to grasp it for almost two centuries now. "Modern physiology is now in a position to incorporate successfully the phenomenon of consciousness,"[40] promised Breuer's teacher, Ewald Hering, using almost the same terms Hallett did. We are still waiting.

But maybe we don't need images of the brain to acknowledge the actuality of FND patients' suffering. As Siri Hustvedt wrote: "The New York Times headline 'Is Hysteria Real?' upholds the conventional belief: if you can see it, it's real and physical. If you can't, it's unreal and mental." We can't see any mental illness: depression, anxiety, or schizophrenia. We can only see how people with these conditions suffer. In the early 2000s, doctors like Stone and Hallett were pursuing brain scanning, experimenting with identifying biological correlates of their patients' symptoms, but it wasn't the brain scans that showed them that the suffering was real. It was the patients themselves, their bodies and their stories, present in examining rooms, that convinced these neurologists that something was happening, something that needed to be attended to, something that could not be ignored.

The patients could not be neglected forever.

In 2010, a group of neurologists including Stone (who identifies himself, at that point, as a "junior" member) wrote a petition to the editors of the *DSM*, asking them to reconsider Freudian notions of functional disabilities. They wrote:

> The name "conversion disorder" refers to a hypothesis based on psychoanalytic etiology. Although long dominant, the conversion hypothesis is now just one of many competing etiological hypotheses and has little supportive empirical evidence. Even the notion that the etiology of these symptoms is wholly psychological may be scientifically incorrect.

For these neurologists, the psychoanalytic theory of conversion was not helpful for most patients, and for many it was not medically accurate. The editors of the *DSM* responded by putting the two diagnostic labels side by side, FNSD and conversion disorder, and by removing from the manual any language that specifically endorsed psychoanalytic conversion theory.

The conversation is still evolving. Across the medical world, there's little agreement on what to call these disabilities, and there are still plenty of doctors who don't regard these disabilities as "real." One final capsule narrative from that 2021 article in *Epilepsy and Behavior Reports*:

> After the ER doctor checked my daughter, I could hear him talking to other doctors outside our room. They were giggling. They tried to make it quiet, but I could tell it was about my daughter. She couldn't walk, and they were laughing at her.

The neurologist Suzanne O'Sullivan is one of the fiercest opponents of this kind of dismissive, reductive attitude toward these patients. Her most recent two books are probably the two most popular books written about functional neurological/psychosomatic disorders (she uses both terms)— the first won the Wellcome Prize, for best medical book in English—and its title describes, as well as anything, the dissolving and shifting consensus around the condition. In the United Kingdom, in 2015, the book was called *It's All in Your Head: True Stories of Imaginary Illness*. In the United States, in 2018, it was *Is It All in Your Head?: True Stories of Imaginary Illness*. As the shift from declarative to interrogative demonstrates, over the last decade even the best writers on the subject have been grappling with how to describe this.

In *Is It All in Your Head?*, O'Sullivan takes a Freudian perspective. As she describes it, circa 2015, medical understanding of conversion disorder hadn't much progressed since the nineteenth century. "For all the shortcomings in the concepts proposed by Freud and Breuer in *Studies*," O'Sullivan writes, "the twenty-first century has brought no great advances to a better understanding of the mechanism for this disorder." In 2015, O'Sullivan saw her patients' struggles in straightforwardly psychoanalytic terms: "Against all logic," she wrote, "people's subconscious selves choose to be crippled by convulsions or wheelchair dependence rather than experience the anguish that exists inside them." By 2021, when she published her next book, *The Sleeping Beauties*, her language had changed:

> What was once called "hysteria" is now referred to by some as a conversion disorder, or, more recently and more aptly, as a functional neurological disorder (FND). . . . In neurology, the word "functional" has increasingly replaced "psychosomatic." Functional is considered preferable because it indicates that there is a problem with how the nervous system is functioning, while disposing of the prefix "psych," which is too often (wrongly) distilled to mental fragility, or even madness.

O'Sullivan wrote *Is It All in Your Head?* while she was a working neurologist at the British National Hospital for Neurology and Neurosurgery. Her work with patients suffering from epilepsy had led to her interest in functional seizures, and this led to an interest in functional disorders more generally.

O'Sullivan's investigation into the phenomenon began when she was put in charge of a group of patients whose seizures could not be managed with standard medication. "It transpired that 70 percent of the people referred to me," writes O'Sullivan, "did not have epilepsy."

> Suddenly I was seeing a greater number of patients whose illness could be more fairly classified as psychological rather than neurological. And each person I encountered had a story to tell, and too often that story was one of a journey through the hospital system that led them to no satisfactory understanding of what was wrong. Few received treatment and few recovered.

O'Sullivan is sympathetic with her patients' plight, and she is deeply understanding of the stigma they face: "Society is judgmental about psychological illnesses and patients know that."

In *Is It All in Your Head?*, O'Sullivan is clear that she's describing the same disorder that Freud and Breuer discussed in *Studies*.

> Conversion disorders were once also referred to as hysterical conversion or hysteria. Over the years the word *hysteria* has become entirely pejorative. Therefore to use the term in proximity to the disorders I describe might be misleading. . . . On the rare occasion that I do use the term *hysteria* in this book, I will be using it in the way that it was used prior to 1900—to mean a significant physical problem beyond the patient's control and with none of the judgments the word currently implies.

The first patient she introduces us to is one she calls Pauline. When she is fifteen, Pauline falls into a strange illness. Her problems are not so different from Bertha Pappenheim's or Hailey Hooper-Gray's—her symptoms are incongruous, inconsistent, and inexplicable. According to O'Sullivan, at first onset of her condition, Pauline felt "tired and plagued by aches and pains." Then "her joints felt increasingly painful." Then "she had difficulty walking." Pauline stopped eating—as did Bertha Pappenheim, as did Hailey Hooper-Gray. She lost all strength in her legs. O'Sullivan met Pauline after Pauline began to suffer seizures, and O'Sullivan was able to diagnose those seizures as psychogenic or functional, to show that they were not epileptic. In *Is It All in Your Head?*, O'Sullivan delivers the conversion disorder diagnosis to her patients, and there are inevitably fights. To her credit, she lets her readers see these fights.

"You think it's all in my head," Pauline says. Pauline can't believe it. "I'd rather have a convulsion than face something unpleasant? Why would I do that to myself?"

"Every week," O'Sullivan writes, "I tell somebody their disability has psychological cause." She introduces us to another patient, Matthew, who suffers "pins and needles" sensations that intensify and change to become complete numbness and paralysis in his legs; and to Shahina, whose hand gets stepped on in a lecture hall, and whose fingers then become completely rigid and useless. Examining her patients, she is able to demonstrate in each case that there is no nerve damage, or muscle damage, that the flesh is all unhurt. In each case, in *Is It All in Your Head?* she suggests that the problems are stress-related, and in each case the patients and their families resist this diagnosis. Shahina's mother writes an outraged letter:

> I would like to complain about the treatment that my daughter received at the hands of Dr. O'Sullivan. My daughter has been severely disabled with spasms of the right hand for some time. Despite the purely PHYSICAL nature of my daughter's symptoms, and <u>based on no evidence that I can see</u>, Dr. O'Sullivan summarily accused her of having psychological problems!! My daughter, who is a law student and extremely reliable, says that Dr. O'Sullivan approached her without warning and advised her that she was imagining her symptoms.

The conversion disorder diagnosis puts neurologists and patients at loggerheads. "Doctors are frightened to face the almost inevitable anger that will occur when a psychosomatic illness is mentioned." The patients have come to the neurologist because they believe their trouble is physiological. When the neurologist then tells them what is *not* wrong with them, they get angry. Conversion theory (as O'Sullivan recounts in *Is It All in Your Head?*) can sound like an accusation. This is something you are doing, an expression of your (unconscious) desire. In *The Sleeping Beauties*, O'Sullivan moves away from this Freudian formulation of the problem:

> In Freud's formulation, every symptom could be tracked back to a specific moment of psychological torment. That viewpoint had such traction that, even today, many people, including a large number of doctors, still regard repressed trauma as the full explanation for all psychosomatic disorders. This has created decades-long counterproductive relationships between doctors and patients, in which the doctor insists that their patient is in denial about an unresolved conflict and the patient's subsequent refusal to accept that viewpoint only goes to prove the doctor's point.

There's a strange ju-jitsu that Freudian dogma performs: the patient tells their story, and then the doctor refutes it. *There's nothing wrong with your body*, says the doctor to the patient in the wheelchair, and furthermore: *You want this.* There's something hidden inside the patient's subconscious, something the patient is not aware of, something the doctor somehow knows is there. *You're hiding a secret.* If only the patient would come clean, would face the repressed memory, things wouldn't be like this. *You know the magic words that can make this stop.* If the patient would only face the unconscious repressed memory, if the patient would only say it, then they could get out of their wheelchair and on with their life. *Say the magic words and this will all vanish.*

Abracadabra. Open, sesame.

This is not to dispense entirely with Freud's powerful vision of the effects of repression and desire. People do repress horrors, and repression can play itself out on the body. There are patients for whom a hidden truth can be spoken, and when spoken, the symptoms can improve. O'Sullivan recounts such a case, the last case in her book, a patient she calls Camilla—Camilla finds the non-epileptic seizures she suffers to be both debilitating and embarrassing. She is put through neurological exam after exam, and despite the frequency of the seizures, it is determined that she does not have epilepsy. No physical cause of her illness is discovered. Camilla asks, over and over, *Why is this happening to me?*

"There's nothing on my mind," she says. "Nothing is bothering me. Any problems I've had in my life I've dealt with."

Her doctors get no good answers to these questions, until, after Camilla is incapacitated to the point that she can no longer work, O'Sullivan presses her, asking, when was the first time she suffered a seizure? In Cumbria, says baffled Camilla, after a very successful business meeting.

Camilla's husband, Hugh, in the room with his wife and her doctor, interrupts. "Darling?" he says. "You know that wasn't the very *first* collapse."

And then it spills out, the thing repressed, the thing Camilla has hidden from her doctors and from herself—the first collapse came after her child (a child she never before mentioned to O'Sullivan) died right in front of her eyes, run over by a truck, the baby carriage squashed underneath the chassis. When Camilla admits this, she finds relief.

Freud and Breuer weren't wrong. This is a way FND can present itself. Cases like Camilla's exist. But, as doctors like Hallett, LaFaver, Perez, and Stone—and O'Sullivan—contend, it's not the only way. All kinds of people suffer functional neurological breakdowns for all kinds of reasons. Not everyone who suffers FND had a particularly significant repressed trauma, and not everyone who has experienced a terrible trauma—not everyone with PTSD—suffers a functional neurological breakdown.

As his theory turned more rigid and doctrinal, Freud invented terms that stripped patients of their authority. If they went to a doctor for help with their trouble, this demonstrated their need for "secondary gain"— the patient went to the doctor because of a neurotic craving for attention. If the patient did not go to the doctor, this was a different neurotic reaction to hysterical illness, called "*la belle indifférence*."

Bridget Mildon, the founder and CEO of FND Hope, the largest FND patient advocacy group, pointed out to me how the Freudian paradigm boxes in a patient: if you go to a doctor, it's for attention, *secondary gain*; if you don't go to the doctor, it's denial, *la belle indifférence*; if you do tell your story, it's by definition incorrect; if you don't tell your story, you're never going to get better.

O'Sullivan is no strict Freudian, not even in *Is It All in Your Head?* She's an expert in seizure disorders, and an empathetic practitioner. "That is how people with psychosomatic disorders feel," she writes, that "their suffering is real but they do not feel believed." Her fights with her patients are frustrating and painful for her. She sends them to psychiatrists and psychotherapists. But, as the medical historian Edward Shorter wrote in a review of her book, "psychiatrists tend to be baffled by such referrals." Psychiatry has been backing away from the treatment of these conditions since the 1960s.

Even as O'Sullivan endorses a Freudian view in *Is It All in Your Head?*, she acknowledges the world of FND research that will form the intellectual framework of her next book. She describes the new fMRI scans and what they demonstrate. "It is now possible to show that although the brains of those affected appear healthy, they have lost the ability to recruit the necessary motor pathways to make the paralyzed limbs move. . . . Psychosomatic illness is not pretending," she writes, "the disability is real." One of her patients, Matthew, sees a psychiatrist on her recommendation, and he comes back with a different way of describing his condition than the one she has offered. "The psychiatrist explained things a lot better than you did," Matthew tells her.

One of the marvelous things about *Is It All in Your Head?* is O'Sullivan's willingness to describe her patient's dissatisfaction with her, and she does so without frustration or rancor. Matthew continues by explaining that his doctor does not call his condition "conversion disorder" but calls it "functional neurological disorder."

"He said the nervous system is like a computer," Matthew tells O'Sullivan, excitedly, "that my hardware is intact and the wires are all in the right place, but I have a software problem that keeps my legs from receiving the instructions to move," and O'Sullivan counts Matthew's acceptance of his diagnosis as a victory:

Matthew had been given a label and an explanation that he could relate to. For any illness the first step to getting better is to accept the diagnosis, and Matthew had learned to do that. That came with firm benefits for Matthew: now he could move forward with his treatment, and he could take steps to help himself. And he had a prognosis. He could anticipate recovery.

This is one of the goals of reframing "conversion disorder" as "FND": to offer patients a description of their illness that does not clash with their own experience of their body and mind, to help doctor and patient collaborate on a narrative with healing power.

"It is priceless to help someone see and understand a page in the open book of his life," wrote Bertha Pappenheim, "so clearly that all of the coming pages will unconsciously be illuminated and appear to him in a new light—to bind him but also to let him become active."[41]

But hearing a distressed patient's story is difficult, and sometimes it's impossible, even for the clearest-eyed, most compassionate doctor—even for a doctor who's a gifted storyteller!—to collaborate on a narrative with healing power.

11

In his 1906 lectures at Harvard, Charcot's student and colleague Pierre Janet described a man who had been in a carriage accident, and though not injured physically, was rendered unable to walk. Janet argued that a person didn't have to be actually hit by a carriage to be crippled by an accident. For Janet, this didn't have to be the result of some repressed long-held secret: it was enough, after a carriage accident, for a person to believe that "the wheel passed over his leg." A person could be crippled by "suggestion," Janet wrote, by "a too-powerful idea acting on the body in an abnormal way."

Dr. Kathrin LaFaver, the neurologist who has run the FND clinics at the University of Louisville Hospital and at Northwestern University Hospital, directed me to a twenty-first-century version of Janet's carriage wheel case: a successful young man who was driving back to his workplace when his car went out of control and crashed, and though he had no discernible injuries to his spine or bones or nerves or muscles, he lost his ability to walk and to talk, and his short-term memory was damaged. The first doctors he saw were dismissive of his complaints, but eventually he found his way to Louisville, where a team of speech pathologists and physical therapists supervised by LaFaver managed to help him achieve a nearly full recovery. This was a rare example of a prominent person who had discussed FND in the news media, and had described himself as an FND patient on his professional webpage, and had even chronicled his recovery on his Twitter feed. Nevertheless, when I asked him if I could include his name in my book, he requested kindly that I please not do so.

FND is not something people want to talk about. Occasionally patients publicize their diagnoses. "Penguins Reporter Rob Rossi Faces Off Against Rare Neurological Disorder" ran an April 2022 headline in the *Pittsburgh Gazette*, and it described the sportswriter's FND, but the condition makes only rare appearances in US media. A February 2022 *Slate* magazine article argued that the so-called "Havana syndrome," the strange set of headaches, twitches, and confusion that has afflicted so many US diplomats, "likely belongs to a category of illnesses known as 'functional neurological disorders.'" In the United Kingdom, there's more awareness. Alison Poole, an FND sufferer, was scheduled to address Parliament about the condition on September 22, 2022, but she was rescheduled due to the death of the Queen.

The most eloquent and erudite FND patient I have found writes under an alias, FND Portal. On FND Portal's website I found the single best, most comprehensive bibliography for my research. Also on the website—along with a list of the leading FND treatment centers in North America—there is a beautiful autobiographical essay, "Cadenza for Fractured Consciousness: A Personal History of the World's Most Misunderstood Illness." The essay is illustrated by pictures of fMRIs of the brain and by the famous painting of Charcot and his *leçons du mardi*. FND Portal puts his experience in the clinical context of Yale neurologist Benjamin Tolchin's *JAMA* study that found doctors "routinely accused [FND patients] of faking their symptoms, disparaged them, and even inflicted minor injuries on them in efforts to 'prove' their symptoms were fake." The Portal, as an FND patient, feels invisible:

> It took me a while to realize that, like Hysteria, I too had become a wandering ghost. Between 2010 and 2017, I traveled to many large hospitals and small clinics, seeing any specialist who might be able to help. Everywhere, doors closed in my face.

He finally makes it to the NIH, and finds himself on display in a seminar room, a show that reminds him of Charcot's work at the Salpêtrière.

Dr. Mark Hallett, the head of the Human Motor Control Unit, sat next to me. He demonstrated in Charcotian fashion that I had "give-way" weakness: my leg would collapse if you pushed on it.

From Hallett, he goes to Mass General, to David Perez. "There are traditional doctors' offices here," he writes, "but also rooms that look more like a Planet Fitness, full of yoga balls, workout machines, and cushioned floor mats." Finally, it's through connections with other FND patients, through hearing their stories, that he is able to cobble together a new identity, without shame.

The so-called "hysteric" of yesteryear held almost no power; they were treated, medically and socially, however society saw fit. They had no platform from which to speak, and indeed were often told they were the *cause* of their disability. . . . But that too has begun to shift. People with FND have harnessed internet platforms to tell our stories and advocate for disability justice. . . . Talking with other people with FND helped me understand: these are common feelings, and I need not carry them alone.

———•=•———

Kathrin LaFaver speaks English with a faint accent that softens her consonants and vowels. She has straight, shoulder-length blond hair. She's direct in conversation, and she's impatient with false categories and simplistic arguments about FND. When I tried to make the distinction between "conversion disorder" and "FND," she called it semantic (though she "vastly prefers" the term "FND"), and when I tried to pin her down on the difference between a "brain network disorder" and a "psychosomatic disorder," LaFaver laughed. She initially aspired to be a psychiatrist but was frustrated by the profession as practiced in the United States.

"It's very in and out," she said of contemporary pharmaceutical-based psychiatry, "treating more on the surface of symptoms."

By chance, in the course of her neurology training at the Mayo Clinic in Minnesota, LaFaver found herself in the FND program and was astonished by what she saw: a wheelchair-bound patient learning to walk again.

"What was really striking to me," LaFaver told me, "is that as neurologists we would generally make the conversion diagnosis in patients like her, and gently tell them this is a psychogenic disorder. You need to see a psychiatrist or psychologist. And that approach would typically lead to the patient being very unhappy. Patients saying things like, 'You think I'm crazy?' It's very hard to actually relay that diagnosis, to make people believe that their very dramatic, extremely disabling physical symptoms can have a psychological etiology."

After her stint at Mayo, LaFaver worked with Mark Hallett at the NIH in his functional movement lab, and then went to Louisville, where she developed her own clinic, where patients worked with speech therapists and physical therapists, along with psychologists and neurologists, and in a one-week in-patient setting, learned the tools to allow them to use their bodies again.

Essentially, this is a motor reprogramming, retraining course, and it does not work for everyone—about a third of the patients in such settings see a great deal of improvement, about a third see some improvement, and about a third don't make much improvement at all. But in many cases, a one-week training can change a life.

"I'm not a neuroscientist," she told me. "I'm trying to be very pragmatic about these disorders. I usually tell patients, 'You have a functional movement disorder. This is a brain-network disorder where you have problems controlling your movements accurately; this happens because there is over-activation of the emotional system, and the different parts of the brain just don't communicate correctly together. However, there are ways we can help you to get the brain in a better balance and retrain control over your body.' My main goal is really to help people, and to help patients get a narrative that makes sense for their lives, so that they can move forward, and get into a treatment that is going to be helpful for them. Essentially, regaining the best possible function for their life."

After her work at Louisville, she started an FND unit at Northwestern University in Chicago. There, she saw a wide spectrum of patients. Some, she says, presented with what she calls "the typical Freudian" disorder—a patient who was sexually abused as a child and suffered consequent physical symptoms later in life. She saw patients traumatized by war—for instance, a medical professional on a navy ship who was extremely isolated and became extremely distressed in a way that triggered her functional symptoms—she became entirely mute. But she also saw people from all walks of life, successful, well-adjusted people who didn't seem to suffer from PTSD.

"What I think I've learned," she said to me, "what others wiser than I have taught me, is that it's not especially helpful after just meeting somebody to make these very simplistic judgments or solutions—to tell someone, 'well, you got divorced last year,' or 'now we have a pandemic,' and so of course now your symptom is related to that cause. People need to find out for themselves."

Feeling strong, Hailey Hooper-Gray could spend her day baking. But then came days when pain stretched across the whole left side of her body, and all she could do was lie in bed screaming. She could find some relief from this left-side body pain by soaking in hot water. The local church in Lake City pitched in to buy her a soaking tub, but sometimes the tub wasn't enough, and she needed medication, prescription morphine.

Every week, twice a week, her mother put Hailey and her wheelchair in a car and drove the sixty-mile round trip for physical therapy, and thirty more miles to and from counseling. But as the FND persisted, as it advanced, the professionals who were helping her began to despair.

"My physical therapist and my counselor both said: you know, I can treat you for recovering from this surgery, but I don't know how to treat this. I can treat you for your PTSD from your medical trauma, but I don't know how to treat this."

Both thought they would be doing her a disservice if they continued working on a problem that they didn't know about or understand. So very soon after Hailey came home from her hospitalization, she had no care at all, except from her family and friends, and no school to attend, except remotely, and that, too, after a time, became untenable. Breuer describes Pappenheim's illness as "persistent somnambulism." He describes Anna O. running away from him to climb a tree. Hailey was a sleep-runner.

"If I ran one way from our house," she told me, "I was running straight into the woods. If I ran the other way I was running through town, and would eventually meet up with the river. I never got very far without passing out and having a seizure, and then I'd wake up and be paralyzed. My dog Abe would run with me, and that's actually how my mom found me a few times. I was unconscious and I didn't know what I was doing, and I cut through some people's property, and I ended up passing out and having a seizure behind their shed. So my mom was driving around, trying to find me and wouldn't have been able to find me, except Abe was with me. I was conscious, but I was paralyzed, and he came and sat next to me, and then he would get up and he would walk back to the road, where if my mom was driving around she could see him. He never left my sight, but he made it so that she was able to find me and he did that a few times. It was absolutely devastating."

A lot of FND patients suffer from something they call "brain fog," and Bertha Pappenheim called her states of semiconsciousness "time-missing." Hailey prefers the term "time-blurring." When she was having a seizure or sprinting blindly through the woods, she had a sense of consciousness but a vague and distant one. As she explained to me, "It's almost as if you're looking through a camera to take a picture, and it's getting into focus, and one second it will be vivid, the most vivid it could possibly be, and other times it's incredibly blurry. You can't even really make out what it is, but you see the same colors and things, and it kind of goes back and forth between those two."

She tried to recover as much of a life as she could. A friend would come over, and Hailey and she would watch *Gilmore Girls*, and sing the theme song at the top of their lungs. When Hailey had a feeding tube, she decorated the feeding bag with words from the novel *The Fault in Our Stars* by John Green. She worked on art projects, including a body-tracing collage that tried to represent all she was going through. But there was no help available from conventional medicine. To this day, it's difficult to find treatment for pediatric and adolescent FND. Online, Hailey's mom, Karen, found a center in California that promised mental health help for adolescents and young adults, including patients with FND. A stay in the Malibu facility cost about what Karen would make in two years, but with financial help from their extended family and their church, they managed to afford it, and Karen and Hailey flew out to LA.

The facility was gorgeous—the former home of a Hollywood celebrity. But the staff didn't know what to do with Hailey. When, on her second day at the facility, her left side flared up in agony, the staff told Hailey just to relax. They were slow to bathe her in hot water and refused to give her medication.

She fell into a seizure. When the seizure passed, staff called 9-1-1 and rushed her by ambulance to a hospital emergency room, scanned for head trauma, and meanwhile the Malibu treatment center called her mother. Hailey was not welcome to return, they said. Her bags were packed. Karen could come by and get the luggage.

"I wasn't willing to try anything else," Hailey told me. "I honestly had no faith or trust in the medical community anymore."

It had been almost a full year since her first seizures, and Hailey had given up all hope when, by chance, Karen heard of a psychotherapist in Boulder who specialized in treating FND patients and who saw adolescents—a friend of a friend had a daughter with FND who had been treated by this therapist in Boulder. The doctor's name was Afra Moenter. Hailey did not want to see her, or even to meet her.

"Let's just have a consult visit," Dr. Moenter said over the phone to Karen.

"I don't want to have a consult visit," said Hailey.

But one night they met on a video chat. Hailey's memory of the conversation, she told me, is kind of blurry. "But there's one moment that's incredibly clear."

"Hailey, this is something that is happening to you," Dr. Moenter told her, as Hailey recounted it to me. "This is not something you are causing, this is not your fault. And I think I can help you."

"The way I like to explain it," said Hailey, "is that she followed the same protocol that any doctor follows, any good doctor follows, when anybody with a knowable or a well-known medical disorder shows up in their office."

Instead of telling her what her problem was *not* ("this is not epilepsy"; "this is not MS"), instead of leaping to conclusions about the *cause* ("this is anxiety"; "this is PTSD"; "she is faking"), Moenter defined Hailey's FND as an expression of a dysregulated nervous system and discussed treatment.

As Hailey put it, Moenter said: "'Let's talk about what *we* can do to get you better'—compared to every other doctor, who was saying: *you're* manifesting, this is a manifestation of *your* anxiety. Which translates to, *this is your fault.*"

Moenter's schedule was full, but in a few months she would have room to treat Hailey.

———

I asked Afra Moenter what I should read to learn more about FND, and the first book she suggested was Charcot's *Lectures on Neurological Diseases.* "When you talk about FND," Moenter told me, "You really have to talk about Charcot, because Charcot is seen as the grandfather of neurology." For Moenter, like many FND doctors I've read and spoken to, her current work is related in a straight historical line to nineteenth-century treatment of hysteria.

Moenter is energetic, stylish, thin, middle-aged, warm, direct, and tremendously confident. She's not particularly fond of Freudian conversion theory (when I mentioned it, she gave me two thumbs down), and she doesn't practice cognitive behavioral therapy, which is the dominant form of talk therapy in most hospital FND treatment centers.

Moenter's work with FND patients emerges out of her training in psychotherapeutic methods that address trauma, the nervous system, and the body. She's interested in the ways that life challenges influence and are influenced by the autonomic nervous system. She wrote her dissertation on trauma, changes to the brain, and the onset of complex partial epilepsy. She's worked with patients suffering from PTSD, Parkinson's disease, and epilepsy. Inevitably, since so many seizure disorders are functional, Moenter's work led her to specialize in treating functional nervous disorders.

"FND is a normal reaction to an overwhelming experience that exceeds the person's ability to cope or integrate what had happened," she explained.

"In the trauma world there's a model that's called 'the window of tolerance,'" she told me. Functional symptoms, she says, come to patients who experience feelings outside that window. These are, she says, "symptoms of a dysregulated nervous system, sensory processing issues, and somatoform disorders." Her work she said, involves "teaching people how to self-regulate their nervous system." She also works with her patients' families, so that they can learn to identify signs of a dysregulated nervous system.

Hailey Hooper-Gray spent two two-week periods in five-day-a-week sessions with Afra Moenter. In Moenter's terms, Hailey learned how to "self-regulate" her nervous system, how to regain flexibility, and not get stuck in overactivation or collapse. Hailey remembers the day she knew she was getting better. She was in a café in Boulder, and a cute guy walked in, and Hailey could imagine herself meeting him, flirting with him. She was becoming part of the world again.

Hailey set out three goals in the beginning of her treatment with Dr. Moenter: to ski again, to climb mountains, and to go back to school. As of this writing, she has achieved all of them, and is going to college in Seattle.

We don't want to believe that someone as strong and as capable as Hailey Hooper-Gray—or as Bertha Pappenheim—can so thoroughly lose control of their own body. I can hear the skeptical reader cry: *Surely there's some degree of intentionality here? Surely all those symptoms had some meaning?* Modern neurology pushes us away from that kind of psychoanalytic

thinking, and if Hooper-Gray's story is in any way atypical of FND patients more generally, it's not in the loss of control of her body, it's in the
completeness of her recovery. Most patients suffer with these problems
for years, or for a lifetime.

We like to think, as Delmore Schwartz once put it, that the ego is
always at the wheel, that we are driving our own bodies, our own selves.
But at the 2022 meeting of the FND Society, Dr. Lisa Feldman Barrett,
director of the Interdisciplinary Affective Science Laboratory at North-
eastern University, reminded her audience that intentionality and agency
(what we think of as *mind*) is only a very small part of the brain's operations. That small part need not be in the driver's seat. The best available technology for examining brains—fMRI scans—corroborates the
patients' description of their experiences. They have lost control.

For hundreds of years, we have been explaining these patients' problems to them, we've been saying that they are malingering, or that their
problems don't "really" exist. In Bertha Pappenheim's case, every story
has been thrown at her except the most obvious: that there was a breakdown in her brain—a functional problem, a software issue, a dynamic
lesion—and that she lost control of her arms, her legs, her mouth, and her
language.

———————

Afra Moenter's vocabulary may come from a different area of training
and expertise, but in so many ways her approach to treatment echoes
current neurological thinking about FND. Like them, she argues for
patient-centered thinking.

"Listen," was her advice on how to treat FND patients, "learn their
language, speak their language." Hailey Hooper-Gray, in that first consult meeting, heard Dr. Moenter saying to her, "It's going to be a lot of
work for you, but let me show you how. Let me hold your hand. Let me
walk you through it"—an introduction not so very different from the
message Kyla Kenney took from David Perez.

One of the crucial factors in successful treatment of FND is patient
buy-in. Kathrin LaFaver sent me several papers that emerged from a
conference at Emory University, a set of seminars in which neurologists,

psychiatrists, and other health professionals from around the world gathered to develop protocols for treating patients with FND. I was struck by a paragraph that ended the introduction of one of those papers, "Diagnosing Functional Neurological Disorder: Seeing the Whole Picture":

> The identification of comorbid psychiatric conditions in the context of the evaluation is frequent and should be addressed as such, avoiding the trap of reducing the explanation of FND to stress, anxiety or depression. It is essential to assess the duration of the functional neurological symptoms and ascertain the presence of previous or concomitant unexplained symptoms in other organ systems. This can further aid in the appreciation of the patient's prognosis and inform the treatment recommendations. It supports the development of a case formulation—the "story"—forged by the therapist with participation from the patient into a narrative that has healing power.

The goal is to see the patient whole, to listen to the patient, and to develop a "story," "a narrative that has healing power." The same kind of language recurred in the paper on which LaFaver was the lead author, "Treatment of Functional Neurological Disorder: Current State, Future Directions, and a Research Agenda." LaFaver and her coauthors write:

> FND needs to be understood within a biopsychosocial, spiritual, and cultural framework. . . . Regardless of the specific intervention, development of a trusting clinician/patient rapport is crucial in order for patients to feel heard and understood and not alone in the process, and help diminish feelings of shame, guilt, and distress.

From the hard-headed world of brain scans and fMRI, there is emerging a new kind of talking cure, a talking cure which, unlike the classic Freudian conversion disorder version, accepts the patient as an authority on their own condition. Someone to be listened to, someone to be heard.

12

In his review of *Is It All in Your Head?* in the *British Medical Journal*, the historian Edward Shorter argues that "O'Sullivan is silent about a huge source of psychosomatic illness, namely the phenomenon of suggestion," and Shorter gives a simple example of what he means:

> Sally begins vomiting and suddenly all the ten-year-olds in the schoolyard start vomiting as well. The public health authorities rush in. There is alarm in the press. An organic cause is never found but everybody is better the next day. It is an epidemic of suggestion that has invested the school yard.

This phenomenon has long been observed. Freud writes about this kind of contagion in *The Interpretation of Dreams*:

> Supposing a physician is treating a woman patient who is subject to a particular kind of spasm, in a hospital ward among a number of patients. He will show no surprise if he finds one morning that this particular kind of hysterical attack has found imitators. He will merely say, "the other patients have seen it and copied it; it's a case of psychical infection."

Elaine Showalter's 1997 book *Hystories: Hysterical Epidemics and Modern Culture* is a review of late twentieth-century cases of what Freud might have called "psychical infection," and Showalter argues that a wide variety of illnesses—she begins with nineteenth-century "hysteria" and cites Anna O.—can be and are spread through culture and media.

> Infectious epidemics of hysteria spread by stories circulated through self-help books, articles in newspapers and magazines, TV talk shows and series, films, the Internet, and even literary criticism. The cultural narratives of hysteria, which I call *hystories*, multiply rapidly and uncontrollably in the era of mass media, telecommunications, and e-mail.

Writing under the influence of historians like Shorter, Showalter argues that "hysteria" should not be considered as "a single, unified affliction." Quoting from the psychiatrist Phillip Slavney's 1990 book *Perspectives on "Hysteria,"* she argues that "hysteria" "was regarded as a disease—an affliction of the mind that was expressed through a disturbance of the body," but has since "come to imply behavior that produces the *appearance* of disease."

Under the capacious umbrella of "hystories," Showalter brings together eating disorders like anorexia and bulimia ("examples of modern hysterical epidemics"); "chronic fatigue syndrome" (whose sufferers generally prefer the term "myalgic encephalomyelitis"); alien-abduction narratives; and even mass social panics, like the 1980s paranoia about satanic ritual abuse in preschools, in which teachers from Texas, California, and New Jersey were tried in court on charges that they donned ceremonial robes and forced young children to drink blood, and then violated the children anally, charges the coached children corroborated in fantastical testimony. Showalter quotes the historian Norman Cohn:

> It is as though units of paranoia hitherto diffused through the population suddenly coalesce to form a new entity: a collective paranoic fanaticism. But these first followers, precisely because they are true believers, can endow their new movement with such confidence, energy, and ruthlessness that it will attract into its wake vast multitudes of people who are themselves not at all paranoid but simply harassed, hungry or frightened.

Showalter is an English professor and identifies herself as "a critic of hysteria's stories." She examines her case studies as if they were a kind of socially produced literature or drama. Her goal, she says, is not to condemn the victims of this "fanaticism," but to sympathize. "I want to emphasize my belief that hysteria is part of everyday life," she writes, and connects personally with her subjects: "Whenever I lecture about hysteria, I cough." She's a neo-Freudian.

> We must accept the interdependence between mind and body, and recognize hysterical syndromes as a universal psychopathology of everyday life before we can dismantle their stigmatizing mythologies. When anti-Freudian zealots make sweeping attacks on psychoanalysis and psychiatry, we can defend Freud's insights and try to restore confidence in serious psychotherapy.

Though nineteenth-century "hysteria" is the focal point of Showalter's book—its beginning and its central theme—she doesn't include a chapter on "conversion disorder" or what we would now call FND. In 1997, for most scholars in the humanities, as for most psychiatrists and neurologists, the condition was not a current concern.

When I first read *Hystories*, I was knocked out by its sweep, style, and scholarship, but in the context of the work of contemporary FND doctors (research unavailable when Showalter was writing), the book's analogies seem unfair. It's unreasonable to conflate on the one hand a crippling illness like the one suffered by Hailey Hooper-Gray or Kyla Kenney and on the other hand a contagious rage, "mass hysteria," hysteria of the kind that led to witch burnings in Salem. The conflation is not Showalter's own.

The problem lies in our language, in the word "hysteria," and in the history of medicine. In his beautiful and masterly 2012 *Hallucinations*—a book I love to assign to my classes—Oliver Sacks juxtaposes William James's 1896 lecture on "demoniacal possession and witchcraft" (page 244) with Freud and Breuer's description of Anna O. (page 245), as if the two were varieties of the same disorder, and Sacks concludes:

Anna's "trance" personality became more and more dominant as her illness progressed, and for long periods she would be oblivious or blind to the here and now, hallucinating herself as she was in the past. She was, at this point, living largely in a hallucinatory, almost delusional world, like the nuns of Loudun [who saw demons] or the "witches" of Salem [whose visions led them to be burnt at the stake].

This kind of connection has become part of the stigma that FND sufferers have to contend with: the notion that they are delusional, paranoid, as if swept up in mass confusion. But this is unfair. A person who suffers functional seizures is only in the most tenuous way analogous to a paranoid parent who believes that his child is being raped by Satan-worshiping preschool teachers. Early in our correspondence, Jon Stone sent me a short video clip from *The Simpsons*:

Teacher: You see, class, my Lyme disease turned out to be [writing on the board] PSYCHOSOMATIC.
    Boy: Does that mean you were crazy?
    Girl: No, that means she was faking it.
Teacher: No, actually, it was a little bit of both. Sometimes when a disease is in all the magazines and on all the news shows, it's only natural that you think you have it.

In the summer of 2022, Stone addressed the problem of the so-called "TikTok Tics" in an essay in the journal the *Conversation*. He was responding to a British television program that argued that Tourette-like symptoms were being spread via social media. According to the TV news, girls stressed out by pandemic lockdowns were transmitting strange symptoms via TikTok videos: they would film themselves cursing and twitching, and the curses and twitches would spread via the videos— girls who watched the TikTok videos would become infected. The news story's argument followed Showalter's terms, as if the Tourette-like symptoms were multiplying rapidly and uncontrollably via media, as if social media was the cause of something otherwise inexplicable.

Stone begins his critique of this story simply: by asserting that functional twitches are not the same as Tourette's, that they sit under the general umbrella of FND, and that such tics and twitches are not uncommon in teenage girls. According to Stone, what the girls were experiencing—tics in which they hurt themselves or others or called their mother "motherfucker"—were nothing mysterious. They were a phenomenon well observed by neurologists. "New tics in teenage girls are hardly ever caused by Tourette's," he argued, and continued:

> Tourette's is a developmental disorder that begins gradually in early childhood. It is more common in boys. Functional tics typically start rapidly and are much more common in girls – although girls do get Tourette's, too.
>
> Functional tics can involve movements . . . that hurt the person who has them, or others, whereas this is rare in Tourette's.
>
> *Coprolalia*, the medical word for the kind of swearing vocal tic seen in the TV show, is rare in Tourette's, and much more common and frequent in functional tics.

There was, Stone argued, no evidence of a new "epidemic" of functional tics among teenage girls, but perhaps there was a slight reported rise in the number of girls coming to neurology clinics with such symptoms. Social media could be a possible factor in such a rise, he argued, but should not be seen as a cause. "We already know that people who tic are more likely to do so by watching others with the same thing," Stone argued. "This is similar to how watching someone yawn makes you yawn or feel sleepy." To say the functional tics were *caused* by TikTok "would be like blaming all cases of stroke on smoking. Sure, smoking is relevant for some, but so are lots of other things—genetics, cholesterol, hypertension and bad luck." The causes of FND are complex. Sometimes, as Stone points out, psychological stress can be a trigger in FND. Sometimes, "it arises as a result of an illness, an injury or even a transient vaccine reaction." It seems that each time FND appears on the public radar, journalists and academics stand drop-jawed with wonder—transfixed by the phenomenon, as if they have seen a ghost.

"Our goal is not to create fear," said the television anchor on News Channel 4 Nashville while reporting on post-vaccine seizures. Their reporter on the scene, Rachel Cardenas, interviewed a patient in her hospital bed. The COVID-19 vaccine had paralyzed her, the anonymous patient said. She said that she was epileptic, but that "this was not a seizure."

"I just started feeling not great." Then she couldn't walk, and she suffered excruciating neck pain. "It just started progressively getting worse, and I started screaming in pain like at the top of my lungs."

She was unable to move from the neck down. Her husband rushed her to the hospital. CAT scan, MRI, EMG, and blood work showed nothing worrisome. By the time she was interviewed for television, she had regained movement of her arms. NO MEDICAL CONFIRMATION THE VACCINE IS RELATED read the chyron at the bottom of the screen.

"As far as why this happened, they don't know," the patient said.[42]

Her suffering was reported as a mystery—possibly caused by the vaccine—but for doctors studying FND, her reaction was predictable.

"I guess those of us who worked in FND for quite a while were expecting this to come," the neuropsychiatrist Timothy Nicholson told the 2022 FND Society conference when he was at the podium discussing COVID vaccine–related seizures. "The whole pandemic environment made it quite likely. Any injury, any accident, any neurological illness is a risk factor for getting a functional reaction, and something about the pandemic and the new vaccines fed into people's concerns—the idea that Bill Gates was implanting microchips in vaccines, all that stuff."

Mild functional reactions to a shot are common, Nicholson reported. In blind studies, roughly a third of the population experienced headache or fatigue in response to an injection of saline solution that was thought to contain the novel vaccine. This is called a "nocebo" reaction, the opposite of a placebo, and given that hundreds of millions of people were getting the vaccine, and that there was great concern about side effects and vaccine safety, it was perfectly predictable that some functional reactions, some nocebo responses, would be worse than simple headaches. It was reasonable to assume, in such a large population, that some people would convulse.

In an April 2021 article in *JAMA Neurology*, David Perez and several coauthors argued that internet videos recording adverse effects of COVID-19 vaccinations "show evidence of rule-in signs consistent with functional movement symptoms, such as asynchronous movements that are variable in frequency and amplitude." The way the patients reacted, the time frame within which the patients reacted, all of these things, for doctors who specialize in FND, were telling. The problem wasn't that the vaccines were causing these reactions. The problem wasn't that the patients were faking. The problem was that the bulk of the medical and media world didn't see these reactions as legitimate, as "real." These seizures were an example of an ancient condition that would have been recognizable to Aretaeus of Cappadocia, to Thomas Sydenham, to Josef Breuer, but somehow for our current medical and media community, they seemed baffling—something to be feared or ignored or both.

This is the way most media covers FND: as something unspeakable, as a story they will not hear. In one chapter of *The Sleeping Beauties*, Suzanne O'Sullivan describes "The Witches of Le Roy," in which a dozen teenage girls in upstate New York, all of whom attended the same high school, were all afflicted in 2001 by the same symptoms.

> Some of the girls had full convulsions, in keeping with dissociative seizures. Some couldn't walk. Over time, the symptoms . . . evolved with each girl ultimately needing a wheelchair when muscle jerks became so violent that they caused them to fall.

As O'Sullivan recounts, the high school called in experts, including the New York Department of Health and the Centers for Disease Control and Prevention, and "the girls were fully investigated and ultimately diagnosed with a functional neurological disorder under the name 'conversion disorder.'" But this diagnosis was unacceptable to the children's parents and community, who appeared on the *Today Show*, scandalized by the suggestion that their children were psychologically ill. The national media took up the case. *Mass Hysterical Outbreak Reported in NY Town*,

CBS News reported. Erin Brockovich—famous from the movie in which Julia Roberts plays her—took up the case. Brockovich was interviewed on ABC News by Dr. Drew Pinsky.

"Did you have the same reactions I did?" Pinsky wondered. "The diagnosis seemed . . . it didn't feel right in your gut, and then it kind of closed the door on further investigation."

The news media was deaf to the diagnosis. As O'Sullivan writes, "The doctors were incorrectly referred to as 'stumped.' . . . News reports repeatedly referred to the doctors as 'baffled.' Even in articles that mentioned the conversion disorder diagnosis, the focus was still on the mystery." Whereas in 1997 the English professor Showalter saw media narratives as spreaders of hysterical panic and disease, in 2021 the neurologist O'Sullivan described media narratives as mystification, distorting the ordinary phenomenon of FND and making it spooky and weird. Even when doctors explain it to us, we refuse to believe it's real.

From culture to culture, symptoms can vary—even in the most basic experiences of our bodies. The anthropologist Margaret Lock argued that "when older women in Japan stop menstruating, they rarely experience the hot flashes and night sweats that are associated with menopause in North America."[43] From epoch to epoch, the experience of the body shifts. O'Sullivan's *The Sleeping Beauties* is devoted to the investigation of socially defined illnesses, afflictions confined to a particular community at a particular time. O'Sullivan's title refers to a sleeping sickness that affected children of refugee immigrants to Scandinavia. "With all of the victims so geographically contained," she writes, "there must be something in their social environment that has created that possibility." In *From Paralysis to Fatigue*, Edward Shorter has argued that people suffer from symptoms that exist within their culture's "symptom pool"—symptoms their doctors will approve of—and for Shorter, this explains the rise and fall of fashionable diagnoses.

> Patients want to please doctors, in the sense that they do not want the doctor to laugh at them and dismiss their plight as imaginary. Thus they strive to produce symptoms the doctor will recognize. As doctors' own ideas about what constitutes "real" disease changes from time to time due

to theory and practice, the symptoms that patients present will change as well.

But just as a culture can be a factor in the etiology of an affliction, so it can also be a factor in an affliction's erasure—people suffer in ways that are outside the acceptable "symptom pool." For most of my lifetime, neurologists, psychiatrists, journalists, historians, and literary theorists have argued that "hysteria" wasn't in the pool of diseases considered "real." Patients appeared with symptoms their doctors rejected. Writers like Shorter and Showalter—as brilliant and learned and careful as people can be—joined with the culture around them, including the medical community, and were unable to see what was happening, to distinguish between the imaginary and the real.

PART THREE

Imagining Freud

13

Recha Pappenheim's new apartment was just a ten-minute walk from Breuer's home. That's where Bertha was living in the winter of 1882. "I would come to see her in the morning, hypnotize her . . . and, once her thoughts were concentrated on the symptom we were treating, I would ask her about the occasions on which it appeared," Breuer writes in "Anna O.," but it's hard to square his account in *Studies* with the existing historical record.

In the story of "Anna O.," these morning sessions are preliminary meetings. The time is used to organize and prepare for the more detailed and intensive therapy at the end of the day. Each morning, according to Breuer, he and his patient focus on a particular symptom (for instance, "visual disturbances"). Anna O. gives Breuer "captions" (in the Luckhurst translation) or "headings" (in the Strachey)—perhaps naming moments in which the visual disturbances occurred, perhaps naming different categories of visual disturbances. I understand these morning sessions as a kind of outline, preparatory for the more detailed therapeutic storytelling at the end of the day.

Then, at sunset, maybe four-thirty in Vienna in January, Breuer appears at the apartment and finds Anna O. in her *condition seconde*, her evening hypnosis. It's in these evening meetings, he tells us, that he attempts to unwind "the thread of memory," to dig deep into recollections of each symptom, going methodically backward through time. Breuer claims that he makes Anna O. recall every instance of every symptom, working in reverse historical order, until he comes to its origin. In this way, according to *Studies*, doctor and patient, from December to June, run through thousands of memories. In "Fraulein Anna O.," they go through 287 different recollections of temporary deafness—and that's just one of the milder symptoms of her "hysteria." In Breuer's telling, it's crucial that she recall each of these instances one by one, backing up through time:

> Yet they were so clearly separated in the patient's memory that if she once mistook the sequence it had to be corrected and the right order re-established, otherwise the presentation would be held up.

Breuer calls this period starting in December 1881, "Gradual winding down of mental states and symptoms until June 1882," but the available evidence suggests that for much of this period Pappenheim was miserable. According to a letter from Recha, Bertha had surgery on her left upper jaw in February, and afterward suffered "momentary linguistic confusion for two whole days." This goes unmentioned in *Studies*. In the middle of March, again according to Recha's letter, "when unusually intense brain activity took place," Bertha's "facial neuralgia" became "persistent and very excruciating." This, too, is omitted from "Fraulein Anna O."

Stranger things happen in *Studies*. According to Breuer, Anna O.'s mind derails and straddles history. In the daytime she lives in the present, in 1882, but every night her mind slips a groove backward, and for her it's 1881 all over again. "She lived through the previous winter day by day," according to Breuer.

> The switch from one state to the other occurred spontaneously but could be very easily prompted by any sense impression that reminded her vividly of the previous year. Holding up an orange for her to see (she had eaten almost nothing but oranges during the first stage of her illness) was enough to cast her back from 1882 to 1881.

She jumps back 365 days into the past, exactly. For proof of this Breuer refers to "a diary kept secretly by her mother." One day, she is inexplicably annoyed at Breuer. He notes that, according to the diary, she was annoyed at him on precisely the same calendar date in 1881. She mistakes a brown dress for a blue one, and Breuer confirms, by looking at the diary, that one year earlier to the day she wore a blue dress, not a brown one.

As Mikkel Borch-Jacobsen points out, there's an awkwardness to Breuer's outdated vision of memory—Anna O.'s memories lurk like buried photographs or phonograph recordings, fixed and immutable, and pop up a year later, perfect and unchanged. There's a music-hall quality to the hypnosis: Breuer's orange is so much like Carl Hansen's magic orb. Recha's diary feels less like a confirming piece of evidence and more like a bit of stage business—like the secret letter at the end of a play that proves that Edmund was up to no good the whole time! The grand finale occurs on the one-year anniversary of the day when Anna O. was carried off, against her will, to the sanitarium in the suburbs of Vienna. After having hypnotized her maybe thousands of times through each of her symptoms' every occurrence, Breuer arranges the room in the apartment so it's like the room in the chalet where Anna O. kept watch over her father. He throws her backward in time, and she produces it all, the mythic sequence: the frozen arm, the fingers that become snakes, the visions of skulls, and the inability to say her Hebrew prayers. She tells the final story, and Anna O. is released from all her symptoms. No more hysteria, ever again.

Maybe Bertha Pappenheim did tell that story to Breuer, about the sick father, and the snakes and skulls and the prayers and the train whistle—perhaps she told versions of it, over and again, through hypnosis—but as Borch-Jacobsen points out, she is at best an unreliable narrator. Sick, drugged, hypnotized, she had been repeating and reconstructing stories about snakes and skulls and invalids and nurses for something like eighteen months, since her first fairy tales. In June 1882, after some eight months of Breuer's pleading with Dr. Robert Binswanger, Pappenheim was finally admitted to the Bellevue Sanitarium in Kreuzlingen, Switzerland, a place where Breuer had wanted to put her since at least October of 1881.

In his letters to Binswanger (collected by Hirschmüller) Breuer does not discuss the miraculous hypnotic memory cure. Mostly, he's concerned about Pappenheim's drug dependence, her "slight hysterical insanity," and his own inability to take care of her. "As you can see," he writes, "a considerable degree of responsibility rests with me." He writes that "in recent months" she's had horrible physical symptoms, "extremely severe convulsions which, beginning as severe chorea minor, increased to rolling convulsions." He says that he gave her varying doses of morphine (I assume in milligrams): up to 0.15 to 0.20 per day ("rather high," writes Breuer). Breuer himself seems shocked by the amount of chloral he's giving her, "rising to 4.00 in recent months (!)"—that's his exclamation point inside the parentheses. "She becomes very insecure and suspicious, at times—as she says—'quite crazy.'"

In the months when Anna O. was supposedly recovering, Bertha Pappenheim was more than a little paranoid: "Confessing at the moment to all kinds of deceptions, genuine or not, occasionally still seeing bits of nonsense such as people suppressing her or spying on her, and the like." When he tried to wean her from the drugs, Pappenheim fell into DTs: "She hallucinated small animals, heard voices, was somewhat inclined to be violent, i.e., she threw a bottle on the floor, and so on."

Again, that "and so on." Writing to Binswanger, Breuer tells a story that's far, far from the easy comfortable resolution of illness that happens at the end of his treatment of "Anna O.," but on one point, he's consistent. He insists to Binswanger that his patient has shown "no element of sexuality throughout the entire illness," and this denial of her sexuality, together with his vague "and so on" hints at upsetting behavior, make me wonder what he's omitted from his notes and letters.

"I am powerless to cope with her agitated state," Breuer wrote to Binswanger, almost the exact opposite of what he argued in *Studies*.

In June 1882, when he left Pappenheim in the Bellevue Sanitarium, he was at a loss to help her, and full of self-reproaches. She would no longer talk to him, and he could no longer understand her. We do not have the letters Binswanger wrote to Breuer, but apparently he thought that Breuer had misjudged and mismanaged the whole case. Breuer defends himself: "Your present contention that her entire illness is an invention is certainly false, even if individual elements are not genuine."

As always with cases of FND, the doctors are asking each other: is this real?

———•———

That same spring, when Breuer was either (a) guiding Anna O. back in time masterfully with his new (and never again practiced by him) hypnotic technique or (b) losing control of Bertha Pappenheim to drugs, seizures, pain, and anxiety, Freud met a girl.

She was a friend of his sisters, and Sigmund met her at his family's apartment in April of 1882. Martha Bernays was at the dinner table, peeling an apple, and somehow this apple peeling dazzled him. She was not rich, but Freud found her beautiful, and she was intelligent and kindly. She belonged to the class, or kind of family, to which he aspired.

On June 16, 1882, when the mythic Anna O. was on the verge of unburdening herself at last of all her hysteria, when the actual Bertha Pappenheim was suffering seizures and DTs and her doctor was incapable of reaching her, that's when Sigmund Freud and Martha Bernays were engaged, secretly. His first gift to Martha was a copy of *David Copperfield*. Every day he sent her a red rose and a poem in Latin or French or Italian.

———•———

How did the story of Anna O. become the theory of psychoanalysis? That's a scholarly question best pursued through close attention to the books Freud wrote in his period of greatest invention, *Studies in Hysteria*, *The Interpretation of Dreams*, *The Psychopathology of Everyday Life*, *Three Essays on the Theory of Sexuality*, and the "Dora" case, *Fragment of an Analysis of a Case of Hysteria*, and also through careful reading of the century of scholarship that has arisen around those books.

How did the story of Bertha Pappenheim become the story of Anna O.? That's a dramatic question, a tale of ambition and seduction, sex and drugs, friendship and betrayal. It's a story of intellectual seduction: how Freud got Breuer, one of the more measured, conventional scientists in

Vienna, to lie in print, to claim he had stumbled on a miracle cure, and to endorse Freud's sexy, radical theory of the human mind.

It's the story of three people struggling to describe a mysterious medical phenomenon. One hundred forty years later, medicine has advanced, but when it comes to the problem that they were pursuing, the facts and evidence remain confounding, and we have nothing that resembles certainty.

"There's so much we don't know," says David Perez of functional neurological disorders, "so many gaps in our knowledge."

———•———

The Bellevue Sanitarium overlooked Lake Constance and was constructed on the grounds of an old monastery. What remains is a substantial villa, almost a castle, four stories tall, built in an Italianate Renaissance style, with a square tower at the center. The patients were wealthy, many of them titled nobility, and there were fancy cottages all over the grounds and an elaborate glass greenhouse.

Binswanger's patients took classes in languages and literature; they exercised and gardened. They were not sequestered from the world, but mingled with the staff and other healthy people—visitors, lecturers, workmen. Pappenheim had a two-bedroom apartment in the sanitarium, and she had a lady companion. She loved Lake Constance. She bathed in the water. There's a picture of her in a handsome bowler hat and a black riding outfit, the jacket cinched wasp-like at the corseted waist, the long skirt covering her feet, in one hand a pair of leather gloves, in the other a long riding crop. Her expression is serious, her cheeks are plump. We have an account of her life at Bellevue from a Dr. Laupus, which is included in Hirschmüller's biography. It mostly describes Pappenheim's addiction to morphine and chloral, her DTs, and her difficulties weaning herself from the drugs. It also says:

> The patient displayed genuine signs of hysteria. She frequently exhibited an almost hostile irritation with regard to her relatives and others . . . stressing bitterly the pointlessness of her residence here. . . . Thus for weeks on end she would be preoccupied with her intention to dedicate herself to hospital

nursing at the very earliest opportunity, but would then reject this idea in favour of other plans. During her last weeks here she was obsessed with the idea of visiting her father's grave in Pressburg. She would frequently keep a silent, tearful vigil for hours at a time before her father's picture. . . . She frequently allowed her phantasies to range freely in escapist dreams.

The most complete account of her illness in Pappenheim's own voice is an undated letter that she wrote in imperfect English in the summer of 1882, in which she declares (I'll leave in her odd grammar and spelling), "I will try to give, as well, as a person who has never made any medical studies, can do, a short account of my own observations and experiences considering this terrible estate." Mostly in her letter, she's concerned with her continued loss of her native language, the pain in her face, her loss of the sense of the passage of time, and her periods of anxiety and depression.

It [the loss of the German language] appears quite suddenly without the slightest transaction in the very moment I recline in my bed, independent from the hour, which I have varied already between 9 o'clock in the evening till 1 p.mn. Two days I had once been obliged to stay in bed for some other littl unease, and then the phase begun at 10 o'clock. For some hours then I ame perfectly unable to communicate anything in German, whist the other languages, which all I have learned later, are present to my mind, and the English I can use nearly to perfection.

When the strong neuralgic pain, from which I am suffering, allows it, I mostly read a French or English book till the happy moment of my recovering German arrives; (what never occured before midnight, seldom past 2 o'clock in the morning.) The whole going on is not accompanied from the slightest physik sensation; no pain, no oppression or giddiness are to be felt. From the point of any such symptoms the whole thing could pass very well without its being from me remarked at all, but as I do no understand my servant nor am I understood, I dayly must learn anew to find myself in the sad, bitter fact.

Consider my humour, my mental and psychic state during this time, there are some observations to be told. In the first 2 months of my sejourn here, I had shorter or longer absences, which I could observe myself by. A strange feeling of "timemissing"; one told me that I used to speak with great vivacity during these absences, but since some weeks there have been none. When I do not read I am laying, not always very quiet, occupied with my thoughts, and ame quite able to govern them; I can reproduce the past and make plans for the future; I only get realy nervous, anxious, and disposed to cry, when the but too well motivated fear to lose the German language for longer again, takes possession of me. When I have society during this phase I feel much easier, but also when I am quite alone I dont fall into heavy melancholic or hypochondric thinking.

There's scholarly disagreement on the nature of her recovery. Richard A. Skues argues that Breuer cured Pappenheim of the main symptoms of her hysterical illness, what we would call now her functional movement disorder: Pappenheim could now walk, she had no weakness in her limbs and neck, and she regained the use of her hands. She was still angry, still estranged from her mother and brother. A letter to Binswanger from her cousin Fritz Homburger expresses this discreetly. She is "deeply attached to her mother," Homburger writes, but "at a distance." He adds that "she is also more attached to her brother when she is separated from him; he thinks all the time that he has the right to dominate her."

Recha's letters to Binswanger reveal a caring parent. "I shall stay in the background so as not to paralyze or spoil matters," she writes. When Binswanger wants to operate on Bertha's face, Recha stops him: "This neuralgia is not a wholly independent condition but is closely connected with her psychic processes."

Bertha stayed in Bellevue for four months, until October 1882, when she went to live with her cousins in the town of Karlsruhe, Germany, about 150 miles north of the sanitarium. Here she went to the opera—she saw *Carmen*—and she enrolled in a nursing course. She wrote to Binswanger: "As for my health, I can tell you nothing which is new or favorable. You will realize that to live with a syringe always at the ready is not a situation to be envied."[44] She was still addicted to chloral and morphine.

In Karlsruhe, she wrote short stories that she read aloud to her cousin Anna, who encouraged her not to be a nurse at all, but to be a writer.

Sometime in December, Pappenheim seems to have experienced a rap-prochement with her mother. She and Recha journeyed together to Frankfurt, Recha's hometown, and then in late January they returned to Vienna.

———•———

It was when Pappenheim was traveling with her mother that Breuer first confided to Freud about the case. Freud at the time was in professional and romantic crisis. In the summer of 1882, he had confided the news of his engagement to his boss Ernst Brücke—maybe Freud was hoping that he'd get a promotion and a salary—but Brücke, "my teacher, for whom I felt the highest possible esteem," told Freud that it was time to leave laboratory research, as Freud remembered it in *An Autobiographical Study*, "strongly advising me, in view of my bad financial position, to abandon my theoretical career." There was not going to be a place for him on the medical faculty at Vienna General Hospital. If Freud was going to get married and support a family, he would have to leave his academic research and become a practicing physician, something that he didn't particularly want to be.

The lab at the hospital was his dream job. His colleagues were mak-ing technical and anatomical advances that would change the course of medicine. To be kicked out of the university was to be kicked out of the higher ranks of science and to undertake the lower rank of a practitioner. As George Makari writes in his great book *Revolution in Mind*:

> German scientific medicine held therapeutics in low regard. Most thera-
> pies could not be scientifically proved and were based on little more than
> hearsay and the scattered experiences of seasoned doctors. . . . Prominent
> leaders at the medical school suggested that the present state of knowledge
> suggested that therapeutics were at best worthless, at worst dangerous.

Freud was twenty-seven years old and not entirely healthy. In a let-ter, he describes himself as "neurasthenic." He suffered migraines and fainting spells and periods of listless depression. He lived part-time in his parents' apartment, and on other nights at the Vienna General Hospital, where his shabby room was decorated with two needlepoint samplers made by Martha: "*Travailler sans raisonner*" (work without reasoning) and "*En cas de doute absteins-toi*" (in case of doubt, abstain). He considered converting to Catholicism—it was a common route ambitious young Jews took toward success. That's how Gustav Mahler got to be the conductor of the opera, that's what Theodor Herzl considered doing—Herzl's first idea for the normalization of the Jews, before he came up with modern Zionism, was a single day of mass conversion with all the church bells in Vienna ringing.

On July 12, "the hottest, most agonizing day of the whole season," as Sigmund wrote to Martha, when he "was already childish with exhaustion," he "noticed that I had need of some uplift" and so, from the stifling lab where he had worked all day, Freud made his way past the famous cafés and the brand-new buildings, the streets filled with manure, flies, and horse-drawn trolleys, through the center city to visit Breuer.

14

Breuer was welcoming but miserable. His wife and children were in the country. "He had a headache, poor fellow, and was taking salicyl," writes Freud. "The first thing he did was to chase me into the bathtub." Freud took off his sweaty summer suit. In the tub, warm water bubbled with scented soap. As he soaked, Freud dreamed of a future where he'd have his own house and maid and porcelain bath ("my thought was, if little Martha was here, she would say, this is how we want to organize things too"). At this time in Freud's life, Breuer was a kind of ideal—the Jewish doctor who despite exclusion from the university was still a leader in experimental neurology. Freud "emerged rejuvenated" from the bath. They ate dinner "upstairs in our shirt sleeves." Breuer must have lent him a clean shirt, a little too long in the sleeves for Freud. They weren't in the dining room, perhaps in a library? Many books and soft old chairs, and low tables and a chess set.

I imagine a bachelor meal of bread and cheese and cold chicken and apricot preserve. Breuer poured wine. He offered Freud a cigar. "And then came a long medical conversation about 'medical insanity,' and nervous illnesses and strange cases." Breuer unburdened himself, talking about Martha's friend, Bertha Pappenheim, "once again." The talk became intimate, and Freud left the Breuer house well after midnight. He walked—his body clean, his suit and socks and underwear still dirty—through the

narrow streets, maybe to his room at the hospital, maybe all the way to
Leopoldstadt, to his parents' place, along the grand, gas-lit boulevards,
from the center of the city toward its edges. The metal tracks of the street-
cars ran through the avenues. The town would have been empty of all life
but the prostitutes, who were everywhere in Vienna in 1882. "The present
generation has little idea of the vast extent of prostitution in Europe before the world wars," writes Zweig in *The World of Yesterday*. "While today
prostitutes are seen in big cities as seldom as horses in the streets, at the
time the pavements were so crowded with women of easy virtue that it
was harder to avoid them than to find them." Zweig described it this way:

> This monstrous army of prostitutes was divided into different kinds, just
> as the real army was divided into cavalry, artillery, infantry and siege ar-
> tillery. In prostitution, the closest equivalent to the siege artillery was the
> group that adopted certain streets of the city as their own quarter. . . . The
> authorities allowed a few alleys there to be used as a market for love. Two
> hundred or five hundred women would sit next door to one another; side by
> side, on display at the windows of single-storey apartments. . . . Itinerant
> prostitutes corresponded to the cavalry or infantry; these were the count-
> less girls for sale trying to pick up customers in the street. Street-walkers
> of this kind were said to be *auf den Strich*, because the police had divided
> up the street with invisible lines, leaving the girls their own patches in
> which to advertise. Dressed in a tawdry elegance which they had gone to
> great pains to purchase, they paraded around the streets day and night,
> until well into the hours of dawn, even in freezing and wet weather, con-
> stantly forcing their weary and badly painted faces into an enticing smile
> for every passer-by.

Freud unlocked the gate to his family's apartment building. He walked
up the creaking stairs. His father and sisters were in bed. Was his mother
awake, anxiously waiting for him? ("Charming and smiling when strangers were about," remembered Freud's niece, "with familiars she was a ty-
rant, and a selfish one."[45]) Freud shut himself in his cabinet—the room
where he kept all his books and took all his meals. He took off his dirty
clothes and wrote to Martha. It's a weird and sexy letter, with him naked

in the bathtub, and then (as he tells her), "I am writing in a more pronounced negligé"—Sigmund Freud at two a.m., in the buff, in his parents' apartment, scribbling out secrets and hints to his fiancée. Breuer has
told him something unspeakable, something "I am supposed to repeat
only 'once I am married to Martha.'" If he ever wrote down what secret
Breuer told him, Freud did that in his journal, a journal that he later
destroyed.

On July 30, 1883, a little more than two weeks after Freud's tête-à-
tête with Breuer, Bertha Pappenheim checked back into the Inzersdorf
sanitarium—the one in suburban Vienna, where the talking cure had
been invented and named. She was a wreck, in worse shape than she had
been with her cousins, complaining about her drug addiction. Breuer visited her in early August and described her symptoms to Freud, and then
Freud wrote to Martha, saying that Pappenheim was "quite deranged,"
and that Breuer wished she might die "so that the poor soul could be
released from her suffering."[46] Breuer swore off treating Pappenheim—or
ever again using the cathartic method that they had stumbled upon. "I
vowed at the time," Breuer wrote later, "that I would not go through such
an ordeal again."[47] For Breuer, the talking cure as they had practiced it
was neither tenable nor entirely effective.

But at the sanitarium Pappenheim improved, and by autumn Sigmund's reports of her to Martha turned increasingly gossipy. In these
letters, he seems less interested in her illness—which he sees as severe
and incurable—and more interested in her sex life. October 31, he wrote
to his fiancée:

It will surely interest you to know that your friend Bertha P is doing
well . . . getting rid of her pains and her morphine poisoning and is
rapidly gaining weight. This I know from a colleague who sometimes
drives out there to substitute for Doctor Breslauer. He is very taken
with the girl with her piquant looks in spite of gray hair, her wit
and her intelligence. I believe that were it not that as a psychiatrist,
he knows acutely what a cross is this to bear, severely hysterical illness, he would have fallen in love with her. But discretion all around
Marty. Also in respect to what I tell you now Breuer too has a very

high opinion of her and has given up her care because his happy marriage threatened to come unstuck on account of it. The poor wife could not bear it that he devoted himself so exclusively to a woman about whom he obviously spoke with much interest. . . . [Mathilde Breuer] fell ill, lost her spirits, until it dawned on him and he learned the reason for it which was of course a command for him to withdraw completely from the activity as a physician of BP. Can you be silent, Marty, it is nothing dishonorable but rather something very intimate and that one keeps to oneself and one's beloved?

From the start, Freud suspected that Breuer was attracted to her, and he always imagined that Bertha Pappenheim cast a spell—every doctor he knew who sat with her fell in love. Martha wrote back:

It has often been on the tip of my tongue to ask you why Breuer gave up Bertha. I could well imagine that those somewhat removed from it were wrong to say he had withdrawn because he was unable to do anything for her. It is curious that no man other than her physician of the moment ever got close to poor Bertha, that is when she was healthy she already [had the power] to turn the head of the most sensible man—what a misfortune for the girl. You will laugh at me, dearest, I so vividly put myself in the place of the silent frau Matilda that I could scarcely sleep last night.

Sigmund's response, on November 4, is full of innuendo:

My beloved little angel, you were right to expect that I would laugh at you. I do so with great gusto. Are you really so vain as to believe that people are going to contest your right to your lover, or later to your husband? Oh no, he remains entirely yours, and your only comfort will be that he himself would not wish it any other way. To suffer Frau Mathilde's fate one has to be the wife of Breuer, isn't that so?

Freud's admiration for Breuer was marbled with jealousy. In *Freud's Women*, Forrester and Appignanesi write, "To Freud, Breuer was the epitome of the medical charmer who worked his way to many cures through sleepwalking." In one letter Freud complains: "Through a lucky deal, not through knowledge or ability, [Breuer] won the game of life and made his fortune." Breuer went to parties at the Palais Todesco, "the house of geniuses and demons," where Franzi Todesco entertained all the men Freud worshiped, Meynert, Brentano, Exner, and Fleischl. This was the Vienna of decadence and genius, the world from which Freud was excluded, the world which—ever since he was a boy dreaming of Hannibal—Freud had wanted to crush.

Bertha Pappenheim remained in the Inzersdorf sanitarium until January 1884. Breuer went out just four days before she was discharged, and he wrote to Binswanger at Bellevue, "I saw the young Pappenheim girl today. She is in good health, no pains or other troubles."[48]

<hr />

The invention of psychoanalysis coincided with the invention of modern antisemitism. People like Breuer, Freud, and Pappenheim lived in a world where Jews faced constant pressure, constant danger. In 1880, the word *pogrom*—which was until then Russian for "destruction"—took on its contemporary meaning, the systematic murdering of Jews, the raping of Jewish women, the burning of synagogues and towns. Survivors of the Russian terror massed on the border of the Hapsburg Empire, but these Jewish refugees were kept out of Austria. The proto-Nazi Georg Schönerer, the "Knight of Rosenau," was elected to the Austrian parliament. Schönerer was, in the words of Carl E. Schorske, "a curious compound of gangster, philistine, and aristocrat." A railroad tycoon's heir who had succeeded at almost nothing until he found his gift for populist politics, he attacked "the Jews" as "the sucking vampire that knocks on the door of the German farmer and craftsman." Schönerer introduced the terms "Aryan" and "Semite" to the Viennese political discourse, as well as yelling to the parliament and street violence to the republic. One of his first moves after he consolidated power would be to keep Russian Jewish refugees out of the Austro-Hungarian Empire, and he based his legislation on the United States' Chinese Exclusion Act of 1882. The Viennese newspapers at the time were full of the Tizla-Eszlar case, medieval accusations of blood libel that were being tried in a modern Hapsburg court. Breuer wrote a friend:

> None of you realizes how badly people such as ourselves are affected by these matters. Nevertheless I prefer not to "bother" my friends with the problems. In all the years my indignation has "boiled over" only twice, over the bloody vileness of the "ritual murders." Yet my friends are astonished by my "fanaticism"! . . . I cannot deny that the general silence on matters which afflict me, and everyone can see afflict me, the trouble everyone takes to avoid discussing all this comes to have a seriously oppressive effect.[49]

Breuer signed his letters "*stirpe judaeus, natione germanu*," a Jewish tree grown in German land, and for him Freud was a little Semitic sapling he hoped to nurture. Frederick Crews paints Freud as someone who participated in the Jew-hatred of the time. Crews quotes letters in which Freud describes one Jew as a "weed" that belongs in a "compost-heap," another as a "*grobber Jüd*," another as a "a typical little Jew with sly features," and another in which Freud rails about "the ardor of the savage, merciless Jew." But in his feelings about Jewishness, as in everything, Freud in the 1880s was a knot of contradictions. He was a Jew uncomfortable with Jewishness, a doctor who didn't want to be a physician, a brilliant researcher who could not find focus.

His work on eel testes had led to his work on lamprey cells, but just as he was getting somewhere in cell biology, he switched focus. As Crews writes, Freud "skipped from one self-contained task to another . . . never crucially testing any of his own hypotheses." From 1883 to 1884, when Pappenheim was in and out of the Inzersdorf sanitarium, when Breuer was doggedly running experiments on the inner ears of birds, Freud began working on a gold-chloride stain for microscope slides, trying to discover a process for better definition of cell walls. Freud was still asking urgent questions—in 1906 when Santiago Ramón y Cajal won the Nobel Prize for his discovery of the neuron, Cajal shared the prize with Camillo Golgi, whose major breakthrough was a stain that made for better microscopic study of nerve tissue. Freud had chased after both of these problems, but he had pursued them with no professional position or support.

He worked his way through the wards of Vienna General Hospital: surgery, dermatology, nervous disease, and ophthalmology. He was promoted from *Aspirant* (an assistantship) to *Sekundararzt*, but all these positions were unpaid, and he joined Theodor Meynert's psychiatric clinic, where he was unhappy. Meynert's masterwork, *Psychology: A Clinical Treatise on Diseases of the Fore-Brain Based Upon a Study of Its Structure, Functions and Nutrition*, was published in 1884, a book that explained the whole of the human mind as something governed by reflex actions, with no room for free will. Makari describes it this way in *Revolution in Mind*:

> The brain, [Meynert] argued, was split into lower and higher cerebral functions, both of which were reflex driven. The automatic, inherited reflexes of the subcortical centers were opposed, controlled, and inhibited by acquired associational reflexes in the higher regions in the cerebral cortex.

The brain, in Meynert's view, was an electrochemical machine that ran like clockwork, with mechanistically connected centers bouncing automatic responses off one another, so engendering human behavior.

In these years Freud wrote detailed case histories—case histories much admired by Oliver Sacks—of a scrofulous boy who died of a cerebral hemorrhage, of an eighteen-year-old with multiple neuritis, and of a man whose curious spinal condition caused him to lose his sense of pain and temperature while retaining his sense of touch. Freud's income came mostly from the charity he got from wealthier men, like Breuer and Fleischl. His fiancée lived hundreds of miles away.

Restless, he changed the focus of his research once more, this time toward drugs. He got some expensive white powder from Merck Pharmaceuticals, and on April 30, 1884, *Walpurgisnacht*, the night when Goethe's Faust made his deal with Mephistopheles, when witches are said to meet on Brocken Mountain and dance with the devil, Freud in his hospital chambers under the samplers stitched by Martha mixed five milligrams of pure cocaine in water and drank his first dose. He loved it.

Cocaine "was an almost perfect remedy against his neurasthenic spells," wrote Siegfried Bernfeld. "Cocaine jacked up [his] mood and capacities from their depressed state to a more normal level."[50] Freud called cocaine his *Zaubermittel*, his magic cure. "I will write an essay on it," he wrote to Martha, "and I expect it will win its place in therapeutics." He planned to "try it out on cases of heart disease, then on nervous exhaustion, particularly in the miserable condition after morphine withdrawal." Cocaine would bring the success he longed for. "We need have no concern about being able to stay in Vienna," he assured his fiancée, "and to possess one another soon." His first experimental subject was himself. His second was his colleague, the brilliant and wounded Ernst Fleischl von Marxow.

Fleischl, tormented by the neuromas in his hand, had become addicted to morphine, which he used to numb his pain. He worked in Brücke's lab, and was about a decade older than Freud. "Our relationship isn't one of real friendship," Freud complained to Martha, explaining that Fleischl made him feel inferior.

> There is always a gap surrounding him, an aura of unapproachability, and when we've been together he has always been too occupied with himself to come near me. But I admire and love him with an intellectual passion, if you will allow such a phrase. . . . I love him not so much as a human being, but as a precious work of creation.

"His disappearance," Freud wrote, "will touch me in the way that an ancient Greek would have been moved by the destruction of a holy and famous temple."

Theodor Billroth had undertaken several operations on Fleischl's hand, shaving back his wounded thumb over and over again until it was just a stub. But it still ached, and Fleischl took more morphine to control his pain. In early May, less than a week after his own first dose of the drug, Freud approached Fleischl with a plan to free him from his morphine dependence: "I proposed cocaine to him, and he has clutched at the idea with the haste of a drowning man." So they entered together in an experiment, chronicled blow by blow by Freud in his letters to Martha. On May 9, Freud was ecstatic: "Triumph, rejoice with me . . . [Fleischl] has taken no morphine for three days, but has substituted cocaine and is in excellent spirits . . . I am so happy." But then on May 12, just three days later, the project crashed.

Fleischl is in such a sad state that I cannot enjoy the cocaine success at all. He continues to take it, and it continues to protect him against the miserable state of morphine use. But he has had such frightful pains in the nights from Friday to Saturday and from Saturday to Sunday that he lay there as if unconscious until 11am. . . . Early Monday I wanted to visit him, but he didn't answer my knocking. Two hours later, the same result. Finally, Obersteiner, Exner, and I pulled ourselves together, got the key from the servant, and went in. There he lay, quite apathetic and not answering our questions. Only after some coca did he come to himself and tell us that he had terrible pains. These attacks afflict the soul; in that state he can only become maniacal or kill himself.

Even as Fleischl was falling apart, Freud had noticed how the drug could numb his own lips and tongue, and when Billroth proposed a new, electrical shock treatment to relieve Fleischl's pain, Freud convinced both doctor and patient to use cocaine as an anesthetic. It didn't work. The radical surgery left Fleischl in agony, addicted to two drugs now instead of one, and, as Makari puts it, suffering "horrifying toxic psychoses."

Freud was blind to it all. On May 14, he gave a lecture on the miraculous curative properties of cocaine, skipping over the horror of Fleischl's hand. On May 23, he wrote to Martha, "The cocaine has stood the test very well." As Crews has demonstrated, even after his failures with Fleischl, Freud wrote articles for profit, paid by pharmaceutical companies, extolling his *Zaubermittel*, both as an anesthetic and as a cure for morphine addiction. He wondered how "little" Martha would handle a "big wild man who has cocaine in his body." But then his research into cocaine came to what Freud felt was a bitter end.

A colleague, Carl Koller, "to whom I had also spoken about cocaine," showed a conference of ophthalmologists how cocaine could function as a painkiller in eye surgery—and it was Koller, not Freud, who got the credit for the discovery. Freud burned with resentment. He stopped working on drugs, just as earlier he had given up on nerve cells and microscopy.

With Breuer's help, he won a fellowship to travel to Paris, and he left town to study with Jean-Martin Charcot. As ever, and despite all his failures, he remained confident in his own genius, telling Martha in his coked-up prose that he expected to go to

> Paris and become a great scholar and then come back to Vienna with a huge, enormous halo, and then we will soon get married, and I will cure all the incurable nervous cases and through you I shall be healthy and I will go on kissing you.

———•———

Breuer, meanwhile, was having problems. On April 8, 1884, Freud reported to Martha that "Breuer has *again* applied for the vacant position . . . in the hospital . . . but he won't get it." This time, Breuer's application for a professorship went all the way to the prime minister. Breuer had no luck. In the end a gentile physician, Dr. Ludwig Langer Ritter von Edenberg, got the job. As the prime minister's note described, Langer had "*incidental* qualities which almost seemed to rule out his fellow candidates from the start."[51] (Ritter's father was on the faculty.)

From the winter of 1885 to the spring, Bertha Pappenheim was again in the sanitarium at Inzersdorf, hysterical, hallucinating, and losing her German.

15

When Freud headed off to Paris in 1884, he was a twenty-eight-year-old virgin, the child of penniless immigrants, a habitual drug user, and a member of a despised minority. He was engaged to be married to Martha but could not go through with it: he had no money and no real prospect of employment. His research showed flashes of brilliance, but he skipped from subject to subject. He didn't get along with the leading psychiatrist in Vienna (Meynert); he had just poisoned and destroyed the one man (Fleischl) most likely to help him move forward in laboratory neurology; his mentor (Breuer) could not even get himself a professorship; and Freud had little interest in becoming a practicing physician. He came to France to work in a pathology laboratory, dissecting infant brains, but when he got there he saw Charcot lecture on hysteria, and Freud was overcome.

It was Charcot's project to find the organic sources of symptoms and disabilities that had no discernible physical cause. By the 1870s, he had identified the anatomical etiology of several previously mysterious diseases, including multiple sclerosis and amyotrophic lateral sclerosis (ALS). He had classified certain distinctive tremors and argued that they be named Parkinson's disease, after the Englishman James Parkinson. Where his

Viennese counterparts kept their focus on laboratory pathology, on the microscopic study of the dead tissue of the brain, Charcot's interest was in clinically observing his patients, looking at them carefully, and defining the nature of their illnesses. His students were the leading neurologists on the continent, among them Janet, Babinski, and Tourette. The hospital where Charcot worked, the Salpêtrière, was a complex of some forty-five buildings, including a massive, seventeenth-century stone structure like a jail. The hospital housed almost exclusively women, about 5,000 in all,[52] some 1,500 of them classified as insane—the mad and broken members of Paris's armies of sex workers and domestics. Charcot's was a museum of female neuroses, and he was the chief curator, and he showed off his collection in public lectures every Tuesday afternoon. These lectures were attended by some of the greatest psychologists in the world (Freud, William James) but also tourists and thrill seekers, people who wanted to see crazy ladies on display.

In 1872, in a reorganization of the hospital wards at the Salpêtrière, the epileptics had been put in the same rooms as the hysterics, and soon all the hysterical patients were having pseudo-epileptic fits. Charcot became fascinated—he thought that the patients' suggestibility was an integral part of their disease, hypothesizing those "dynamic lesions" in the hysterics' brains. Charcot identified four stages of hysteria, and according to Rachel Bowlby these stages shaped the way that Breuer and Freud conceived of the progression of the disease in *Studies*. (In a letter to me, Crews disputes this.) Charcot had his patients photographed in characteristic hysterical postures. For writers like Elaine Showalter, these are "elaborately framed and staged," their poses "suggest the exaggerated gestures of the French classical acting styles." But doctors treating FND see these pictures differently. Afra Moenter, the psychologist in Boulder who treated Hailey Hooper-Gray, sometimes shows patients the pictures that emerged from Charcot's studies, as these demonstrate that her patients' symptoms aren't strange and idiosyncratic—their seizures and postures aren't their own invention; they have been observed since the dawn of photography.

Charcot became interested in hypnotism, in the ways that through hypnotic suggestion paralysis and tremors and other functional symptoms could be induced. Only hysterics, in Charcot's view, could be hypnotized.

Every Tuesday, in his strange, misogynistic, scientific burlesques, Charcot brought these women into crowded lecture halls. As Freud describes it in a letter dated October 21, 1885:

> At ten o'clock, M. Charcot arrived, a big man of fifty-eight, wearing a top hat, with dark, strangely soft eyes (or rather, one is; the other is expressionless and has an inward cast), long wisps of hair stuck behind his ears, clean shaven, very expressive features with full protruding lips—in short, like a worldly priest from whom one expects a ready wit and an appreciation of good living.

He hypnotized his women and had them display their symptoms. His subjects became famous. Blanche Wittman was his star, a celebrity hysteric, and the most famous actress on the continent, Sarah Bernhardt, came to see the show.

> Some of them smelt with delight a bottle of ammonia when told it was rose water, others would eat a piece of charcoal when presented to them as chocolate. Another would crawl on all fours on the floor, barking furiously when told she was a dog, flap her arms as if trying to fly when turned into a pigeon, lift her skirts with a shriek of terror when a glove was thrown at her feet with a suggestion of being a snake. Another would walk with a top hat in her arms rocking it to and fro and kissing it tenderly when she was told it was a baby.[53]

When Freud was in Paris, Charcot was lecturing on male hysteria, on trauma and suggestion, on the ways ideas could affect the body. Freud was amazed.

A weird little chaste, hairy man wandering around Paris, working in a smelly lab, dissecting baby brains, Freud describes himself in one letter as "a poor, young human being tormented by burning wishes and gloomy sorrows." He complained in letters to Martha "that nature has not granted me that indefinite something which attracts people," and he felt this lack "has deprived me of a rosy existence." When he went to the theater to see Molière plays, he thought of them as "French lessons." When he went to the Louvre, it was to the Assyrian and Egyptian rooms. "For me," he wrote, "these things have more historical than aesthetic value." He disapproved of French sensuality and was not interested in food or art or music or fashion. But what he saw in the Salpêtrière electrified him.

> Charcot, who is one of the greatest of physicians and a man whose common sense borders on genius, is simply wrecking all of my aims and opinions. I sometimes come out of his lectures as from out of Notre Dame, with an entirely new idea about perfection.

"He exhausts me," Freud wrote to Martha, "when I come away from him, I no longer have any desire to work at my own silly things . . . no one else has ever affected me in the same way." Freud reveled in the beauty of Charcot's hysterics' performances. "Each of his lectures is like a work of art." Charcot's approach to the study of disease shook Freud, partly because of its drama and partly because its method differed so profoundly from the neurology he had known in Vienna. In Brücke's lab, the emphasis had been on the observation of dead tissue. At the Salpêtrière, Charcot experimented with the whole bodies of his prisoner-patients, with the way the patients' minds affected their bodies.

At a party, Freud dosed himself with cocaine for courage and approached his new hero. Later, he would claim that he spoke to Charcot about Bertha Pappenheim—"but," as Freud wrote in *An Autobiographical Study*, "the great man showed no interest in my first outline of the subject." Nevertheless, Freud emerged with a job: he returned home as Charcot's German translator, intent on bringing the new Parisian science back to the world of Viennese anti-vitalism.

In April, a small news item was announced by the *Neue Freie Presse*: "Herr Dr. Sigmund Freud, Docent for Nervous Diseases at the University, has returned from his study trip to Paris and Berlin and has consulting hours at I, Rathhaus No. 7, from 1 to 2:30." His wealthier friends had lent him money to open the practice; Mathilde Breuer fixed the plate to his office door with her own hands.

On September 13, 1886, Freud finally married Martha in a civil ceremony in her hometown, Wandsbek. A religious ceremony followed the next day, but Freud would not allow any Jewish tradition in their new home. For Martha, according to one of her cousins, "not being allowed to light the Sabbath lights on the first Friday night after her marriage was one of the more upsetting experiences of her life."[54] On October 15, Freud lectured on male hysteria at the Vienna Society of Physicians. If he was courting controversy and hoping to make a splash, Freud found only skepticism and boredom. Meynert asked for one example of male hysteria, just one, in Vienna. Another of Freud's old supervisors was still more dismissive. "I was unable to find anything new in the report of Dr. Freud because all that has been said has already long been known."[55] If he thought he was going to conquer Vienna with the new French thinking, he was wrong. "He fell into disgrace, as it were, with the faculty," remembered Julius Wagner-Jauregg, one of Freud's school friends.[56]

He had a pregnant wife and a struggling practice. He fought with Martha's brother about money—Eli Bernays was married to one of Freud's sisters, and Freud thought Eli was cheating him out of his wife's inheritance.

On Sunday, January 30, 1887, the Freuds attended a dinner party hosted by Emma Pappenheim, Bertha's cousin. According to Skues, the dinner celebrated the engagement of Emma's husband's cousin, Betti Berger, to the musicologist Guido Adler. Bertha was there with her brother Wilhelm.

That night, Martha was anxious about her old friend. She wrote to her mother: "Bertha is quite like before in her essential character; in her appearance she has aged very much; her hair is almost completely gray and the sparkle has completely gone from her eyes."[57]

Pappenheim met Martha's new husband. As he was a nerve specialist, Freud might have been exactly the kind of person Pappenheim wanted to avoid in company. But for Freud? As he recalls in *An Autobiographical Study*, Breuer had "repeatedly read me pieces of [her] case history," and these readings "accomplished more toward an understanding of neuroses than any previous observation." At the same time, the end of her story was a secret: "over the final stage of this hypnotic treatment there rested a veil of obscurity, which Breuer never raised for me." She was his wife's sick and sexy and hysterical friend—he had thought of her when watching the half-naked women faint in Charcot's lecture hall—and he had been meditating on Bertha Pappenheim for years, since that dinner at Breuer's home.

In the grand palace of his mind were combined all continental knowledge of the psyche, French and Viennese thinking, clinical and pathological, and of all the cases he knew, hers was the one by which he was most fascinated. There she was across the table from him, his dream girl. I imagine that he kept staring at her, between his bites of Tafelspitz and sips of Grüner Veltliner wine, and then looking away when she caught his gaze.

Two days later, on February 1, Pappenheim visited the Freud apartment. In a letter to her mother, Martha wrote, "Bertha announced herself directly for the other afternoon here for tea, and in fact she came yesterday with her cousin Anna. Both were very sociable, and plump Willi collected them." Throughout the winter, Pappenheim was a regular guest at Martha's kaffeeklatch. She stopped by again, when Martha was pregnant, in May of 1887, and Martha in her letter to her mother was quite concerned:

> At midday yesterday Bertha visited me for a moment, but she is quite miserable again: after 5 in the evening she gets into one of her states and is then quite useless. During the whole day she is smart and well, but apparently does not eat anything at all again – that is so terribly sad isn't it?[58]

From June to July 1887, Pappenheim was back in the sanitarium at Inzersdorf, anorexic, insomniac, hallucinating, suffering pain, and if I understand Martha Freud, continuing descents into her *condition seconde*. In 1888, she left Vienna and moved to Frankfurt with her mother. In 1889, she anonymously published her first collection of stories, *Kleine Geschichten für Kinder* (*Little Stories for Children*). One of these, "The Pond Sprite," goes something like this (I have condensed it here, and in doing so, reshaped it):

> It was a February night. Footsteps crunched gravel along the abandoned promenades at the edge of a city. Wind rippled the surface of a garden pond. Snow clouds blew through the sky. A little sprite, enticed by the

music of a distant party, emerged from the water, only to find herself face to face with a decorative gargoyle.

The gargoyle had sneering lips. A barren metal pipe poked out of its mouth, a tube from which in the summertime water spouted. The sprite dove back down, but when a window from the far-off ballroom was thrown open, the sound of the strings and trumpets summoned her to the surface once again.

It was forbidden for any water sprite to enter the human world, but the music drew her toward the dance. Slipping away from the fearsome gargoyle, she tiptoed through the reeds at the far end of the pond and made her way across the gravel paths. Through the drawn curtains and steamy windows, she could see the couples twirling in time. Entranced, the pond sprite flew—a trace of fog in the snowfall—and she alit on the terrace in the form of a beautiful girl.

In the ballroom, blooming camellias bunched together in vases. Palm trees grew in pots. Her hair shimmered. Her neck and fingers were adorned with silver and pearls. She had only one desire, for a dancer to come and choose her, to lead her in a dance. A tall, bearded man approached. His eyes were blue and sympathetic. She followed his steps. When he asked her name, she found herself speechless. When he thanked her, out of her mouth came the sound of rushes and of breaking ice.

With a start, he recognized the green of her eyes, the marmoreal whiteness of her flesh. His blue eyes filled with fear. She ran down the stairs and out the door past the footmen. The cold bit her shoulders, the gravel bit her feet. She staggered to the water's edge, the wind breaking her hair to crystals. Her feet below the surface of the water melted. Her body crumpled. Her back turned to frost. Snow blanketed the lawn, leaving white caps on the eyebrows of the sneering gargoyle. From his pipe came snowy laughter.

But February doesn't last forever. One March morning, when all the ice had gone, a little green plant bloomed at the edge of the pond, right where she had fallen—a snowdrop.

Most people who write about Pappenheim's first decade in Frankfurt agree on three things: (1) that she transformed from a helpless, drug-addicted young woman to a powerful advocate and organizer; (2) that there's very little hard documentation of her life between 1888 and 1900; and (3) that, nevertheless, they have the tools to make her transformation explicable.

Freudians tend to pathologize her politics—she went into activism against the sex trade because of her troubled psychosexuality. Feminists tend to politicize her illness—in her hysteria she was fighting against the patriarchy, just as she was in her activism. Daniel Boyarin, the Berkeley historian of religion who sees Pappenheim as a "foremother of lesbian feminist separatism," writes that "the hysteric grew into the feminist, because being a feminist 'cured' the hysteric."[59] Melinda Given Guttmann, the Pappenheim biographer who (like Boyarin) sometimes performed dressed as her heroine, argues that her breakdown was a "creative illness," a process that allowed her to "transform the inner self in order to transform the world." There's a more mundane explanation for her entry into politics: she was drawn into it by her family, her friends, and the people she met at her synagogue and congregation in Frankfurt.

16

Frankfurt was a smaller, quieter city than Vienna. It was, historically, a banking center. There were five Rothschild mansions in the city, and some of the Rothschilds were cousins by marriage to Bertha's mother, Recha Pappenheim, née Goldschmidt.

Initially, Bertha and Recha rented an apartment on Leerbachstrasse, in a neighborhood in which many wealthy Jews lived. The building in which they lived is gone—the whole Jewish ghetto of Frankfurt was razed in World War II—but you can still see neighboring apartment houses like it, dignified nineteenth-century buildings, white stucco with brown trim, five or six stories tall, with terraces overlooking the street. Recha was fifty-eight, returning home after forty years in Vienna. The previous decade of her life had been a war with her daughter Bertha. The war was now over. That first Friday night, I imagine, the two women dressed and went together to worship in the synagogue of Recha's childhood—so different from her dead husband's Schiffschul with its congregation of (I quote here from the liberal Austrian-Jewish newspaper *Die Neuzeit*) "hot-headed Hungarians, Pressburg liars, lunatics, fanatics, and warmongers." Recha and Bertha found their seats in the women's section. Bertha was twenty-nine. The crazy *dybbuk* that had invaded her body seemed gone, and so were the syringes. Recha looked around. The faces were strange, but the temple smells and songs were as they had ever been. Maybe, Recha thought (or so I imagine her thinking), there was still a chance for her daughter to begin again, normally, to put all the Austro-Hungarian medical madness behind her and find a nice man, a widower, maybe. (There's a dream that Pappenheim recounts in a letter, of two men visiting the apartment on Leerbachstrasse, Herr H. and Herr S., who smelled like jackals.) Mother and daughter walked home after the services. No riot of prostitutes on these streets. No bustling Viennese cafés. How strange it must have been for Bertha, to be alone at night in her new bedroom, to start life again in early middle age. Did it ever come again at night, that dreamy feeling, or the sense that she would lose the use of her native language? Restless, did she feel the urge for chloral to help her sleep? She was up all night writing, working on her fairy tales. Their second Friday in the city, maybe, they visited relatives for sabbath dinner.

The Rothschild mansion closest to their apartment was owned by Max Goldschmidt-Rothschild, Recha's cousin. In a townhouse on Emil-Claar Strasse, across from the gardens, lived Louise Goldschmidt, who had been born in Prague and had married into the family. (Louise had married her own uncle, a financier, who among other things invested profitably in the building of American railroads.) A few blocks from the Pappenheims' new apartment was another cousin, Anna Edinger, whose father Moritz Goldschmidt had been a banker, and whose husband Ludwig was a painter, a hypnotist, a philanthropist, and the leading neurologist in the city. Louise Goldschmidt and Anna Edinger were roughly Bertha's age.[60]

Boyarin writes about Pappenheim's "solid, rugged, masculine appearance," but Samson Schames, who painted her, recalled Pappenheim's vanity, particularly when it came to her hands. One friend described Bertha as "delicate and fragile," another said she combined "a masculine mind" with "feminine beauty and charm."[61] She had left Vienna partly because, as her cousin Paul Homberger wrote, her hysteria was "common knowledge" there.[62] I'm guessing her ambitions at this point were modest: to write her stories and to live with her mother.

Ludwig Edinger, their cousin's husband, had studied with Charcot in Paris. Later, he would found an institute for neurology in Frankfurt, but in 1888 he was (as far as I can tell) unaffiliated, not so different from Breuer, a brilliant Jew who married rich and sustained his own research through his wife's money. A gynecologist friend secretly delivered embryos to the house, and Ludwig anatomized their brains in his bedroom.

The Edingers had a new baby, Fritz. (He would become a neurologist, like his father; and then would be murdered by the Nazis in the Sobibor extermination camp.[63]) The candles were lit. The blessings were recited. Anna Edinger was a member of the Israelite Free Women's Association. She had just founded the Frankfurt Women's Education Association. Louise Goldschmidt supervised a soup kitchen, feeding immigrant Jews from Galicia. Later, Pappenheim would write about "the necessity to adjust the commandment to help your neighbor from overblown philanthropy and blind senseless spending of money to sensible action. The congregation at Frankfurt AM fifty years ago offered a rich and challenging place for such an effort." She volunteered at the soup kitchen her cousins funded, and there she began to do things she had never done before: to peel potatoes, to wear an apron, to spoon porridge into a refugee child's bowl. As one of her charges, Helene Krämer, remembered later:

> This period meant a complete revolution in her life . . . with total renunciation of her former habits. . . . She did justice to the many demands which the new sphere of activity imposed on her. She increased her manual skills, mingled with the children . . . and participated . . . in all kinds of housework.[64]

As she turned thirty, she was for the first time in her life independent. She could walk the streets by herself, home to work, and back. But outside she had to guard her dignity. As Zweig writes:

> An unmarried woman of her age had been "left on the shelf," and a woman left on the shelf became an old maid. The humorous journals, with their shallow mockery, made fun of old maids all the time. If you open old issues of . . . the humorous press at the time, it is horrifying to see, in every edition, the most unfeeling jokes cracked at the expense of aging, unmarried women.

Pappenheim taught sewing classes to refugee children. She ran a story hour. By 1895, the year of *Studies'* publication, she was the orphanage's director. According to Krämer, her goal was:

> To protect young people and to bring them up as proper people and good Jews. For this purpose it seemed to her necessary to preserve the utmost simplicity, in contrast to what had been the custom until then. Thus, the food was often too Spartan and simple, and we would have been happy for her to soften the unflinching strictness which she showed in her demands on us.[65]

In 1896, under the pseudonym P. Berthold, Pappenheim published *In the Junk Shop*, a collection of nine stories, each told from the point of view of an abandoned object in a secondhand store.

"You must wonder how I got here," a coffee mill says to an old cigarette case.

The mill's brass shines, but her side is dented and her handle is gone. Once, the mill says, she had a sheltered, dignified life—in a bustling kitchen where an old cook took her down twice a day, polished and cleaned her after use, and put her back in her place beside a handsome mortar and pestle, who would lean his long rod against her at night and murmur, "I love you." But that life didn't last: the kindly cook left, and a careless kitchen maid took charge, a girl carrying on all kinds of wanton intrigues. One day, the girl received a postcard from a lover who had jilted her, and, furious, the girl shoved the card into the coffee mill and cranked until the paper blocked the gears and the handle snapped.

"That's life," says the grandfather clock.

17

Freud's house filled with babies, born faster than one every two years: Mathilde (named for Breuer's wife) in 1887, Martin (named for Charcot) in 1889; Oliver in 1891, Ernst in 1892, Sophie in 1893, and Anna in 1895. Freud was so broke, according to Peter Gay, that he could hardly afford cab fare to pay house calls. Effectively exiled from the world of Viennese brain science, he found himself a new confidant and friend, an eccentric German-Jewish internist from Berlin, Wilhelm Fliess.

Fliess met Freud through Breuer when Fliess was visiting Vienna, and the two men fell for each other. They shared the same fascinations: hysteria, sex, cocaine, and the interrelation of body and mind. They posed for a photograph: two messy-haired, bearded, unsmiling medical men, both Jews in their late thirties.

"If he gave me bisexuality," Freud later wrote to Marie Bonaparte, "I gave him sexuality before that."

All we have is Freud's side of the correspondence—Freud either hid or destroyed the letters he received from Fliess, and then Anna Freud suppressed or censored much of her father's writing to Fliess. But all of Freud's letters to him were finally published in 1985, in *The Complete Letters of Sigmund Freud to Wilhelm Fliess, 1887–1904*, edited by Jeffrey Moussaieff Masson.

Fliess saw an anatomical parallel between the structure of the sinuses
and the structure of the vagina and the womb. He believed that all kinds
of neurotic illnesses, especially in women, were caused by something that
he called the "nasal reflex neurosis." Fliess's first course of treatment for
any psychosexual problem was cocaine applied to the nostrils; the second,
electrically shocking the nose; and the third, surgery: the removal of the
patient's turbinate bones, the nasal conchae, the long, thin, curved bones
that flare from the middle of the face into the breathing passages. The
"bad practice" of masturbation, Fliess wrote, could "only be finally cured
through an operation on the nose." He believed that menstrual pains
were caused by masturbation.

"Women who masturbate," he wrote, "are generally dysmenorrheal,"
and "it is to be noted that the middle turbinate bone seems to play a role
precisely in the mechanism of uterine bleeding." Through these operations, Fliess thought he could defeat all pleasure and pain associated with
female sex. "If one completely removes this segment of the middle turbinate bone on the left," Fliess promised, "which can be carried out with
suitable bone forceps, the stomach pains can be permanently cured."[66]
He believed that monthly cycles affected both men and women, and he
developed complex numerological theories, based on the numbers 23
(days of supposed male periods) and 28 (female). He developed a formula,
$x \times 23 \pm y \times 28$ (as Frederick Crews points out, this equation can be used
to generate any positive integer), and with this, Fliess understood everything. "The date of death is menstrual," he claimed.

On the afternoon of March 24, 1899, my wife's sister Melanie R., began
to have labor pains, and six hours later her daughter Margaret was born.
On the same afternoon my wife's period began, and, as we later learned,
it was to be her last period [before becoming pregnant]. So one sister had
continued the pregnant state of the other. This is more than a simple pattern. Behind it lies a hidden law of nature determining relationships. For
if one continues 280 days from March 24, that is, 10 times 28, one comes
to December 29, the very same date on which, 4 years earlier, my eldest
son came into the world. (December 29, 1895). And 20 years earlier, on

December 29, 1879, my only sister became suddenly deathly ill with chills and died thirty hours later.[67]

In the crucial years of Freud's intellectual development, between 1887 and 1900, when he was working through *Studies* and toward *The Interpretation of Dreams*, Fliess was the man to whom Freud sent his drafts and theories, and to whom he wrote almost daily.

In the collected letters to Fliess, Freud complains about his sex life; he and Martha were "now living in complete abstinence," he wrote in one letter. "Business is not good," he wrote in another, "my practice . . . barely keeps us alive." He confessed his drug dependence ("I need a lot of cocaine") and his insecurities ("I have not learned enough to be a medical practitioner"). He boasted. The other neurologists in Vienna, he tells Fliess, "look upon me as pretty much of a monomaniac, while I have the distinct feeling that I have touched upon one of the great secrets of nature." He bitched about Meynert, "who in his customary impudent-malicious manner spoke out authoritatively on a topic of which he knows nothing," and spilled a lot of ink complaining about Breuer. "Breuer is an obstacle to my professional progress in Vienna. He dominates the very circles on which I had counted." All the while, to his face, Freud continued to flatter and cultivate his old mentor. When Freud's translation of Charcot appeared, he inscribed a copy to Breuer: "To his, before all others, most highly esteemed friend, Dr. Josef Breuer, secret master of hysteria and other complicated problems, in silent dedication, the translator."

Throughout the early 1890s, Freud was afflicted with cardiac palpitations, "the most violent arrhythmia, constant tension, pressure, burning in the heart region; shooting pains down my left arm." Fliess thought that Freud's cardiac complaints were related to his nose ("you still explained it as being nasal") and suggested that they be treated with cocaine. Freud replied:

I kept the nose under cocaine, which one should not really do; that is, I repeatedly painted it to prevent the renewed occurrence of swelling; during this time I discharged what in my experience is a copious amount of thick pus; and since then I have felt wonderful, as though there never had been anything wrong at all. Arrhythmia is still present, but rarely and not badly.

Both Breuer and Fliess suspected that Freud was suffering from nicotine poisoning from cigars,[68] but no one seemed to suspect that the heart problems might be related to Freud's drug use.

"Dearest Friend," Freud calls Fliess, or "my beloved friend," or "Dearest Wilhelm," "Carissimo Guglielmo," "Diamonie," and "Dear Magician." "I still don't know how I won you," Freud tells Fliess, and later, "you altogether ruin my critical faculties." Freud described their meetings as "congresses" and looked forward to seeing Fliess as if to "the slaking of my hunger and thirst." At some points the line between self and other vanishes. When Freud offers advice to Fliess, it seems he's talking to a mirror: "Announce the forthcoming investigation, describe the anticipated result as that which it really is, something new; show people the key that unlocks everything, the etiological formula." His coked-up attention veers wildly, from Fliess's work, to his own health, to his developing theories:

> Recently, I too encountered something like crossed reflexes. Furthermore, a short time ago I interrupted (for one hour) a severe migraine of my own with cocaine, the effect set in only after I had cocainized the opposite side as well, but then it did so promptly. I see a good possibility of filling yet another gap in the sexual etiology of the neuroses. I believe I understand the anxiety neuroses of young persons who must be presumed to be virgins and who have not been subjected to abuse. I have analyzed two cases of this kind; it was a *presentient dread* of sexuality, and behind it things they had seen or heard or half-understood—thus, the etiology is purely emotional but nevertheless of a sexual nature.

When Freud looked back on the relationship later, in a letter to Sándor Ferenczi, he saw the romantic nature of the affair and the heartbreak, and understood that his intimacy with Fliess was a crucial moment in his coming into his own.

You not only noticed, but also understood, that I *no longer* have any need to uncover my personality completely, and you correctly traced this back to the traumatic reason for it. Since Fliess's case, with the overcoming of which you saw me occupied, that need has been extinguished. A part of homosexual cathexis has been withdrawn and made use of to enlarge my own ego.

The affair with Fliess ended with a terrible row, and with it something died in Freud, "the need to uncover my personality completely," i.e., his need for intimacy. After Fliess, he was never so open with a human being again.

The bromance, the eccentricity, and the misogyny of it all can distract us from the correspondence's profundity. "Sigmund Freud did not so much create a revolution in the way men and women understand their inner lives," writes Makari. "Rather he took command of revolutions that were already in progress." But he did so at first from a position of near isolation. In a busy intellectual city, he was alone, or would have been if not for Fliess. To Fliess, Freud could say anything.

Their correspondence begins with the discussion of cases in which Freud has difficulty distinguishing a patient's "incipient organic and neurasthenic affections," i.e., whether or not the patient's symptoms were functional.

She suddenly could not walk, but apart from heaviness in the legs complains of no other sensations—there is none of the pulling and pressing in the muscles, the manifold pains, the corresponding sensations in other parts of the body, and the like.

Freud sent Fliess drafts of work in progress, including pieces of *Studies*, and diagrams of the psyche as he was beginning to conceive of it, with the x-axis being mind-body ("somat-psycho boundary") and the y-axis being the line between consciousness and unconsciousness ("the ego boundary"). He sent chapters of his *Project for a Scientific Psychology*, whose "intention" was "to furnish a psychology that shall be natural science: that is, to represent the psychical processes as quantitatively determined states of specific material particles."

The house was full of children. His medical practice consumed Freud's days. "Fueled by cocaine," Makari writes, "Freud sat down around eleven in the evening and labored deep into the night as he sought to integrate physics, biology, neurology, and psychiatry." He was reacting with and against Charcot's Parisian school, and Meynert's Viennese hard science, and he was influenced—crucially, according to Oliver Sacks—by the English neurologist John Hughlings Jackson. Instead of Meynert's brain map of specific centers, Freud proposed a brain that worked in more complex and diffuse patterns, "with *systems* for achieving cognitive goals," as Sacks summarizes it, in an essay about Freud as a neurologist, "systems that had many components and which could be created or greatly modified by the experiences of the individual." For Freud, the brain's workings were malleably and complexly interwoven. The connections between the physical organ of the brain and the human experience of the mind were subtle and indirect. In *On Aphasia*, in 1891, he wrote:

> The relationship between the chain of physiological events in the nervous system and the mental processes is probably not one of cause and effect. The former do not cease when the latter set in . . . but, from a certain moment, a mental phenomenon corresponds to each part of the chain, or to several parts. The psychic is, therefore, a process parallel to the physiological, "a dependent concomitant."

Freud dedicated *On Aphasia* to Breuer, but Breuer didn't want to be associated with any of this. As Freud complained in a letter to his sister-in-law Minna, Breuer "was very much embarrassed by [the dedication] and said all kinds of incomprehensibly bad things about [*On Aphasia*], remembered nothing good; at the end, to mollify me, [he offered] the compliment that 'the writing is excellent.'" As his connection with Breuer waned, his connection with Fliess deepened.

Freud sent one of his patients, Emma Eckstein, to Fliess for a consultation. In the doctors' minds, Eckstein's complaints were associated with her menses and her supposed masturbatory bad habits, and therefore with her nose. Fliess cut the turbinate bone out of Eckstein, and afterward her face swelled grotesquely. Bits of blood and bone came out of her nostrils.

Freud believed that these symptoms were somaticized expressions of her repressed sexual longings. This was in 1895, just as *Studies* was being completed. Her wound began to fester, and stink. Freud was in the room when Dr. Ignaz Rosanes cut open her face. Freud describes it to Fliess this way:

> There still was moderate bleeding from the nose and mouth; the fetid odor was very bad. Rosanes cleaned the area surrounding the opening, removed some sticky blood clots, and suddenly pulled at something like a thread, kept on pulling. Before either of us had time to think, at least half a meter of gauze had been removed from the cavity. The next moment came a flood of blood. The patient turned white, her eyes bulged, and she had no pulse.

Freud ran from the room and vomited. Rosanes managed to bring Eckstein back to life. The story of Eckstein's surgery is recounted, obliquely, in *The Interpretation of Dreams*. It's in one of the early sections of a dream interpretation drawn from Freud's self-analysis, in a passage called "The Dream of Irma's Injection." It's an elegant, abstract interpretation, the very first dream in the book; the interpretation is that it was a dream about a misplaced anxiety, and the conclusion is moral exculpation.

The true story behind Irma's injection wasn't known until the 1980s, with the publication of the uncensored letters to Fliess. I remember my father when he had read the truth. I see him in my mind's eye, younger than I am now, red-faced and shouting. We're in his bedroom. I am in there, asking him for something, probably money. He has a book open in his left hand, and his right hand is a fist and it's pounding and pounding on the pages.

Freud was a neurologist—a researcher and practitioner—for over almost twenty years before he began to focus on psychoanalysis. Sacks hazards that in early private practice, Freud saw "presumably a mix of patients . . . some with everyday neurological disorders such as strokes, tremors, neuropathies, seizures, or migraines; and others with functional disorders such as hysterias, obsessive compulsive conditions, or neuroses of various sorts." As Freud points out in *An Autobiographical Study*, his turn toward the psychological, functional disorders was pragmatic and financial. That's where the patients were, where the money was, in "the crowds of neurotics" in Vienna, writes Freud, "whose number seemed further multiplied by the manner in which they hurried, with their troubles unresolved, from one physician to another." It was through Breuer's referrals that Freud began treating some of the richest women in Europe. To his protégé, Breuer sent Fanny Moser, who appears in *Studies* as Frau Emmy von N., the second case study in the book, the one that follows Anna O.

Fanny Moser was born Fanny Sulzer-Walz in 1848, and when she was young and beautiful she had married Heinrich Moser, a fantastically wealthy designer of watches and railway carriages who was nearly forty years older than she. When Heinrich Moser died, the children of his first marriage accused Fanny of having poisoned him, a case that was never settled, and around which evidence mysteriously disappeared. According to Appignanesi and Forrester, Fanny Moser "was, at least in many circles, so surrounded by scandal, that when she visited health resorts and spas, she sometimes forbade her children to tell people their name." Her "energetic salon life," Appignanesi and Forrester report, "included her taking a succession of lovers, frequently the personal physicians whom she had in the house." She was addicted to morphine, but Freud, apparently, saw none of this. In *Studies*, he presents her as a woman with "a flawless development of character and a purposeful way of life," a woman who demonstrated "moral seriousness in the execution of her duties." He extolls her "love of truth" and "personal modesty" and as with Breuer's description of Anna O., he claims that in Emmy von N., "the sexual element . . . was completely absent."

Her symptoms, like Anna O.'s, affected her speech, her perceptions, and her limbs—pains in the legs, hallucinations, and a speaking voice that was full of tics and clicks. She lived in Zurich, and Freud took eighteen-hour train rides to her estate, and he laid his hands on her forehead, applying pressure, before conducting with her what he began to call (publicly, for the first time, in print in 1889) "the cathartic method of J. Breuer."

As early as October 24, 1887—either directly through Breuer or on the recommendation of Breuer's colleague, the gynecologist Rudolf Chrobak—Freud was introduced to Anna von Lieben, who in *Studies* is called "Frau Cäcilie M." In the book there's no single chapter devoted to her, no complete history of Cäcilie M.'s treatment, but hers is a case that informs all the rest. Freud calls her "a highly intelligent woman to whom I am indebted for much help in gaining an understanding of hysterical symptoms." "I got to know her," Freud writes, "far more than any of the other patients in these *Studies*." In one letter, he referred to her as "my former patient and teacher."

Peter Swales's research into Anna von Lieben's life—his proof that she was the mysterious Frau Cäcilie M.—changed the way that *Studies* has been understood, and I depend on Swales here: Anna von Lieben was born in 1847 as the Baroness Anna von Todesco, to an ennobled Jewish family of industrialists, bankers, and silk merchants. She grew up in the Palais Todesco in central Vienna, a block-long mansion built on the model of a Medici palace. When Anna was a child, Brahms and Liszt were guests at the Palais. Johann Strauss met his wife there. Dark-haired, heavy-featured, and plump, she was a painter and a poet. She married a banker, Leopold von Lieben. Her hysteria involved a lot of pain—facial neuralgia, pains in her feet, and a piercing headache between her eyes. She abused morphine, slept only in the day, and subsisted largely on caviar and champagne. She required that a professional chess player be stationed outside her bedroom door all night. Sometimes, she took on two players at once. According to Swales, "It is said that Anna was able to stick a knitting needle through her arm—possibly when she was in a state of trance; and presumably without any pain or blood." In 1888, she lived a five-minute walk from the Freuds.

Her children distrusted Freud. They called him "*der Zauberer*," the magician. As he did with Fanny Moser, Freud adopted a "pressure technique," putting his hands on Anna's forehead while she lay in her *chaise longue*, thereby getting her to relax and speak freely. In one session with Freud, Anna von Lieben recalled a time when her husband insulted her, and the insult had felt "like a slap in the face." She spoke those words, and then, voilà, her face pain vanished.

At the height of their treatment, Freud visited Anna twice a day. He went to her house morning and night, going through her symptoms, traumas, and memories, several hundred recitations of several hundred memories, each session focused around a particular symptom, seeking its root in trauma and finding its origin so that it could disappear. This archeological work that Freud took on with Anna von Lieben does not appear in any of the cases in *Studies in Hysteria*—but it seems very much like the work that Breuer claims to have done with Anna O. in the last months of her treatment.

Breuer struggled with the composition of "Anna O." It took years for Freud to persuade him to collaborate, and to publish the account. In *An Autobiographical Study*, Freud writes, "I could not understand why he [Breuer] had so long kept secret what seemed to me an invaluable discovery." For about a century after *Studies'* publication, Freudians have asked the same question about Breuer that Freud asked: *What took him so long?* Freud's answer has long dominated the historical conversation: that Breuer was hiding an embarrassing secret, and therefore didn't want to write it down.

But imagine the situation from Breuer's point of view. He wasn't an expert in hysteria. He had never pursued the talking cure again after 1882; his scientific focus in the 1890s was on the inner ear. According to Hirschmüller, "Breuer spent years, mostly evening nights at home in a small closet or connecting room, engaged in laborious dissection of hundreds of fish, frogs, birds, and mammals." He was busy studying otoliths, tiny particles of calcium carbonate, the little stones that rub against the tiny hairs of the utricle, and thereby allow all vertebrates from fish to humans to perceive the force of gravity. He debated some of the great minds in Europe—including the physicist-philosopher Ernst Mach— trying to grasp the precise nature of the rotation of liquid within the aural ampullae. For Breuer, as for most researchers in Vienna, the stuff Freud was doing wasn't serious. And when it came to Pappenheim's case, Freud was asking Breuer to revisit the memory of a therapeutic failure, an embarrassment.

Breuer recognized, as almost no one else did, Freud's genius. In one letter to Fliess, he writes, "Freud's intellect is soaring: I struggle along behind him like a hen behind a hawk." But Freud also writes about "battles with my esteemed mentor," and as Crews describes it, Breuer worried that Freud was nuts. Freud saw Breuer as the secret master, the one who held the key—by attaching Breuer's respectable name to the "cathartic method," Freud could make it respectable. For Peter Swales, when Freud began to advertise "the cathartic method of J. Breuer," Freud was trying "to force his mentor's hand."

By 1894, Bertha Pappenheim had left Vienna. Billroth, Brücke, and Meynert were all dead. Breuer, past fifty, perhaps accepted that he would never get his professorship. Freud kept pressuring, pressuring, for the collaboration, and reluctantly Breuer relented and agreed to publish. In June 1892, Freud wrote Fliess, "Breuer has declared his willingness to publish jointly our detailed theory of abreaction, and other joint witticisms on hysteria." In this collaboration, Breuer tried to temper some of the extremes of Freud's thinking. Freud wrote to Fliess in July of 1892, "My hysteria has, in Breuer's hands, become transformed, broadened, restricted, and in the process has partly evaporated." They worked together spasmodically. In June 1894, Freud declared, "The scientific contact with Breuer has stopped." But in April of 1895, he told Fliess, "The book I am writing with Breuer is progressing." When Breuer appeared publicly with Freud, his ambivalence was obvious. "[Breuer] was supposed to give a lecture in my class on Saturday, but he got stuck three times and gave up with apologies. I had to take over for him." Was it "Fraulein Anna O." that Breuer was reading to Freud's class? If so, in public, Breuer couldn't get the words out of his mouth.

Breuer's admirers have trouble accepting the fact that he lied on Freud's behalf. Hirschmüller complains that "if we are not to impute base motives to Breuer, the only feasible explanation" for Breuer's false claim that his patient was cured by the talking cure "is that he . . . assumed that he had been completely successful in eliminating that element in the hysteria that was accessible to psychotherapy." But I don't think we have to impute base motives to Breuer, just ordinary human complexity, mixed motives, and relative weakness in the face of the tectonic force that was Sigmund Freud.

Breuer was a complicated man: a devoted husband who became fascinated by a charming patient, a laboratory researcher trafficking in mystic theories; if he was a proto-feminist (as Louis Breger describes him), he was one who sent masturbating girls to Fliess for bone-removing surgeries. In his relationships with both Pappenheim and Freud, Breuer extended himself sympathetically, paternally, toward someone he wanted to help, and in both cases he got burned.

As with all of this, the evidence is scant, the facts are murky. The first eighteen months of the Anna O. case study correspond so closely with Breuer's contemporaneous Pappenheim notes that it seems a good bet that, twelve years after treating her, Breuer went out to the Kreuzlingen to consult them. But the notes drop off abruptly at the point when the narrative becomes implausible—and that at that point in the story, Breuer acts on Pappenheim in much the way that, for Swales, Freud acted with Anna von Lieben. As Borch-Jacobsen points out, their hysterias closely mirror one another: "Anna von Lieben's symptoms included a facial neuralgia, losses of sensation, and even a temporary inability to speak German, exactly as in Bertha Pappenheim's case." For Borch-Jacobsen, "there is good reason to suspect that Anna von Lieben . . . had heard about Bertha Pappenheim's treatment," and his implication is that—in some kind of dutiful pantomime—Freud with Frau Cäcilie M. reenacted the dance steps originated by Breuer and Anna O.

But for me there's a simpler explanation. We know that Breuer didn't want to report the end of his failed treatment, and Freud needed Breuer to announce that his "talking cure" had been a success—so, it seems plausible to me that more than a dozen years after he treated Pappenheim, Breuer obliged his collaborator by completing the story of Anna O. not with a true history of her drug addiction and his failure, but as it might have been, as the kind of success that Freud wanted—even needed—to have been achieved: the success he claimed to have achieved with Cäcilie M.

In January and February of 1886, Freud visited Charcot at his residence in Paris. In *An Autobiographical Study*, Freud says that he discussed the case of Bertha Pappenheim with Charcot, and that Charcot had confided in him that the cause of all hysterical cases was sexual. According to Peter J. Koehler, Freud worked fitfully on a single essay for the next six years: one that attempted to distinguish between "organic" and "hysterical" cases of paralysis. James Strachey speculates that Freud may have completed the first two sections of the essay by 1888. These first two sections deal with paralyses that were caused by damage to the brain and by damage to the spinal cord. For paralysis caused by injury to the brain, Freud offers the term "representation paralysis," and he argues that "hysterical" paralysis is like "representational paralysis" in that these cases "never affect single muscles (except where the muscle concerned is the sole instrument of a function)." Freud cites the work of the English neurologist Robert B. Todd, who had argued that "the hysteric drags the leg like an inert mass instead of performing the circumduction with the hip as does an ordinary hemipelagic." Hysteria was like an idea, a performance of paralysis, Freud saw, rather than a specific physical immobility.

In the third part of the essay, Freud takes up paralyses caused by damage to the nerves, by lesions to them. Here, he begins to question Charcot's neurology and his notion of the "dynamic lesions" in "hysteria." Freud wonders:

> What, after all, is a dynamic lesion? I am quite sure that many who read M. Charcot's works believe that a dynamic lesion is indeed a lesion, but one of which no trace is found after death, such as an oedema, an anaemia or an active hyperaemia. These, however, although they may not necessarily persist after death, are true organic lesions even if they are slight and transitory. . . . I . . . assert that the lesion in hysterical paralyses must be completely independent of the anatomy of the nervous system, since *in its paralyses and other manifestations hysteria behaves as though anatomy did not exist or as though it had no knowledge of it.* [italics his]

The fourth part of the essay was written, according to Koehler, some seven years after the visit to Charcot, roughly at the same time Freud and

Breuer were outlining their new conception of the disease, and it's here that Freud writes about paralysis without any neurological lesions: "For that purpose I only ask permission to move on to psychological ground— which can scarcely be avoided in dealing with hysteria." He wrote these sentences over the course of years that he worked with Anna von Lieben and Fanny Moser, and it is here that Freud's thinking left the stable precincts of the body and embarked on his journey into the whirl of the symbolic and dynamic mind.[69]

18

Studies in Hysteria entered the world quietly. It took thirteen years before its first printing of 626 copies sold out.[70] Reviews were mixed. "I am afraid that many hysterics will be encouraged to give free rein to their fantasy and invent stories," one critic wrote. One hundred forty years later, Breuer's studies of the inner ear are mostly forgotten, but *Studies* remains a standard text in the history of Western thought. I have to admit, I loved the book. It consoled me in my grief after my father was gone—just the seduction of good writing, of Freud's narrative voice, of daring minds at work on wildly difficult problems.

After the "Preliminary Statement" and the confusion of "Fraulein Anna O.," the book's opening acts are over, and the real show begins. Freud is among the great doctor-writers of his time, or any time. He can conjure a patient's character, can make us feel her anxieties, and also his own efforts and struggles. He brings the reader into the drama of a medical case, building tension and complexity, and guiding it all to satisfying resolution. "I myself still find it strange," he writes, "that the case histories I write read like novellas and lack, so to speak, the serious stamp of science." But Freud must know he's good at this. He gives us Frau Emmy von N. in the flesh:

> Her face bears a tense, pained expression; her eyes are screwed up and cast down; she has a heavy frown and deep naso-labial folds. She speaks as if

it were arduous, in a quiet voice that is occasionally interrupted by spastic breaks in her speech. When she speaks she keeps her fingers, which exhibit a ceaseless agitation resembling athetosis, tightly interlaced.

When Freud writes about her hallucinations, he builds her terrors intimately, from the ordinary thought to the phantasmagoric, drawing the reader into Emmy's twisted perception of the world:

She explains that her fear of worms comes from having once received a gift of a beautiful pin-cushion. When she wanted to use it the next morning hundreds of tiny worms crept out, because the bran, which had been used as stuffing, was not quite dry. (A hallucination? Perhaps it did actually happen.) I ask her to tell me some more animal stories. When once she and her husband had gone for a walk in a park in St. Petersburg the entire pathway to the pond was so covered with toads that they had to turn back. There have been times when she was unable to shake hands with anyone for fear that her hand might change into a frightful animal.

Freud gives us Emmy's voice, which goes, "Keep still!—Don't say anything!—Don't touch me!" or "I don't want any antipyrin injections, I would rather keep my pains." We get her background, as if she figured in a novel by Turgenev. "Her family is originally from Central Germany, but the last two generations have resided in the Baltic Provinces of Russia where they have extensive estates." Freud sets the scene, a sanitarium, with doctors and nurses, baths and gynecologists, dogs in the garden, books all around, a Faradic brush for electric massage of her frozen leg, and a couch with a leather bolster, a divan.

He himself is a character, full of doubts and foibles. He forgets to bring towels to the massage table, he tells lies to his patient, his hypnotism doesn't work. In the early case histories—in "Frau Emmy von N."—Freud is trying to repeat the French methods, and he fails. But in later case studies, and inspired by Breuer, Freud forgoes hypnosis and suggestion and moves toward the talking cure.

Emmy von N. is the first pancake, the one you throw out because the griddle hasn't gotten quite hot enough. Freud writes, dolefully, "I did, in fact, fail to pursue the analysis either far enough or systematically enough." In this case, he is learning his trade and his method, and the cure doesn't quite work out in the end. "Since this visit in May 1890 my news of Frau Emmy has gradually become sparser." There is a melancholy touch to the final sentences. "And so I relinquished my exclusive prerogative [to be her doctor] in writing."

Emmy's functional symptoms are a lot like Anna's: hallucinations (again, snakes), difficulty in speaking (she can still speak German, but she makes weird clacking noises), and weakness in some of her limbs and paralysis in others. As with Anna (or Hailey Hooper-Gray, or Kyla Kenney, or some of the patients described in O'Sullivan's book), her symptoms shift over time; they seem to move around within her body, now in her mouth, now in her leg, now in her eyes. She can't eat, she can't drink, she suffers insomnia, and her moods swing with the hour of the day: she's sad every day before sunset. Her mind, like Anna O.'s, is broken into "two states" and "the two states were entangled and yet unaware of each other."

The patients in Freud's next three case studies, Miss Lucy R., Katharina, and Fraulein Elisabeth von R., all have varied symptoms. Lucy R. is "in low spirits, tired and complaining of a muzzy head, together with a loss of appetite and stamina." She is plagued by the odor of burnt pudding, and she can't smell anything else. Katharina is afflicted by "breathlessness":

"It comes on me all of a sudden. First of all it comes down like a pressure on my eyes, then my head gets so heavy and it makes this roaring sound, it's unbearable, and I'm dizzy so that I think I'm going to fall over, and then it presses on my chest so that I can't get my breath."

Elisabeth von R. has a limp, the limp doesn't follow any pattern that comports with a physical injury, and Elisabeth acts like the limp isn't a problem—*la belle indifférence.*

The range of symptoms here is wider than the one described by O'Sullivan in *Is It All in Your Head?*, but there's nothing that wouldn't fit under the umbrella term of FND, and in each of the three studies—the cases of Lucy, Katharina, and Elisabeth—Freud traces the hysteria back to a sexual problem, a repressed desire or trauma. He compares his analytic sessions to chapters in a thriller. The breaks between sessions build up the story's suspense:

> The interruption that is dictated by incidental circumstances of the treatment, such as the hour being late and so on, often occurs at the most awkward points, precisely when we might be able to approach a decision or when a new theme emerges. These are the same difficulties that spoil anyone's reading of a novel serialized in a daily newspaper, when the heroine's decisive speech or, say, the ringing out of a shot is immediately followed by the words: "To be continued."

He's so excited! He's having fun listening to these patients and decoding their problems, and as the book goes on, the stories get racier and darker and increasingly melodramatic.

Katharina is a "sullen-looking" young servant whom Freud has encountered on his visit to a mountainside inn. She asks for Freud's help because she's having her attacks of breathlessness, and she wants to know why. Freud explains to her: "I'll tell you where your attacks come from. Once during that time two years ago you saw or heard something that embarrassed you very much, that you would rather not have seen."

"Heavens, yes," says Katharina. "I saw my uncle with the girl, with Franziska, my cousin!"

The analyst digs deeper. Eventually it comes out. The horror, the repressed memory, is not what her uncle was doing with her cousin, but what this same uncle has done to her:

> He [the uncle] stayed in the bar, drinking and playing cards; she [Katharina] started to feel sleepy and went early to the room that they were sharing upstairs. She was not sound asleep when he came up, but then she fell asleep and suddenly woke up and "felt his body" in the bed. She jumped

up and reproached him. "What are you up to, Uncle? Why don't you stay in your bed?"

In the story Freud tells, Katharina escapes unmolested, and retains her innocence.

When asked subsequently if she did know what he [her uncle] wanted of her, she replied, "Not at the time," it had only become clear to her much later. She had resisted because she didn't like having her sleep disturbed, and "because it just wasn't nice."

The confession relieves her of her hysterical breathlessness—but the contemporary reader can't help but wonder: *What actually happened between Katharina and her uncle?*

The fact is, Freud substituted the word "uncle" for the word "father." On his mountain idyll, he encountered a girl who asked for his help and told him that her father was a rapist, a sexual predator, a man who had attacked her and was now going after her cousin. Freud claims to have cured her "breathlessness," but does he do anything about the rapist with whom she is still apparently living?

In the last case study, "Fraulein Elisabeth von R.," Freud's narrative and theoretical powers find their fullest articulation. He describes his patient's strange limp:

She walked with her upper body bent forward, but without using any support, in a manner that did not correspond to any of those recognized as pathological and which, in any case, was by no means strikingly bad.

He examines the affected leg and is surprised.

When . . . the hyperalgesic skin and musculature of the legs was pinched or pressed, her face took on a peculiar expression, more that of pleasure than pain, she cried aloud—I couldn't help thinking that it was as if she were being tickled voluptuously—her face became flushed, she threw back her head and closed her eyes, her trunk bent backwards.

He describes the crucial moment of Elisabeth's life—the memory that leads to her hysteria—with the economy and clarity you'd find in a perfect short story:

> There now followed her memory of the arrival in Vienna, the impressions made on them by relatives who were expecting them, the short journey from Vienna to the nearby summer resort where her sister was staying, the arrival there in the evening, the path hurriedly crossed through the garden up to the door of the small garden pavilion—the stillness inside, the stifling darkness; that her brother-in-law did not come to greet them; then they stood in front of the bed, saw the dead woman, and in that moment of dreadful certainty that her beloved sister had died without having taken leave of them, without her last days having been brightened by their care—at that same moment another thought flashed through Elisabeth's mind, a thought that had now presented itself again unavoidably and came like a bolt in the dark: now he is free again, and I can become his wife.

Elisabeth is in love with her dead sister's husband, but cannot admit it to herself, that's Freud's conclusion. Freud looks at Elisabeth and thinks: "the little mask reveals a hidden meaning." And he offers his famous metaphor for getting to that meaning: "We like to compare it to the technique of excavating a buried city." He tells Elisabeth that "she would never get rid of her pains as long as she kept anything secret."

A struggle ensues between them, in which the secret is unearthed, but the patient is unwilling to face facts. She rejects Freud. Despite this rejection, she is cured—against her will, he has revealed the buried city. The pathogen is abreacted, and in the denouement, Freud spies Elisabeth at a social gathering.

> In spring 1894 I heard that she would be attending a private ball, to which I could also obtain an invitation, and I did not let the opportunity escape me of seeing my erstwhile patient fly past in a lively dance. Since that time she has, by her own inclination, married a man unknown to me.

Elisabeth von R., whose real name was Ilona Weiss, did not notice Freud at this ball. For her, Freud was "just a young, bearded nerve specialist" who tried "to persuade me that I was in love with my brother-in-law, but that wasn't really so."[71]

I can't escape a feeling that I have through much of *Studies*: that the patients are more important to the doctors than the doctors are to the patients. This is especially true for Bertha Pappenheim—Anna O. meant the world to Freud, the first ship in his armada, but for Pappenheim, Freud was the husband of an old friend, the colleague of a doctor who had tried and failed to help her. Freud was someone whose theories—if they interested her—she found appalling and unworkable in her business of saving young women's lives.

After "Fraulein Elisabeth von R.," Freud steps off the page, and Breuer comes on for his essay, "Theoretical Issues." This is the solo-Art-Garfunkel part of *Studies* and, lest we get too excited, Breuer warns us at the start, "Originality is the least claim in what is to be put forward over the following pages."

Throughout, Breuer wants to steer a middle course. He rejects both physiologically reductive and psychologically reductive thinking about hysteria. He doesn't want to say hysteria is all in the body, in the cells of the brain. He's not going to try to describe psychology in neurological terms. But he doesn't want to say that hysteria is purely psychological, either. He dismisses the notion that "all hysterical symptoms are ideogenic." According to Breuer, who in his low-key way can be quite racy, saying that hysterical symptoms come from thoughts is as if one were to argue that "because ideas and perceptions very frequently give rise to erections, we assume that [ideas and perceptions] alone do so." A man can get a hard-on from thoughts, he argues, and from physical stimuli, too, and likewise for hysteria, it's both somatic and psychological.

Breuer is writing in a genre more congenial to him than the case study, and we get a better sense of how balanced, how wise, how modern and eclectic and antidogmatic, and also how honest he can be. He reviews the ideas of the thinkers under whose influence he and Freud wrote: Binet,

Charcot, Janet, and Möbius. Breuer sees, more vividly than Freud did, the stress and brutality that conventionally honorable Viennese bourgeois women suffered in their intimate lives: "It is surprising that the wedding night does not have a pathogenic effect more frequently since very often it is regrettably not a matter of erotic seduction but of rape." Breuer does not accept Freud's idea that all hysteria is ultimately sexual in nature, but he sees that sex can cause trauma, and sexual trauma can cause pathology. He describes a boy who was molested: "On his way home from school he had gone into a urinal where a man had held out his penis to him and asked him to take it in his mouth . . . from that moment on he was ill." Breuer describes "hysterical symptoms of a traumatic origin," and he agrees with Freud that hysteria "for the most part . . . involves ideas and processes related to sexual life." But here again, Breuer won't go to extremes: "I do not believe, though, that the genesis of the psychical splitting would be anything like exhausted by the half-understood processes listed above." In place of the hardware/software analogy, Breuer chooses the thing he knew that was closest to a computer network: an electrified apartment building:

> But if the basis of hysteria is an idiosyncrasy of the entire nervous system, the complex of ideogenic, psychically determined systems are raised up from it, like a building from its foundations. And it is a *multi-storey building*. In the same way that the structure of a building like this can be understood only if one differentiates the floor plans of the various storeys, so, I believe, the understanding of hysteria depends on taking into account the various kinds of complications in the ways the symptoms are caused. If one disregards this and attempts to undertake an explanation using one single causal nexus, a very large number of unexplained phenomena will always be left over; it is just as if one wanted to enter the various rooms of a multi-storey house into the plan of a single storey.

Breuer refuses to make any sweeping claims. "I would not take the process in Anna O.'s case to be generally valid." According to Breuer, under the surface of every normal person, "the person who is quite free from 'nerves,'" there may well exist "the 'nervous' person for whom the slightest occurrence is cause for palpitations and diarrhoea." Breuer had no urge to construct a grand theory, no desire to conquer the world, and so, in the pages of *Studies*, his voice is overmatched by Freud's.

———⋅———

The last section of *Studies* is the one in which the student becomes the master, and though this section has a modest title, "On the Psychotherapy of Hysteria," it's in this fifty-page essay that Freud begins to sketch out his theory of the human mind: the mind in a constant struggle, on the one hand, to perceive itself, and, on the other, to hide from its wounds and urges.

In "On the Psychotherapy of Hysteria," Freud is drawing on, and distinguishing his thinking from, two groups of ideas. On the one hand, there's French thinking about hysteria, associated largely in Freud's eye with Charcot and Janet, hysteria as a physiological condition, a somatic condition, usually hereditary—the patient has inherited a problem with the brain. On the other, there's the vision inspired by the process worked out between Breuer and Pappenheim, hysteria as a psychological mechanism, something caused largely by ideas—he's also, as he writes the book, moving away from hypnosis.

Technically, Freud is at a midpoint. He likes to press the patient lightly on the forehead, so as to help the patient attain an associative state: "When the patient is lying in front of me, applying pressure to the forehead or taking his head in my hands proves to be the most comfortable action for my purpose, and the action is most conducive to suggestion." But "the talking cure"—"the cathartic method"—is the opposite of the kind of suggestion that would be performed by a hypnotist. Instead of giving the patients commands under hypnosis—*Stop coughing. Speak German. Move your legs!*—the doctor lets the patient do the talking. Instead of implanting a healthy notion, you remove the sickness. The sickness, in this case, is not physical but mental, not somatic but psychological. For Freud, hysterics can be physically healthy. There is nothing wrong with their actual nerves. Then, Freud attacks Breuer.

Breuer is wrong, Freud argues, hysteria is not hypnoid, it's not separate from the healthy mind, it's in the working of the normal mind. The case of Anna O. was written under an outdated system of thinking since it "was never considered by its observer from the perspective of sexual neurosis and has now simply become unusable in this respect." For Freud, the etiology of hysteria has to be sexual. "I have not encountered any genuine cases of hypnoid hysteria," he writes. Freud's intellectual model has begun to move from Koch's immunology toward Aristotle's poetics. The mind as a place of drama. The idea in the "Preliminary Statement"—that the hysterical memory is a foreign body within the dark recesses of the mind—begins to develop into a more complex conception of consciousness.

> An in-depth portrayal of the workings of the inner life, such as one expects to be given by novelists and poets, together with the application of a few psychological formulas, does allow me to gain a kind of insight into the course of a hysteria.

It's *Oedipus*, but it's also *David Copperfield*. It's the story of people trying to be both the hero and the narrator of their own lives. Freud struggles for words and for metaphors. He offers several compelling but contradictory images, different ways to envision the layered, competing forces of the psyche. He compares the mind to a sedimentary buildup of layers; a binder of folders containing many papers; and then this binder of papers is at the core of a circle of developing layers; the binders of papers are a book that's like the earth's magma, with volcanic eruptions of thought, and the earth's crust struggling to hold the magma down.

> Our pathogenic psychical group . . . cannot be cleanly extracted from the self, its outer strata pass over into parts of the normal self on all sides and ultimately belong just as much to it as to the pathogenic organization. . . . The inner strata are increasingly estranged from the self, yet the point at which the border of the pathogenic material begins does not become visible. The pathogenic organization does not really behave like a foreign body but more like an infiltration. In this comparison, the resistance must be taken as that which is doing the infiltrating.

The trauma becomes part of the self, the effort not to know the trauma becomes part of the problem. Character is conflict, the formation and deformation of character comes in our willingness and unwillingness to remember and to understand—and this struggle to perceive and not to perceive oneself is the drama of life. Freud touches that exact spot where scientific medicine meets the novel of self-discovery, and reading it, I feel the stark chill of recognition.

You can believe me or not, but after I closed the book, I got up from my recliner, and there it was, on my desk, the envelope my dad had given me on the night before he died, with his word, *Chochum*, written in Hebrew, in transliteration, and then in translation: "WISE MAN." I don't know how I'd missed it all those weeks. Maybe, like Bertha Pappenheim, I'd been suffering a negative hallucination.

PART FOUR

Imagining Ourselves

19

When I was a little boy, I was sickly. My heart was deformed, and if I exerted myself I'd turn blue: not enough oxygen coming to my lips and my face. I spent a lot of time being carried by my father, and I think this is still my fundamental memory of him, with my arms wrapped around his forehead, my legs on his shoulders, my feet in the air, and my nose taking in his smell. My heart defect was corrected when I was five years old, in 1971, in what were still the early days of open-heart surgery. The brilliant surgeon who operated on my heart, Dr. James Malm, was the man who had learned how to fix kids like me, and he made this discovery just a few years before my birth.

After the surgery, I was hospitalized for eleven days, and twice a day I got penicillin shots in my thighs. The penicillin was thick and painful going in, and I remember the feeling of terror and tension as the nurse with the rattling cart approached my curtained-off hospital bed. The very last time they were going to give me the shot, I rebelled. I was skinny, small, confined to a bed and a wheelchair, but I fought with everything I had, and it took a nurse to hold down each of my legs, and a nurse to hold down each of my arms, and my dad held down my head. Screaming with rage, I looked up and saw him beaming. I was so mad at him, but in retrospect I understand his joy. All his wishes for his child had been granted. I not only survived heart surgery, I came out fighting. My dad could not stop laughing.

It happened that as my father was dying, I was finishing a book, a memoir and medical history titled *The Open Heart Club*, all about people born with heart defects. Heart surgery started with kids like me, kids with malformed hearts, and I was in the first large cohort of pediatric heart patients to be saved, and—fairly or not—as I moved from that book to this, it was my thinking about heart surgery and congenital heart disease patients that often guided me as I thought about patients with functional neurological disorder.

In *Is It All in Your Head?*, Suzanne O'Sullivan draws a distinction between "illness" and "disease." In this view, *disease* is what I suffer, an identifiable organic problem, whereas *illness* is what plagues FND patients—or as she called them in 2015, patients suffering psychosomatic conditions, or conversion disorder.

> Illness is not the same as disease. Illness is the human response to disease. It refers to a person's subjective experience of how they feel but does not assume underlying pathology. . . . A person can have a disease and not be ill. For example, a girl with epilepsy has a disease, but if she is not having seizures and the epilepsy is asymptomatic she is not ill. A person with a psychosomatic disorder, on the other hand, is ill but does not necessarily have a disease.

This distinction describes the essential, stereotypical exchange at the doctor's office. The patient comes in, feeling ill, and unsure of the cause. The doctor examines the patient, offers a diagnosis, and names the disease—the underlying pathology. As O'Sullivan's stories demonstrate, in cases in which patients are told that their illness is psychosomatic, in cases where the doctor says there is no underlying disease, the process short-circuits. The patient is suffering, but the doctor says the suffering is only subjective. It's all in your head. Please leave my office. Find a psychotherapist. The patient feels betrayed.

Neurologists who offer the FND diagnosis (O'Sullivan included) have been trying to remedy this problem. The doctor can examine the patient and find rule-in signs for the disorder, and offer a positive diagnosis, and plan a course of treatment. In the case of FND, the lines between "illness" and "disease" blur. When we consider a "functional" disorder to be a "brain-based" condition, the "subjective experience" and "underlying pathology" become mutually reinforcing: the way the patient experiences their body affects the way the patient's body fails them. That circularity at first glance seems unusual and specific to FND, but it fits with my own experience of disease, of illness, of living with a malformed heart.

"Biopsychosocial" is a modish word these days, used all throughout medicine (my gerontologist friend rolls her eyes at the word), and that makes sense: everything is biopsychosocial. The biology of human suffering isn't comprehensible outside of the way it's experienced (psychologically) and understood (socially). For me, it's impossible to separate the underlying pathology of my heart disease from my subjective response to it. There are times I deny my symptoms even as they're happening, times that I imagine symptoms when they're not there, and times when the stress of the outside world exacerbates my symptoms, even provokes them. My experience of congenital heart disease is profoundly psychosomatic.

I have my own version of *la belle indifférence*—the pretense that nothing strange is happening to my body, even as it's breaking down. Since I was born, I have had a disease (in O'Sullivan's terms), but I have tried, all my life, never to let on that I was ill. In high school and college, I devoted most of my spring and fall afternoons to sports, though I would never be as fast or as strong as my friends and teammates and competitors. The first time I needed a replacement heart valve, when I was in my early thirties, I ignored my doctor's advice and turned down the option of surgery until it was nearly too late. My subjective response—to delay surgery—weakened the muscle wall of my right ventricle, aggravating my underlying pathology. The second time I had a failing valve, in my forties, I ignored it again and went on a four-day hiking trip in the White Mountains, climbing the tallest peaks on the east coast of the United States. I didn't want to be ill, or to let my disease interfere with my experience.

Sometime between these two heart valve replacements, I suffered a life-threatening attack of arrhythmia—and I disregarded that, too. I was sitting in the sun with a friend at work, eating an ice cream sandwich, when suddenly it came on: ventricular tachycardia, the big lower chambers of my heart pounding as if I were running a sprint while I sat there chatting in front of the Stony Brook University library. I did not go to a hospital, I did not call 9-1-1; instead I continued with what was then my two-and-a-half-hour commute home from work to Brooklyn. I walked across campus to the train station, my heart thundering in my chest all the way. I rode the Long Island Railroad, never flagging down a conductor to say that I might be dying, and then with my heart still banging like Keith Moon on my ribcage, I took the subway to Grand Army Plaza and climbed the stairs to our walk-up apartment. Up the stairs I went, heart going BOOM BOOM BOOM, when each step might have killed me, to our little apartment where my pregnant wife was making dinner, and my dad was waiting for me—he'd been babysitting our baby daughter, but he wouldn't leave until he got a glimpse of me—and when I opened the door, I didn't hug him. If I had hugged him, he might have felt my madly beating heart, might have called for an ambulance, might have tried to save my life. I might have had to admit that I was weak, that I was, in O'Sullivan's terms, diseased. It was my response, my subjective experience, just as much as the underlying pathology, that nearly killed me.

For my heart book, I interviewed other adult congenital heart patients and found that they had precisely—precisely—the same experiences as I did, the same *belle indifférence*, all struggling with disease, all trying to fool themselves and everyone around them by ignoring all signs of illness. I met an elementary school teacher, an adult congenital heart patient like me, who was attacked at work one day by ventricular tachycardia (the same arrhythmia that almost killed me), the big lower chambers of her heart running the last yards of a marathon sprint while the rest of her was proctoring a fourth-grade test. She walked up and down the rows of her classroom, monitoring her pupils' math quiz, and kept going and going and going through the day, taking them down to the cafeteria for lunch and then back up the stairs, pretending all was fine, just like me, right up to the ambulance ride and the shock paddles in the emergency room. Dr. Ali N. Zaidi, who works with both adult and pediatric patients with congenital heart disease, told me that this is typical among his patients.

Even when they are floridly sick, experiencing heart failure, they believe that they are well.

"I say, 'How are you feeling,' and they say they're feeling fine. They don't grasp the severity of their situation because they've been living like that for so long. That's their normality."

The human response to disease, as often as not, is to ignore it. "They were all in good health," writes Tolstoy of his famous dying hero. "It could not be called ill-health if Ivan Illych sometimes said that he had a queer taste in his mouth and felt some discomfort in his left side." Most of us would rather wish illness away than face it. That's what Denis Johnson's narrator in *Jesus' Son* thinks, when he is working in a nursing home, wheeling along a man whose body is fixed in a horrible rictus. "No more pretending for him! He was completely and openly a mess. Meanwhile the rest of us go on trying to fool each other."

When I read critics, say Borch-Jacobsen, who argue that Bertha Pappenheim was pretending, feigning illness when in fact she was healthy, I think: What's "pretending"? What's "healthy"? What could Breuer have meant when he said Anna O. lived in "perfect health," what is *that* if not the act that we perform when we try to fool ourselves, and to fool others, and to pretend that we're not mortal, vulnerable, dying? And so many of us, when in the grip of illness, perform dramas, seek attention, some kind of "secondary gain"—sympathy, affirmation of our suffering. I wrote a book about my heart condition, was paid an advance for it, appeared on public radio and in bookstores talking about it—if that's not *secondary gain*, what is?

Patients can only perceive what's in the range of their experience, and they act according to habituation, and they sometimes hide and sometimes show their vulnerability. Meanwhile, doctors' perceptions—their ability to make out the shifting and murky borderline between illness and disease, between the "human response" and the "underlying pathology"— are limited by the tools at their disposal and by their collective knowledge. When I was doing my research into cardiology, I got to speak with Dr. Abraham Rudolph, the first man ever to use a cardiac catheter to diagnose a heart defect in an infant. Dr. Rudolph was in his nineties when I spoke with him, charming, modest, and generous with his time. When we spoke, I was eager to learn about the relationship between diagnostic technology and clinical practice—how using catheters led to cutting open hearts. Naively, I expected Dr. Rudolph to tell me a story of progress and increasing clarity, better images leading to better surgeries, but that wasn't how he experienced his sixty years in his field.

We talked on the phone. Rudolph had a self-deprecating giggle and a trace of a South African accent, and he didn't want me to be so optimistic about medicine. He described his life's work as if it were a series of errors and corrections, a constant struggle of practice against dogma. In an email after our final phone call, he surprised me by quoting Salman Rushdie: "Facts are hard to establish and capable of being given many meanings. Reality is built on our prejudices and ignorance, as well as our perceptiveness and knowledge." Rushdie wrote this about magical realism in fiction. Abe Rudolph wanted me to know that it applied to his life in cardiology. He wanted me to understand that on account of his breakthroughs in diagnostic technology, children had died. Babies who would have survived had they been left to heal on their own had been put into his care, and had been catheterized by him, and after he'd discovered the holes in their hearts, the babies had been put on operating tables and died unnecessarily in botched experimental surgeries. That was what concerned him, not the millions of lives he'd saved. "Pathology," even in something as seemingly straightforward as a hole in the heart, can be hard to establish, and "human response," both a physician's and a patient's, is riddled with prejudice and ignorance. We want certainty from medicine, but that's not always what we get. In Lorrie Moore's story "People Like That Are the Only People Here," a mother and father are talking about their child's recent cancer diagnosis.

> "It's bad enough when they refer to medical science as 'an inexact science,'" says the Mother. "But when they start referring to it as 'an art,' I get extremely nervous."
> "Yeah. If we wanted art, Doc, we'd go to an art museum."

Patients with the most obviously diagnosable disease experience and present their symptoms through the vague haze of fear and denial, doctors perceive those symptoms through the always-improving, ever-shifting lens of medical understanding, and this doesn't mean that any patient is faking or that any doctor is blind, only that actuality can be very difficult to grasp.

"Health is tolerant of ill health," wrote the great pediatrician and psychiatrist D. W. Winnicott. "In fact, health gains much from being in touch with ill-health and all its aspects." But this kind of acceptance is very hard to accomplish.

Not only have I pretended to be healthy when in fact I was ill, I have also hallucinated pain and illness when there was no underlying problem. In my chest is an implanted device, a little metal multipurpose intelligent machine that monitors my heart. It works as a pacemaker when my heartbeat gets too slow, and as a defibrillator should my heart suddenly start beating too quickly—it will deliver sixty joules of electricity to the chest to shock me out of arrhythmia, a little bomb going off under my ribcage. They put it in me after my lunatic journey on the train from Long Island. One night, years ago, the device performed poorly, and my arrhythmias were acting up. I got shocked nine times over an eight-hour period, from about ten at night to about six a.m. All night long, every time I relaxed, the machine fired. For years after, I would hallucinate those shocks, just as I was drifting into a dream. I'd lie down, and on the cusp of sleep—*whammo*! The hot flash of electricity under my ribs—but it was just an illusion. These kinds of phantom shocks are common among people with implanted defibrillators. I met one patient whose implanted defibrillator had been removed after a heart transplant, but still—even with no device in her chest—she kept on experiencing the hallucinatory explosions. Functional symptoms affect the diseased as well as the healthy. "We must accept the interdependence of mind and body," Elaine Showalter wrote.

My state of mind and the state of the world around me affect my cardiac health. Through the stress of my wife Marcia's illness I suffered arrhythmias, subtle flutters in the upper chambers of my heart, runs of rapid beats that could last for hours. The doctors and technicians knew about her cancer, and they were sympathetic, and there was an obvious implication in their nods and pauses—the scars in my much carved-up heart muscle leave me vulnerable to arrhythmia, but they are only one factor in a given instance of dysfunction. The psychological and social stresses in my life are factors, too. But the intersections are unpredictable. I suffered no arrhythmias on the day Marcia was diagnosed, or on the day she died, but my heart went into one of its craziest runs, once, at a faculty meeting where some of my colleagues behaved badly, and I was enraged, and it was like the muscle of my heart was keeping time with the spastic firing of the synapses in my brain.

From her letters, and from the reports of Binswanger and Breuer, it's pretty clear that Pappenheim could not understand what was happening to her, that she did not always see the line between her affliction and her response to it, between her symptoms and her intentions. Breuer knew that his own understanding was limited.

Was the pain in her face "functional" or was it "organic"? To what extent did the drugs prescribed to her exacerbate her problems? Did she start speaking in English as a private language with her doctor, and if so, at what point, if ever, did her loss of German become involuntary?

Whatever Breuer's errors and deceptions, his innovations emerged from an extraordinary capacity for empathy. His vision was profound, and the questions he raised are ones that we are still asking. How does the mind affect the body? How does memory process trauma? Freud attacked these questions radically, bracingly, daringly, and heroically. A century later, we continue to reckon with his work. Right now, there are people all over the globe limping, suffering tremors, falling blind, losing their voices, tumbling into seizures, paralyzed below the waist, all of them without a conventionally diagnosable underlying biological explanation, many of them unable to talk to doctors no matter what approach the doctors take. We do not know the cause, we struggle to seek the cure, and we are stuck (like everybody else) within the limits of our prejudices and perceptions.

Me too.

When I talked to FND patients, and I shared my idea with them— that we were kindred, FND patients and congenital heart patients, inhabitants of the same medical borderland—they were quick to disabuse me of my vanity.

"The difference is," and the same words, more or less, came out of the mouths of several patients, "you go to a doctor and they help you. We go to a doctor, and they tell us that nothing's wrong."

———•·•———

"I started FND Hope because I was angry," Bridget Mildon told me.

Mildon, who with her husband raised three kids and ran two businesses—an auto parts shop and a hardware store—in Salmon, Idaho, is the extraordinary patient who is founder and director of FND Hope, the global FND patient advocacy group. She has been fighting and talking and collaborating with neurologists and psychiatrists for the last dozen years, and as the world's leading FND patient advocate, she is regularly included in medical conferences and panels, consulted on publications, and invited to lecture at hospitals and universities.

Mildon is the closest thing I can find to a contemporary Bertha Pappenheim: a patient who influenced the way her illness is named and discussed. She has a mane of blond hair and a broad, strong face, the face of an implacable pioneer, the kind unintimidated by a mountain lion or a drought. But she has a cheerful smile, and she becomes emotional describing the plight of her fellow sufferers. Her symptoms began gradually in 2008. She thought it was all caused by problems with her back, and that her symptoms would just all go away. But they didn't.

At her parents' house on Fourth of July weekend, she began to have headaches. She felt "brain fog," that typical spaciness that many FND sufferers experience, what Pappenheim described as "clouds." As they drove home, her symptoms worsened. "My face started to droop, and that's when we thought I was having a stroke." They dropped the children at home. "I live in a small, small town," she told me. "A little tourist town. Walmart's like two and a half hours away."

Mildon began to suffer seizures, very brief thirty-second seizures that looked like epilepsy. From a little rural hospital she was flown to Eastern Idaho Regional Medical Center, where she was monitored more closely. Mildon was strapped to a gurney, and as she was being led out of the hospital toward the ambulance that would take her to the University of Utah's hospital, one of her doctors leaned down to her and said, as kindly as possible: "I'm so sorry that I wasn't able to help you, and I hope whatever this is you'll be able to recover from it."

"I remember just thinking," she told me, "why would I not get better?"

She spent a week at the U of U epilepsy center. As the illness intensified, she lost her ability to walk and to speak. She began to suffer paralysis. She suffered weakness all along the left half of her body.

There were days she could stand, days she could walk, but she had no agency—no capacity to control her most basic movements. "I remember the physical therapist coming down and helping me walk down the corridor. I remember her saying, 'Right, let's turn and go back,' and I just stood there for a minute and I looked—I knew what she meant, but I don't know how to do it. I had no idea how to turn around."

There was a suggestion that she suffered conversion disorder. "We don't think you have epilepsy," the doctors said, and left the room. Later, a nurse who was not fluent in English came into her room and told her that she was being discharged.

"We think this all will just go away," her doctors told her.

She was now seven hours from home, suffering periodic seizures and was unable to walk. Bridget and her husband got in their car—they had no choice—and drove back to Salmon. It was all in her head, or so she was being told.

Back home, Mildon considered the Freudian diagnosis that had been suggested and began to wonder what terrible secret trauma could have converted subconsciously into such self-obliterating symptoms. Was there some horrible event she had repressed, some unspeakable thing that had happened to her as a child, that she had forced deep down into her subconscious—was she now wrestling with a phantom rapist who had attacked her when she was young?

"It made me question myself," she said. "It made me question my family. I started to ask my parents, 'Did you—did something happen to me that you're not telling me? At a young age that I don't remember?' And of course my parents said, 'Well, no.'" But their flat denials gave her no resolution. "It makes you start digging for skeletons in your closet that don't exist, and it starts to make you crazy," Mildon told me. Trying to describe that awful, ragged period of doubt and introspection, her language broke down. "It's like this quest to find the truth, but yet what is—I don't know what is truth!"

Her symptoms progressed. She was home, confined to her bed, out of work, unable to mother her children, with no prospect of treatment. There was nothing to do but go on the computer. She started playing *Farmville*, started going on Facebook. It was a way for her to practice using her fingers and eyes, and it was a way for her to connect with people. Exhausted in bed in eastern Idaho—Salmon is the home of Sacajawea; to find it, put your finger on the 45th parallel, right between the continental divide and the Frank Church Wilderness—Bridget Mildon began to connect with patients who suffered the same symptoms that she did, to learn about the doctors who were studying those symptoms.

She went back to the movement disorder clinic at the University of Utah. The neurologists had her run down a hallway. Many FND patients who have difficulty walking find their gait problems resolved when they run, but not Mildon—her legs collapsed under her. She had a new diagnosis, dystonia (a disorder involving the contraction of the muscles)—but the conversion disorder label was still there on her chart. The doctors in Utah referred her to the NIH, and Mildon flew across the country to Washington DC. Mildon underwent batteries of tests. She sat in a seminar room with doctors and fellows who questioned and examined her. Yes, they said, she had dystonia. And yes, some of the symptoms seemed functional, but others did not. It wasn't until more than a year later that she heard from the NIH again.

"They asked when I could go to DC. I said: I can leave tomorrow."

The doctors in Washington took her off the drugs she had been taking to control her seizures—she was on Sinemet, a dopamine-promoting drug often used to treat Parkinson's disease, a drug that had given Mildon some relief from the worst of her afflictions. At first in DC she was doing fine, but during one test—when she was at a computer terminal, responding to prompts on a screen—her blood pressure dropped, and suddenly she began to seize. She went back on the Sinemet and found some relief. After she returned to Idaho, Bridget was suffering terribly. In her journal, which she shared with me, she wrote: "I continue to have a sharp chest pain that is like a knife cutting to my back. Knowing there was nothing anyone could do I curled up on my bathroom floor clutching my chest and trying to stay calm." She received a book in the mail from the NIH, *Overcoming Functional Neurological Symptoms.*

"I started reading it," Mildon told me, "and I saw that there was a 13 percent success rate for cognitive behavioral therapy with functional patients, and I thought: Are you flipping kidding me?"

In her journal she wrote: "Will I be here 5, 10, 20 years, beating my head against an FND wall?" The book seemed to present 13 percent improvement as an advance in treatment—at the time, it was, and treatment has advanced since then—but for Bridget it was an outrage.

"I'm betting my whole life on this, and I'm getting in this trial program, I'm hoping this is going to cure me—and it's a 13 percent success rate! I'm like, is this some kind of joke? I was furious." The more she read, the more she felt dismissed.

She received a phone call from Dr. Alan Carson, the Edinburgh psychiatrist who is one of the coauthors of *Overcoming Functional Neurological Symptoms*, and who remains one of the world's leading specialists in treating FND.

Mildon remembers telling Carson, as politely as humanly possible, that she hated the book, that she found it condescending, and that she thought it should be pulled off of the shelf. They fell into a conversation. Carson wanted patient input. He wanted patients to have a voice in the way their story was being told. Mildon looked at the website created by Carson's colleague, Jon Stone—neurosymptoms.org—and on the night of April 12, 2012, she began creating her own website, one where patients, not doctors, would describe and discuss their condition.

"I worked on it until about five o'clock in the morning," she told me. "The sun was coming up. I thought, I've got to get to bed." But before tucking herself in, she decided to check in with the Facebook friends she had made who also were suffering FND. "I messaged my friend Nikki and I said, don't tell anybody but I did this last night. Have a look at it, tell me what you think. . . . About three minutes later I see her tag me and post, 'Hey, Bridget created this website! You guys should all look!'" The site wasn't ready, it was just an experiment, but it was now beyond her control. "It just sparked energy. Everyone was messaging me." People had advice, suggestions, edits to her site. "I created the site, but the site was ours. Everyone was contributing. I told them: write your story and send it to me, and I'm going to put it on there." It was April 13, 2012. "That's the day we had a voice. I remember when a woman posted from Australia, writing, 'We are doing it! We are all coming together through hope!'"

Mildon wrote to Jon Stone. "I am quite surprised at the amounts of anti-depressants, pain killers, and tranquilizers many of these patients are on," she told him. "They talk about the extensive therapy they do (physio and psych) yet very few seem to be significantly better." In her letter, Mildon considered the history of the disease, and she quoted Mark Hallett:

> Freud's ideas about this situation stimulated a whole field of thought and therapy, but psychoanalysis has had its day and does not speak to the massive problem we are now facing. In fact, psychoanalysis was so influential that it essentially stopped other lines of investigation. There is now a new interest in the subject in various places around the world, and it is clear that one group of leaders is in Scotland.

When Stone read Bridget's letter, he was responsive.

"We had really good conversations," Mildon told me. "I'm still surprised at how good he is at listening to changes."

Stone wanted to include patient voices in his work, and Mildon's was the loudest voice. "I wanted her on our side," he told me. "And I wanted to be on her side, too." He discussed terminology with Mildon, and she helped him.

"One of the things she was saying," he told me, "Was, why call it functional neurological *symptoms*? If you've been in a wheelchair for twenty years, you haven't just got a *symptom*. You've got a disorder. That really stuck with me."

He was amenable to dropping the S from FNSD, to make it FND.

"I sometimes joke with audiences that my entire research career is just based on opening books from a hundred years ago," Stone told me.

Our conversation took place in March 2022, and we were on Zoom, and I could see through his laptop into his office in Edinburgh. A neat bookcase, a hook to the left in the shape of two human legs (as if a tiny body had disappeared into the wall, leaving only the pants and shoes), and a trombone hanging from that hook.

Stone was wearing his work clothes, a sports jacket and an Oxford shirt open at the collar, and an ID badge hanging around his neck. He'd just bicycled back from the hospital to his home, a thin-faced man with messy short-cropped gray hair, glasses, weary eyes, a narrow mouth that went easily into laughter, very much the picture of the tireless intellectual he is. ("Oh dear," Stone teased me when he saw my description of how he looked on a Zoom call, "I seem to have become a visual cliché!") I have tried to run down all the papers he has published, but he seems to be putting them out at a rate of one every month, papers on the history of hysteria, on the state of brain scan research, and on the best ways of talking to patients. I couldn't keep up.

Stone traces his interest in FND partly back to his childhood. He was a boy with a stutter. He experienced dissociative states. "A lot of children have dissociative experiences when they're growing up," he told me, "experiences which they can't really communicate. It's really common." Young Stone suffered "daydreaming type of experiences, often quite intense. I found them fascinating. A little bit scary, but in an exciting way. Eventually they stopped, and I couldn't get them anymore and I remember feeling quite sad. And then thinking what were they?" What he describes in his childhood isn't so far from what Breuer called Anna O.'s "*condition seconde*," and what she herself described as "clouds."

In medical school, Stone's stutter recurred. Any time someone asked his address, he couldn't say it out loud. Maybe this experience led to natural empathy with his patients. Stone doesn't claim any special kinship with FND patients, but doesn't see them as an alien species, either.

"As a neurology trainee," he told me, "I was seeing loads of these patients, and I was just horrified by how neurologists were treating them. I couldn't understand it. Why were they being so mean to these people?"

He wrote his doctoral thesis on illness perception. He would go to patients' houses and investigate their lived experience of diseases, and when he started working as a neurologist, he brought this interest in patient experience to his practice and research. He found himself in weekly meetings, where difficult cases would be presented to a group of physicians.

"A bit like Charcot," he told me. "The patient comes in the room. They get examined in front of everybody, we all give an opinion." The most difficult, the most mysterious cases were often functional disorders. "Quite regularly, patients would present with FND. And quite often, when the patient had gone and the consultants were sitting around—a lot of men in my specialty, some of whom had a tendency to be macho—they'd be laughing about the patient. They'd say, 'Bogus!' It was as if the patient was probably someone who's just putting it on."

His colleagues' lack of interest confused him. He began applying the illness perception literature to cases of FND. Whereas 56 percent of patients with multiple sclerosis admitted that their disease was affected by stress, only 24 percent of the functional patients said the same. This, for Stone, seemed both unexpected and perhaps connected with the stigma around their disorders. The MS patients had been told that they had a legitimate disease, and they were able to discuss the psychological aspects of their condition. The patients diagnosed with psychosomatic illness had been told that their problem was imaginary, and they had responded accordingly, with indignation—by refusing to have their conditions dismissed, by insisting on the physical nature of the disease, and by fighting with their doctors' implication that the condition was "all in their heads."

At the time, there was very little current neurology literature on functional disorders—neurologists had been sending these patients to psychiatrists for a hundred years. So Stone read over the old literature, and looked at the patients in the examining room, and the problem to him seemed infinitely complex.

"I thought, well, there's a lifetime's work there. And something you'll never get completely to the bottom of." He has no doubt but that the patients who became his focus are the same kinds of patients who had fascinated neurologists of the nineteenth century. "The patients are very recognizable from the old descriptions," he told me. "The specific nature of the appearance of the physical symptoms has barely changed at all. People with seizures who are falling down and shaking all over, people dragging their leg in a certain way or having tremors, or jerky movements, dystonia. I have plenty of slides where I show it—look, here's a picture from 1880, and here's a patient now. It's the same thing. What happened was, in many ways, that we lost the knowledge that was out there," he said. "The neurologists lost interest because they viewed it as a psychiatric disorder. The psychiatrists lost interest because they didn't see the patients or thought the neurologists had got it wrong. So it appeared to disappear."

As Hallett described it—in the piece quoted in Bridget Mildon's letter—the Freudian explanation of conversion disorder had devoured all neurological research and explanation of the problem, and as Freudian dogma receded, the patients fell into a void—neither psychiatric nor neurological, not a legitimate illness at all.

Stone is not anti-Freudian—some of Freud's descriptions resonate well with him—but he doesn't see *Studies in Hysteria* as the best nineteenth-century work on FND, and for Stone, that's because of the book's small sample size, its leaps of logic, and its lack of careful descriptions of the patients' bodies and complaints. "More like reading a work of fiction about the disorder than a scientific book." The problem is that Freud's explanation oversimplified things and became overwhelmingly influential.

"Freud gives it a nice simple hydraulic framework," he told me. "Squash down some trauma, and out pops your symbolic symptom. That's the answer. No need to think about it anymore. Just need to get to the root of the trauma, there you go."

There are ways, he hastened to add, that Freud had been essential. He emphasized Freud's notion of "the idea of paralysis," the way that idea afflicted the patients' bodies. But for Stone, Janet and Charcot offer far better, clearer analysis of FND than does Freud. Could Anna O. in fact have been suffering from a physical malady, something other than FND? Of course it's possible.

"We haven't got drawings and pictures of Anna O.," he reminded me. But there's no obvious reason to assume that Breuer made a misdiagnosis.

By the time Stone talked to Bridget Mildon, he was working to reshape world opinion on functional neurological disorders. He had been publishing for years. He was active in the group petitioning the *DSM*. He had worked on brain scan studies. He was building his website so there would be a quick and easy place for patients to get information about their condition. As he was working through these things, he was thinking about patient experience, thinking about dialogue.

He was eager to work with Mildon. He looked at her website, she looked at his. She asked him to drop "symptom" from the diagnosis, and to leave it at FND. He advised her to continue to move toward patient narratives, patient experiences.

Still, even as they collaborated, Bridget Mildon's body was breaking down.

"I could hardly talk," she remembered. "I could maybe talk for about three or four minutes, and then I would just be done. I was exhausted. That year I was in the hospital like fifteen times. I had two or three surgeries. My gallbladder just quit working. Sometimes my EKGs were abnormal, sometimes they were fine. Then I had started having other bleeding problems and a partial hysterectomy which then went bad. They had to hospitalize me again. My body was just literally shutting down. It just was not healing from everything. The doctors couldn't figure out what my body was doing. It wouldn't metabolize medications like normal bodies do."

Even as she was corresponding with Stone, and building FND Hope, and working as an advocate for all FND patients, Mildon had gotten a new diagnosis, a diagnosis that had nothing to do with conversion disorder.

Mildon suffers from Sneddon's syndrome, a progressive disease of the arteries. Sneddon's syndrome is a rare, treatable, and dangerous condition, affecting about four in every million people in the general population, mostly women in their twenties and thirties. As a result of the disease, Mildon had, over the years, been suffering a series of mini-strokes. The truth was that FND ought not to have been her primary diagnosis. The label of psychosomatic illness had obscured a progressive, devastating condition. Now that medication has gotten her vascular disease under control, Mildon's work is full time as a patient advocate, as the person in charge of FND Hope. And when I asked if she still thought of herself as an FND patient, she offered a complicated answer, walking that treacherous line between organic and functional illness, describing for me the same shadowy territory that the old cardiologist Abraham Rudolph described: of facts, perception, misunderstanding, and meaning. For Mildon, the line between "illness" and "disease" is a fabrication, and the distinction between "underlying pathology" and "patient response" is fairy tale. If only, she says, doctors would have listened to her from the start.

"Patients like me are routinely told that it is they themselves who cannot be trusted," she wrote in an essay on the website Mad in America. "Imagine a world where we allow for medical uncertainty." Mildon does not see her doctors as her enemies, but she does see medical dogma—its rigidity and its demand for authority—as potentially dangerous.

> All illness is integral to the human experience. Each patient's narrative of what they are experiencing—whether or not understood or agreed upon— is still their experience. There is most often no reason for a physician to not trust a patient or to dismiss their account of what and how they are experiencing illness.

Afflicted with her mini-strokes, she was terrified and panicked, and the doctors' assertion that all her symptoms were imaginary or psychogenic only exacerbated that fear and panic, and all this aggravated her troubles. Some of her symptoms were no doubt functional, she says.

"This illness, FND, wasn't created in or discovered in a lab," Mildon told me. "This is something that is created basically at medical conferences. It was created out of people's perception of other people's illnesses. It was based off of medical hunches rather than science, and science ceases to be science when we're no longer seeking the truth, when we're only trying to validate our own perception of what another person is experiencing. We build worlds out of our own perceptions. Go back to hysteria. Hysteria actually included a lot of other illnesses. It included dystonia, it included epilepsy. Recently another doctor gave me an FND paper that spent two pages talking about 'hysteria.' I threw it back at them. I just said we're not going to endorse this. FND Hope isn't going to endorse it. It's enough already! In some ways hysteria isn't FND, because hysteria was everything we don't understand about medicine. Hysteria was: *We don't know what's going on, so you get lumped in this bucket.*"

——•◦•——

Within this context, diagnosis and description can be difficult.

"It's challenging to overcome hundreds of years of dualism in a twenty-five-minute neurology appointment," Stone told me wryly, "especially when you've got six other patients waiting outside."

So much of the language that he has helped develop over the last decades is pragmatic language, language built on thinking about bridging that gap between patient and doctor, trying to construct a meaningful story, a way that people can describe and understand and recover from their own disabilities. Getting people to be able to discuss their illness, to imagine it, and achieving rapport with the patient is crucial. Stone's paper "Functional Neurological Disorder: The Neurological Assessment as Treatment" appeared in the journal *Practical Neurology*, and it tries to model dialogue that can help patients conceive of their condition without stigma.

Doctor: Tell me about that spaced out feeling in your own words. Don't worry about sounding silly. The more detail you can give me, the more I can help.

Patient: Well, it was a really strange feeling—it was like floating and people around me were really far away. It was horrible.

Doctor: How long did it go on for?

Patient: It must have been a couple of minutes.

Doctor: Was it scary? Did it get scarier as time went on?

Patient: Yes, it was frightening—it felt like I was going crazy . . .

Doctor: Actually, what you are describing is called dissociation—it's nothing to do with going crazy. It's a trance like state that people often have when they develop symptoms. . . . I'll explain later.

The goal in conversation is to normalize the doctor-patient relationship, to make the problem comprehensible to the person suffering it. And though Stone offers a sample script in that particular paper, he insists that every conversation between doctor and patient has to be personal and specific, has to be particular to the patient in the room.

"A lot of doctors have read stuff I've written," Stone told me, "and they do parrot it now. They say, 'You've got a software problem, not a hardware problem.' And sometimes it works but sometimes it doesn't." The point of Stone's hardware/software analogy, he says, is not that it contains any magic power, or that it's so exquisitely precise, but that it is a pragmatic way of communicating a difficult thought, quickly, to an anxious patient. "I know the brain's not a computer," he said. But the analogy allows patients to grasp the nature of their disabilities. "In clinic, you're sitting in front of people with paralyzed legs and seizures, trying to find ways to talk about this. And describing these as psychosomatic problems, that clearly was not working. It was immediately translated in patients' heads as: you think I'm crazy."

The computer analogy is not the only way, or necessarily the best way, to talk about FND. Each explanation, Stone says, has to be tailored to the appropriate situation. He's not particularly enthusiastic about the word *functional*.

"It's the least worst term," he told me. "But it's helpful for patients. More helpful than 'psychogenic.'" The term, he says, is useful because it focuses on the mechanism of the symptom rather than the etiology, and that's helpful in treatment. Another reason to value the designation *FND*, for Stone, is that it is a term that patients have been able to accept, to rally around. "I've decided that it's fine."

He seems uneasy with the role of doctor as final, absolute authority, and seems happy to shift some of that authority over to patients, to work with them in finding effective ways of explaining their conditions. When I spoke to him, he laughed at himself, and maybe at me, too.

"A man writing about how to explain hysteria, it's the ultimate sort of mansplaining, isn't it?"

You can hear Bridget Mildon's story and conclude, *Aha! The world's leading FND patient advocate was misdiagnosed, so maybe it's all a problem of misdiagnosis.* But that's faulty logic. All kinds of patients with all kinds of disorders are misdiagnosed, all the time. What Mildon saw—what outraged her—was the way that patients with "psychosomatic symptoms" are treated, which is to say: as if they are not worthy of doctors' care, as if they are hysterical.

In "Functional Neurological Disorder Is a Feminist Issue," a March 2023 article in the *Journal of Neuroscience, Neurosurgery, and Psychiatry*, brain researchers from the world's leading universities—including Stanford, Cambridge, and the University of Vienna—are joined by a variety of coauthors in health care, including a patient advocate, all of them women, to declare:

> The history of FND, in some ways, mirrors the history of women in society. It is a history laden with inequalities, dismissal, and injustice which cannot be undone. Now, patients with FND do not need pity, but parity. . . . This is a call to action. We support and urge careful and appropriate use of this diagnosis to support and empower those affected by FND so their symptoms and sufferings can be recognized and validated. We call for respectful models of clinical care and an end to dismissive and harmful language and behavior toward people with FND. We call for a shift in approach to FND . . . to move away from dualist models of mind and body. We call for parity for FND among other neurological disorders.

The history of Anna O. is central to the history these experts are describing. Whether Pappenheim in fact suffered FND or like Mildon had some other undiagnosed condition, her ghost still haunts doctors' offices all over the world. A patient with FND comes in, and the specter of Anna O. reappears, calling hysterically for the doctor's attention in the same way that in Freud's myth the hysterically pregnant Anna O. called out for Breuer's attention.

One step in beginning to dispel this ghost might be to consider the actual Bertha Pappenheim, not the myth, and to try to see her whole.

20

On February 4, 2009, the patient I will call Emma A. was crossing a street in suburban Washington DC when a pickup truck hit her. Emma thrust her hands against the truck's hood. The bumper hit her left knee, fracturing it. She was flung backward. Emma, a gymnast in middle and high school, flew back, tucking her body reflexively. She landed on her right ankle. The ankle twisted and broke. Her head hit the asphalt.

I talked with Emma over a period of three years, in person, on Zoom, on the telephone, and through email. In our first conversation, this traffic accident was the beginning of her FND story. As we moved together through the years, and as Emma moved through several FND treatments, her story deepened. I have argued, throughout this book, that it is crucial for doctors to listen to patients' stories. Emma A. taught me just how difficult that can be. It's not always clear for a patient where or when or how mind and body first became unglued.

After her recovery from the traffic accident—a concussion and two broken bones—Emma got the H1N1 virus. Then a urinary tract infection that she could not shake. She was prescribed Levaquin (levofloxacin) for the infection, and when that didn't work, Macrobid (nitrofurantoin), then ciprofloxacin. Emma was engaged to be married. A data analyst, she had become unemployed in the financial crisis of 2008. She was also taking Strattera (atomoxetine) for her attention deficit hyperactivity disorder.

Emma is attractive, and when I met her she appeared fit and healthy, with a slim but solid, even athletic, build and a mass of dark, wavy hair. I read her initially as white, but she's biracial. Her father was a public relations executive, a Black man living in a white world, her mother a white woman, a flight attendant. In August of 2010—after the accident and the UTI and the weeks of unsuccessful antibiotic treatments—she woke one morning before dawn to find that something, in her words, "was taking over my body."

"I started moving really slow," she told me. "It was bizarre. It was almost like my body was moving in slow motion. And then I lost my ability to speak. I knew what I wanted to say, but I couldn't articulate it. It would just come out as—" and here she made a consonant-free groan, almost a retching sound.

Her husband—then her fiancé—took her to the hospital. He had to drag and carry Emma, holding her under the armpits. Her ability to speak was intermittent. She could talk to the ER doctor, but, as she said to me, "of course, every time the doctor left, the voice would stop." The hospital ran some tests. Emma started to feel better. She was sent home. Over the next week, she got sicker.

"I started having chest flutters where I felt like I was going to faint. I started having brain fog. I was having these terrible headaches. And then the scariest thing happened. It was early in the morning. I was sleeping. And then all of a sudden my body was stiff as a board. I couldn't move anything. All my muscles were contracted. I couldn't relax my body."

The doctors who saw Emma in the emergency room recommended that she see a neurologist. Her neurologist offered some possible causes of her symptoms: Lyme disease, an autoimmune condition, low-level seizures triggered by the concussion. But all tests proved negative, and having ruled out all other possibilities, the doctors diagnosed her condition as psychosomatic.

Emma's parents were with her when the neurologist said, as Emma remembers it, "There is nothing wrong with you. It's all in your head."

On the doctor's recommendation, Emma consulted with a psychotherapist. On her third visit to the psychotherapist, she related a story that her mother had told her. When Emma was a small child, she had suffered symptoms very similar to the ones she started suffering in 2010. At three years old, she had had a double ear infection, and after the infection started to clear, little Emma began walking oddly. She started holding her arm bent, so the hand would hang loosely. Her speech changed. Little Emma was hospitalized for a week. Her pediatric doctors performed a spinal tap and several scans—but everything came back normal. By the end of the week, she was improving. She was sent home from the hospital, and in a few months, she recovered completely.

In Emma's mind, and in her mother's, the two bouts of illness were similar and, potentially, similarly associated with infection and antibiotics. When she related the story to her psychotherapist, he took a different view. "He told me that maybe I was having these symptoms as a toddler, maybe they were psychosomatic symptoms because I was jealous that my mom had had another baby. I was like, 'No.'"

This was not how Emma understood her relationship with her mother. Her working mom was rarely ever home. "I remember her calling from the airport to say that she loved me, and giving me hugs over the phone, and that was really hard for me." After her brother was born, her mother was home all the time. Her brother's birth came with the gift of her mother's presence. And so Emma told her doctor that she didn't know if she could agree with his assessment. Still, she wondered: if he thought her illness when she was three was psychosomatic, did that mean he thought that her current symptoms were?

"He said he didn't have enough info," Emma told me.

Her symptoms continued to overwhelm her. She stopped seeing the psychotherapist, who, a few weeks later, wrote her general practitioner, indicating that he thought her disease was psychosomatic. A pattern was established. She suffered crippling, terrifying symptoms, she went to the ER, the ER doctors sent her to neurologists, the neurologists recommended psychotherapy. Every neurologist said it was stress related.

"That made me really upset," she told me. "It was almost stressing me out more. What am I stressed about? I was engaged, but I wasn't planning a huge wedding. The wedding was about thirty people. Work was normal stress, but less stressful than the last job. I was like, *I don't know what this is.*"

Emma had a good but inconclusive visit with one of the top movement specialists in the DC area, Dr. Laxman Bahroo, at Georgetown. She went to Johns Hopkins and saw another neurologist. She came—as many FND patients do—armed with a stack of notes on her illness.

"What have all the other neurologists said?" the Johns Hopkins neurologist asked.

"They've said it was psychosomatic," she told him, "that it was just stress, but I don't believe that. I'm not overly stressed about anything right now, except for this situation, which is freaking me out."

"You better hope you're psychosomatic," Emma remembers the doctors saying. "Otherwise you have an incurable condition."

"That kind of broke me," Emma said. "I refused to see a neurologist for another year."

She had one child, a boy, in 2013, and then another boy in 2015. When she started nursing her children, she went off of Flexeril (cyclobenzaprine), the drug she'd been prescribed for her dystonia. Emma went back to work. The year 2016, she told me, was the hardest year of her life. Her husband fell into a deep depression, and she was caring for a toddler and an infant. She started suffering a sudden clenching of muscles all over the right side of her body, and had difficulty with speech and with walking. She tried to power through, to take care of the kids, her husband, and to do her job.

In 2016, she again consulted Dr. Bahroo, the Georgetown movement specialist she had seen first in 2010. As Emma remembers it, this second time she saw Dr. Bahroo, "he sat down, looked me straight in the eye, and said: 'I'm going to refer you to the NIH, and I strongly recommend you go.'" (Bahroo likes to be as direct as possible with his patients. "They would rather have some unknown, unheard-of disease that we don't know how to manage," he told me, "than have a functional neurological disorder.") In the intervening six years, between the onset of her illness and the birth of her kids, the world of medicine around conditions like hers had transformed, and Dr. Bahroo was aware of these developments. He sent Emma to the National Institutes of Health, where Mark Hallett's team was at the forefront of a revolution in the way patients like her were understood and treated.

———◆———

In his lucid and enlightening 2006 memoir, *In Search of Memory*, the Nobel laureate Eric R. Kandel writes: "The new biology posits that consciousness is a biological process that will eventually be explained in terms of molecular signaling pathways used by interacting populations of nerve cells." This is a long-held dream of neurology, to understand the mind through the study of the brain. Embedded in this dream is an assumption: that consciousness can be reduced to the work of neurons, that the brain and the mind are one.

Freud believed this, too, or at least he once wrote that "all of our provisional ideas in psychology will presumably one day be based on an organic substructure." For more than a century, neurologists have been expecting this synthesis, promising that it is right around the corner.

Not everyone outside of neurology concurs with this assumption. The Dalai Lama, for example, has written that this view of mind-brain identity is "a metaphysical assumption, not a scientific fact," and you don't have to be a religious person to agree. Contemporary philosophers argue about whether the "self" even exists, whether or not the "qualia" of the self are illusions; about whether the self is a process, an ongoing construction whose sources lie both inside and outside of the individual brain; about whether it is even possible to understand human consciousness from within human consciousness. There isn't, right now, a broad medical, philosophical, or biological consensus definition of *self* or *mind* or *consciousness*—how individual thought arises from language and social life and gray matter and gonads and food and wine and coffee and family and companionship and everything else that contributes to our being.

Through the study of FND we begin to see the interaction of various brain networks and how they can potentially misbehave, but we are also forced to confront how bogglingly complex are the intertwined relationships—how thought is embodied, how bodies can be transfigured by thoughts, how body-transmogrifying thoughts can be triggered by complicated personal history and circumstance, how thought can move from body to body and alter bodies as it moves. The distinction between *mind* and *brain* is vexed. Some writers believe that functional symptoms are necessarily related to emotional states and can be explained as such. In *Is It All in Your Head?*, O'Sullivan explains functional symptoms this way:

> If I am nervous my hands shake—that is my body changing physically in response to an emotion. When we are frightened our hearts race. When we are upset tears flow from our eyes. These are all examples of the ways in which each of us has experienced physical symptoms when there is nothing physically wrong. These sorts of physical responses to distress are normal everyday responses to fears and upsets. But for some people physical reactions to emotion can be more dramatic and disabling than these simple examples.

"At the milder end of the spectrum," the psychiatrist Alan Carson writes in *The Handbook of Clinical Neurology*, "FND starts to merge with normal function. We have all stood outside an exam hall with our stomach tied in knots, a highly unpleasant experience, but few of us would think of this as a clinical disorder." From time to time, my low back goes out. On the day of my childhood best friend's memorial service, I could not bend at all from the waist. But that's not the same as FND. As Alan Carson says, it's impossible for someone who doesn't have FND to know what it's like to suffer from the condition—to be in the grip of functional symptoms so extreme they seem to rob the patient of selfhood, of agency.

The *DSM* categorizes functional neurological disorders within the broader class of "somatoform disorders," which can include (as well as back pain), functional GI issues, sexual impotence, body dysmorphia, and hypochondria. But FND *isn't* hypochondria, and the connection is as misleading as it is clarifying. "The two most common psychosomatic symptoms are fatigue and pain," Suzanne O'Sullivan writes, and these are symptoms that defy the line between soma and psyche, between object and subject. Fatigue and pain can't be felt or measured by anyone other than their sufferer, and they don't exist unless and until someone feels them. As the philosopher Elaine Scarry wrote in *The Body in Pain*: "To have pain is to have certainty; to hear about pain is to have doubt."

Just as we can never ignore our own intense physical pain, we can't ever know another person's. Our language, like our perception, is limited. Virginia Woolf put it this way:

> English which can express the thoughts of Hamlet and the tragedy of Lear has no words for the shiver or the headache. . . . The merest school-girl, when she falls in love, has Shakespeare, Donne, and Keats to speak her mind for her; but let the sufferer try to describe a pain in his head to a doctor and language runs dry.

Extreme pain lands you in a linguistic and social desert. In pain, you howl. As Scarry points out, we describe pain by imagining the instrument that might be causing it—a *hammering* pain, a *burning* pain, a *stabbing* pain—the pain itself has no name. "Physical pain does not simply resist language but actively destroys it," she writes, "bringing about a state anterior to language, to the sounds and cries a human being makes before language is learned." This fits with the accounts of so many FND sufferers: a sense that their situation is unspeakable, and that no one around them can understand what's happening to them. For a doctor, without diagnostic equipment to verify a cause, it's much, much easier to say "bogus" and to turn away than it is to attend to the patient and to try to understand.

The novelist Siri Hustvedt's *The Shaking Woman* is a narrative of her own functional neurological symptoms and of her quest to name and understand them—shaking fits that attack her, fits her doctors fail to cure or explain. Hustvedt's shaking attacks happen when she is in front of people, lecturing. She writes, in a sentence that spoke for most all the FND sufferers I've met: "It appeared that some unknown force had suddenly taken over my body," and describes her fits this way:

> My arms flapped. My knees knocked. I shook as if I were having a seizure. Weirdly, my voice wasn't affected. It didn't change at all. Astounded by what was happening to me and terrified that I would fall over, I managed to keep my balance and continue, despite the fact that the cards in my hands were flying back and forth in front of me. When the speech ended,

the shaking stopped. I looked down at my legs. They had turned a deep red with a bluish cast. . . . The shaking woman felt like me and not me at the same time. From the chin up, I was my familiar self. From the neck down, I was a shuddering stranger.

Her fits lead Hustvedt on an odyssey through neurological and psychoanalytic diagnosis, and she finds no one who can characterize her symptoms to her satisfaction. She meets a psychotherapist who wonders if she's suffering "conversion disorder," that is to say, if she is "hysterical" (Hustvedt plays with the word), but Hustvedt is not comfortable thinking of her symptoms as exclusively psychological, uncomfortable with the phrase "no organic cause." How can such obviously embodied events be caused by something that is not part of her? "Unless you believed that ghosts, spirits, or demons swooped in from heaven or hell to take control of a person's body, how could it be argued that this wasn't an *organic, physical* phenomenon?" In a neurological exam, there is insufficient evidence to explain her shaking fits—but she doesn't need a brain scan to tell her that her shaking is *real*. Hustvedt searches her past for sources of trauma, for events that paralleled her shaking, but in the end comes up with more questions than answers. "I feel I have one—a self—but why? Is it everything that lies within the borders of my body? Not really. When I shook, it didn't feel like *me*." Like Scarry's sufferer of extreme pain, Hustvedt is left without words to describe the sensations that overwhelm her. "The shaking woman is certainly not anyone with a *name*," she writes. "She is a speechless alien who appears only during my speeches." Hustvedt ends up attacking "the mind/body problem," which, she writes, "created the distinction between psychiatry and neurology: sick minds versus sick bodies." This distinction has to be rethought, Hustvedt argues, but it's hard to do so with our current vocabulary. She quotes the neurologist Joseph Le-Doux: "The problem is that it is not clear how the changes at the neural level relate to those at the psychological level." We can't explain how the psychological emerges from the neurological, or how neurological symptoms emerge from personal history. Freud wrote that the "the Ego is first and foremost a body Ego." A condition like Hustvedt's challenges that embodied foundation of the consciousness, and her meditations lead not to an answer or an explanation, only to the dissolution of her comfortable definition of selfhood.

In a 2012 article in *Neuropsychiatry*, Jon Stone, Alan Carson, and their colleague Jo Perthen describe Oliver Sacks's 1984 *A Leg to Stand On* as a book about "a functional/psychogenic leg paralysis following injury." Sacks at age forty, in 1973, is hiking in the cliffs and mountains of Norway. High on the mountain, far from civilization, he encounters a bull, the bull charges, Sacks flees, and falls, and breaks his leg, ruptures it at the knee, so badly that the joint bends backward. Splinting his leg with his umbrella, scooching on his backside, he manages to make it some way down the mountain, and at dusk—just as he is in despair of ever being found—Sacks is saved by a pair of reindeer hunters. He is flown to London, where the knee is surgically repaired. He sits in his hospital bed with the leg in a cast for eighteen days (today, no doctor would keep such a patient in bed for so long after knee surgery), and then—

"*I knew not my leg*," Sacks writes. "It was utterly strange, not-mine, unfamiliar. I gazed upon it with absolute non-recognition." As in the case of Hustvedt's shaking body, Sacks's leg separates from his self. "There was absolutely no sensation whatever . . . it looked and felt uncannily alien—a lifeless replica attached to my body."

For Stone and his coauthors, this is FND. As they see it, Sacks's memoir offers "a unique insight into a genuinely experienced" but fairly common event: "Sacks's description has numerous features in keeping with a diagnosis of function paralysis, also called psychogenic paralysis, conversion disorder . . . and (at the time he had his injury) hysterical paralysis." But for Sacks in 1974, this complete alienation from that leg is undiagnosable. The loss of feeling in his leg, loss of agency over the leg, leads to "a dark night of the soul." He describes the alienation from his leg as a "scotoma," a neurological term for a blind spot, and puts it this way:

> The word "hell" supposedly is cognate with "hole"—and the hole of a sco-
> toma is indeed a sort of hell. . . . The organic foundation of "reality" is
> removed, and to this extent one falls into a hole—or a hell-hole, if one per-
> mits oneself consciousness of this (which many patients, understandably,

and defensively, do not do). A scotoma is a hole in reality itself, a hole in time no less than in space, and therefore cannot be conceived of as having a term or ending.

For Stone, Carson, and Perthen, Sacks's trip to hell is in many ways the experience of the typical sufferer of functional paralysis:

The onset of Sacks' symptoms coincides with factors that have been associated with functional paralysis, an "organic" injury (in this case causing leg weakness) a physical injury, pain, fear, and a general anesthetic. In a systematic review of 869 patients with functional motor symptoms, in 133 studies we found that 37% were reported in association with a physical injury.

In the new discourse of neuropsychology, there is no unspeakable mystery to Sacks's condition or experience—there are words for it, and statistics, and a treatment. Sacks, in his hospital bed in the mid-1970s, has no such comforting language or context. As with so many FND sufferers, he is thrown into what Stone and coauthors call "diagnostic limbo." His loss of function is incompatible with conventional physiological explanations: "postoperative inability to move his leg could not be explained on the basis of his orthopaedic injury or any structural neurological lesion." He sits in his bed in terror. Sacks (like and unlike Woolf's sufferer of the headache) struggles to find a name for his pain. He writes of his leg: "It had no place in the world." He quotes Thomas Hobbes: "That which is not Body is no part of the Universe . . . and since the Universe is all, that which is not Body is Nothing and Nowhere." He turns to John Donne: "He ruined me, and I am rebegot, / Of Absence, Darkness, Death; things which are not." In this wordless, nameless suffering, Sacks yearns for the thoughts of a sympathetic doctor. He writes:

Desperately now, I wanted communication, and reassurance . . . I myself needed to communicate above all with my physician and surgeon: I needed to tell him what had happened to me, so that he could say, "Yes I understand."

But—as with most physicians facing such sufferers in the late twentieth century, as with so many of the doctors Emma A. saw—Sacks's doctor refuses to engage. Sacks was forty years old at the time of injury; if not yet the most famous neurologist in the English-speaking world, he was already a pedigreed doctor, with degrees from Oxford and UCLA, and the author of *Awakenings*, perhaps his most famous book. But when faced with Sacks's symptoms of functional paralysis, his surgeon addresses Sacks as if the neurologist-patient were a child, as if Sacks had no authority at all on his injury or even his own body—the same way their doctors talked to Hailey Hooper-Gray and Kyla Kenney and FND Portal and Emma A.

> "Nonsense, Sacks," he said sharply and decisively. "There's nothing the matter. Nothing at all. Nothing to be worried about. Nothing at all!"
>
> "But . . . "
>
> He held up his hand, like a policeman halting traffic. "You're completely mistaken," he said with finality. "There's nothing wrong with the leg. You understand that, don't you."

For Stone, Carson, and Perthen, this is unsurprising, even typical. "Sacks' frustration in finding a health professional to understand his frightening symptoms is common, as is his [own] rejection of a psychological component to the problem." His doctors believe his problem is all in his head, and Sacks, like so many patients I've met, doesn't accept that psychoanalytic explanation. In 1974, Freudian dogma reigned. At the time (as Stone, Carson, and Perthen put it), "the conception of a hysterical symptom was a symbolic event induced by intrapsychic conflict related to a psychological trauma." But for Sacks, this psychoanalyzing of his knee joint makes no sense—his alienation from his leg is not symbolic, has nothing to do with any converted expression of any repressed traumatic event. The trauma is the loss of function, loss of agency:

> I couldn't "think" how to contract the quadriceps anymore. I couldn't "think" how to pull the patella, and I couldn't "think" how to flex the hip.

I had the feeling that something had happened, therefore, to my power of "thinking"—although only in regard to this one single muscle.

He has lost some central aspect of himself: "I felt that I wasn't really 'trying,' really 'willing'—because all 'willing' is willing something, and it was precisely that *something* that was missing," and this leads Stone and his coauthors back to James Paget's 1873 observation: "She says, as all such patients do, 'I cannot;' it looks like 'I will not;' but it is 'I cannot will.'" Sacks has lost his sense of will, and so the separation of self from limb sparks an existential crisis. This was "not just a lesion in my muscle," he writes, "but a lesion in me." Lying in the hospital bed, he looks down at his leg in its cast and thinks:

The more I gazed at that cylinder of chalk, the more alien and incomprehensible it appeared to me. I could no longer feel it as mine, as a part of me. It seemed to bear no relation whatsoever to me. It was absolutely *not-me*—and yet, impossibly it was attached to me—and even more impossibly, continuous with me.

This is the Kafka-horror of it, the Gregor-Samsa-into-a-bug horror of FND, the transformation from self to other, the lack of language to describe it.

I had to relinquish all the powers I normally command. I had to relinquish, above all, the sense and affect of *activity*. I had to allow—and this seemed horrible—the sense and feeling of passivity. I found this humiliating, at first, a mortification of my self—the masculine, ordering self, which I had equated with my science, my self-respect, my mind.

Where her fits drive Hustvedt to a reconsideration of the relation of mind and body, Sacks begins thinking about the relation of doctor to patient. Sacks fashions a neologism, *patienthood*, to describe his condition—he uses the word again and again in the book—and for him, his functionally paralyzed leg is the epitome of "patienthood": it's a condition of voicelessness, of not having an explanation, not being able to attend to oneself, and of simultaneously not having anyone *attend* to him. "How often had I myself," he writes, "as a physician, mysteriously stilled the apprehension of my patients—not through knowledge, or skill, or expertise, but simply by listening." But Sacks doesn't get this kind of attention from his doctor. His doctor tells Sacks: "I can't waste time with 'experiences' like this. I'm a practical man. I have work to do."

It's very strange. Pierre Janet in 1906 saw "hysterical paralysis" as "essential to the study of illness," and Sacks writing in 1983 saw his functional paralysis as encapsulating the condition of being a patient—and yet for the medical establishment for most of the twentieth century, these "experiences" were a waste of time, weren't *real*. They were not to be attended to by workaday physicians—the "practical" surgeon's reaction is typical.

The cure comes when Sacks stops thinking about the leg. "He was excessively aware," write Stone, Carson, and Perthen, "excessively attending" to his leg, and his recovery happens through redirection of attention. As they further express:

> Very typically for a patient with functional paralysis, [Sacks] found that the more he concentrated on moving an affected limb, the harder it was to move. Distraction and rhythmic techniques, such as those provided by music, are sometimes effective tools to enable movement (indeed this is the basis of Hoover's sign and the tremor entrainment test).

In the hospital, Sacks begins thinking, not about the leg, but about music. A friend brings a radio to the hospital, and so Sacks finds Mendelssohn's violin concerto playing involuntarily in his mind during physiotherapy, and the rhythm of the piece takes over his motions, and the effect is almost magical: "suddenly, without thinking, without intending whatever, I found myself walking, easily-joyfully, with the music. . . . In this self-same moment, the leg came back." He leaves the hospital, walking with a limp, and only loses the limp when a helpful surgeon plays a trick on him: the doctor sends Sacks to a swimming pool (Sacks likes to swim), where a lifeguard trips Sacks, and suddenly, floundering in the water, he regains full, glorious control of his leg: "I got out of the pool—and found I walked normally." His paralysis is not psychoanalytic, but it is attention-based and a failure of agency, a blow to his very selfhood. For Sacks:

> In a sense my experience had been a religious one—I had certainly thought of the leg as exiled, God-forsaken, when it was "lost" and, when it was restored, restored in a transcendental way. It had, equally, been a riveting scientific and cognitive experience—but it had transcended the limits of science and cognition.

He finds, in the aftermath, that his experience is not unique. In a center for recuperating patients, he meets a number of people who have gone through the same drama, the same alienation, the same isolation, the same trip into a medical and linguistic hell-hole.

Sacks presents his story as a mystery, but Stone and his colleagues use *A Leg to Stand On* as part of a solution. They give the book to their functionally paralyzed patients, and "patients we have recommended the book to have found it helpful to see their own unusual depersonalisation symptoms described so skillfully, and also that recovery is possible with the right approach." The book, forty years after it was written, becomes, for Stone and Carson's patients, what Sacks in another context describes as the medical "miracle of attention and care." It offers their patients just what Sacks asked for: "communication, and reassurance, a doctor to hear them." When Stone gives *A Leg to Stand On* to a patient with a functional paralysis, he is in a sense saying to that patient, "Yes, I understand."

This is a different kind of talking cure from the one Anna O. described, and for so many doctors treating FND, this kind of clarifying story is a crucial first step in treatment: to offer a narrative with healing power. But for most patients, that attention, that narrative is not enough to cure them, nor is their own storytelling. For so many patients, FND is a hard story to tell.

Emma still worked in Washington DC, but only part time. At her desk, she was afflicted by what she described to me as "random symptoms." "It would usually be my hand. Or my stomach. Muscles would start contracting around my mouth." After she put the kids to bed at the end of a workday, she regularly suffered what she termed a "body crash," a full-body dystonic episode. She was out, lying on the couch, for an hour or two. No matter how her husband shook her, she was unresponsive. On the morning of their NIH appointment, they left after the traffic died down for a 10:30 meeting.

The NIH is a sprawling campus, and they got lost on the way out of the parking lot. She carried a folding cane in her bag, but on arrival she was not using it. A nurse tested her blood pressure and vital signs. A young neurologist examined Emma. He asked her to tap her fingers together, pointer, middle, index, pinkie—but she never got that far. As soon as she tapped her first fingers, her hand muscles tightened.

The doctor seemed impressed.

Other tests also triggered her dystonia. Emma was asked to run. As soon as she stopped, her legs seized up. The exam lasted some two hours, and then her case was presented to Hallett and his team. Emma and her husband waited. She signed a video waiver, then was led into a conference room. There was a table at which every chair was filled, and a set of chairs in a ring around the wall, each chair with another medical professional. A member of the staff filmed Emma while Hallett examined her in front of his colleagues. Emma found Hallett kind, attentive, and careful. "I thought it was good," she told me. "People seemed really interested." Hallett asked her to squeeze his finger. Emma warned him that it might trigger her symptoms, and when she did squeeze, the dystonia came. He had her run and stop, and again her muscles seized. Someone asked if Emma experienced pain with her symptoms. No, she told them, no pain. And then she left the room while they discussed her.

Finally, one of the junior neurologists returned to discuss her case. Emma was exhausted by that point in the day, and she had taken her folding cane out of her bag and was using it for support. His first question, as she remembers it, was, "Do you think this is related to stress?"

"I was so frustrated by that question!" Emma told me, her voice rising. "If you guys want to diagnose me with a stress-related condition," she wondered, "then why didn't you have me meet with a psychiatrist?"

He explained that she was young to be having these symptoms. The doctors at the NIH ordered an additional MRI test—Emma had had a scan of her brain, but they wanted to test her neck and back, to rule out multiple sclerosis. Because of her history of concussions (one when she was young, and the one from 2010 when she was hit by a truck), she did not qualify for any of the NIH studies.

"Kind of a bummer," Emma told me.

In her discharge papers, however, was a diagnosis. Hallett's team referred her to Kathrin LaFaver, who was at the time at the University of Louisville. Emma packed her bags and headed to Kentucky, to visit an FND clinic.

"I felt heard for the first time," she said of her visit with LaFaver. "I felt like there was no judgment. It was just acknowledgment. Yes. *What you are feeling is real, it's not all in your head.* And for the first time in a long time, I felt hope. And that was a really amazing experience." She met with other staff of the Louisville FND clinic: a psychologist and a physical therapist. "They told me that FND affects the whole brain," Emma said. "It's not just neurology or psychology. It's both. They told me that they have found it's more effective when it's treated by a whole team."

This was a crucial formulation and allowed Emma to include her broader life experience in her understanding of her condition—physical stressors, psychological stressors, and personal history. Behavior, neurology, and psychology were all deeply intertwined.

"I can go back to my old self!" she thought.

But that wasn't what happened. Her insurance company declined to reimburse her for treatment. There was no justification for in-patient care, the insurance adjuster declared, the patient should be able to find comparable treatment closer to home. But in 2017, there was no specialist in FND near her, no one outside the NIH, which had excluded her from its studies. What followed were years of struggle, years of attempting to find an appropriate specialist. She joined with FND Hope and befriended another woman about her own age who suffered similarly to Emma, and who, like Emma, was committed to getting better. I will call this young woman F.R.: she thought that her own FND was a result of trauma, that the root causes of her disability were in the adverse effects of her childhood.

"When we first started talking, in 2019," Emma told me, "I was a hard *no*, that my trauma had *no* impact on my FND."

In August 2020, Emma suffered a disabling, monthlong flare. She was trapped on her couch. Every time she tried to move her legs, she convulsed. Sometimes her legs wouldn't move at all.

This is around the time when I met Emma, on Zoom. In our first interviews, Emma told me a little bit about her childhood traumas, about her mother flying into rages when she was little, grabbing her by the shoulders and shaking her. She talked about her father drinking too much. Both parents, she admitted, had their share of mental health problems. She also told me that her mother encouraged her to share her feelings, to let all her feelings out, and that her father accompanied her to doctor visits. She did not tell me that, for years, he had been banished from her life, or that when she was a young adult, her therapist had recommended against her ever reconnecting with him.

In September 2020, he came to visit, and he witnessed one of her full-body crashes. What Emma and her husband had normalized seemed an emergency to him. He began working the phones, trying to find an expert who could save his child. It happened that he had a connection at the Mayo Clinic—a friend's college roommate was a doctor at Mayo, and this person connected Emma's father to Dr. Jeffrey P. Staab, chair of Mayo's Department of Psychiatry and Psychology, and one of the country's leading FND specialists—a member of the Board of Directors of the Functional Neurological Disorder Society. Yes, they would see Emma.

Her husband drove her all twenty-two hours from Virginia to Minnesota. By the time they got to Rochester, he was twitching from exhaustion.

"Mayo was probably the most amazing experience," Emma told me. Everyone knew what FND was. Everyone knew that she had it. Emma was seen by a neurologist who in Emma's husband's words, "demonstrated total mastery of what she did"—this neurologist could play on Emma's body, triggering symptoms and then distracting them away. She met with a psychiatrist, a member of Staab's team, who explained the four possible treatments for improving the lives of FND patients with movement disorders: (1) cognitive behavioral therapy (CBT); (2) occupational and physical therapy; (3) talk therapy, for those who were working through post-traumatic stress disorder; and (4) medications to treat other comorbidities—like depression, anxiety, or PTSD. It was recommended that she start CBT while back at home, to work through her complex PTSD, and to schedule a week-long inpatient course of occupational and physical therapy at Mayo.

"When doctors say, 'Oh, it's just stress,' that is very unhelpful," Emma told me. That kind of language minimizes the problem, and it shifts the burden off the doctor and onto the patient. "Some of my FND is from emotional stress, but there's other things, too," she explained soon after that visit to Mayo. "There's an amount of stress that can be put on your body that your central nervous system cannot tolerate. Like if you get hit by a truck. If you have a concussion. Swine flu. An infection that doesn't go away. Impact over impact over impact within a single year." In response to this intense stress, Emma believes, the neural pathways in her brain began misfiring. "My body or brain has been conditioned for a decade to use the wrong pathway, a glitchy pathway." Once that happened, Emma told me, it was very hard to come back from it.

Her insurance declined to cover her cognitive behavioral therapy, she told me, and Emma did not pursue the possibility of CBT further. "They did want me to do CBT," she told me, "but I haven't done it, because for the majority of people it does not work. From what I've read in the groups, CBT is especially helpful for people who don't feel their feelings. I feel my feelings too much." The most valuable thing Emma brought home from Mayo was a simple one-page handout on diaphragmatic breathing, a piece of 8½- by 11-inch white paper with a few dozen sentences in twelve-point type.

Breathing!

- Focus on breath. Breathe in through your nose, out through your mouth.
- Complete when you find quality of movement is going away.
- On the days when you have "bad moments," return back to the basics of breathing.

<u>One big phrase I want you to remember: Quality over quantity!</u>

- Do not push through poor movements. Stop and reset!
  - ☐ If you keep pushing through poor movements, you may have a harder time breaking out of that movement pattern.

<u>Stop before it starts.</u>

- Reset with breathing, then carry on.

<u>Know you will have your good days, and your days with "bad moments."</u>

- You have the self-management strategies to regain control over your movement patterns and get back on track.
  - ☐ Tools are progressive muscle relaxation, diaphragmatic breathing, and additional movements with breath.

"I'm almost always in fight-or-flight mode," Emma told me. "The breathing exercises lower that fight-or-flight response. Breathing gives my body the ability to find the correct pathway. It's kind of like building a muscle up, so that the brain will automatically use the correct pathway instead of the glitchy one."

It had been so difficult to get a diagnosis, and to find a center where she could receive appropriate treatment, but even once that had been achieved, it was hard to schedule a time when she could actually visit Mayo for a week and receive treatment. It wasn't until August 2021 that Emma finally made her trip for an outpatient stay.

She flew to Rochester with the friend she had made online, the FND patient I'm calling F.R., who was in remission from her symptoms and who could help Emma around Rochester, and around the Mayo Clinic.

The treatment Emma received at Mayo was focused on basic exercises to help her achieve control over her body, to recapture her agency over her movements. Under the supervision of Dr. Margaret Moutvic (who has recently retired from Mayo), Emma worked daily, intensely, from nine in the morning to three in the afternoon, with a physical therapist and an occupational therapist.

The focus of FND treatment at Mayo is on functional movement disorders—tremors, for instance, or gait disorders like Emma's—not seizures or sensory disorders. The goal is to help the patients learn to eliminate maladaptive motor patterns. In a single week, the idea is "to teach the patients management techniques," as Dr. Moutvic explained it to me, "not to cure the condition." There's no expectation that someone like Emma will return home free of symptoms.

The first day, Monday, was spent on a series of baseline tests. Her therapists watched her move her fingers. They had her turn her head side to side, and up and down. She sat and stood and walked. The therapists pointed out that Emma was frequently holding her breath. Emma tended to breathe shallowly, from her chest. The therapists wanted her to breathe from deeper in her body. A chest breath corresponds with panic, they taught her. A deeper breath can ease the body.

"I realized that I wasn't breathing long enough for my body to fully relax," Emma told me.

Dr. Moutvic explained to me that one goal at Mayo was "to normalize the condition," to help patients understand that a functional movement disorder is an ordinary thing, roughly "as common as a migraine headache."

As the week went on, Emma took on more complex actions in physical therapy. First breathing, then breathing and walking, then walking ten feet and turning around, and then sitting and standing and walking ten feet and turning around, and then picking things up while she was walking: there were colored cones, and she had to select them in order of the shades of the rainbow. The therapist started asking questions while Emma walked—integrating the breathing and movement with cognitive tasks. Every time her symptoms were triggered, Emma would have to stop and reset and then continue. In occupational therapy, she worked on simple domestic things, like folding laundry, remembering to breathe while doing chores. By Wednesday, she was no longer limping. She could get up and walk normally.

"I didn't use my cane at all," she told me.

On Thursday, there was a street fair in Rochester, with vendors and bands, and during lunchtime she and her physical therapist went there, and though Emma avoided the thick of the crowd, she felt empowered and capable. She was used to crashing with exhaustion in the late afternoon, but now her fatigue was bearable. She went out to dinner with F.R. Sometimes they ordered in, and in the hotel room they would sit and chat.

"Mayo is amazing because you leave your life behind," she told me. No kids, no chores. She didn't worry about money or family. "No stress," she said. On the last day, the occupational therapist had her write out goals: one- to three-month goals, and six- to nine-month goals. One of Emma's goals was to practice her breathing every day. Another was to take a walk, by herself, around the lake near her house. A third was to do half a grocery run.

She had learned at Mayo to take things slowly, to break problems into parts, not to be too ambitious. She asked her therapist, were the breathing exercises something she'd have to do for her whole life? "Yes," her therapist said. "Because there is no cure."

While she was having these conversations in the clinic, she was talking to F.R. The two women saw parallels in their family life and in their FND. They talked about growing up with the stress of their parents' mental illness, and Emma began reflecting on the traumas of her childhood—awful, awful stories that she had not fully shared with her doctors, and that she had not shared at all with me.

And then she had to leave Mayo. The techniques she had learned helped her navigate the airports, but back at home, life was waiting for her: the school supplies had to be bought, the laundry had to be done. Emma posted her list of goals on the refrigerator. She took her walk around the lake. She managed to shop a little. But there are moments in a mother's life when diaphragmatic breathing isn't possible. The kids played out in front of the house with a garden hose, and the younger one came in soaking wet, screaming, "I HAVE TO GO TO THE BATHROOM!!!!"

"I wouldn't say I'm dystonia free," she told me when I checked in after her trip to Mayo. "There are times where I catch myself having symptoms. I can be walking the kids to the bus stop, and then I notice that my toes are curled, that I have been limping the whole way from the house to the bus stop—I don't even realize when there is dystonia in my foot, because it's just so normal for me. There's a big difference between *getting better* and *being well*."

About a year and a half after her return from Mayo, I sent Emma these pages to fact-check. That was when her story unfolded anew for me. She had joined a therapy group for children with narcissistic parents. She was working with a therapist on "emotional freedom techniques," sometimes called EFT tapping, a form of acupressure in which the therapist applies touch to the patient's body, and through the pressure the patient recalls the traumas of their childhood. I couldn't help but be reminded of the nineteenth-century pressure techniques that Freud experimented with.

Emma is adamant on this: she does not want to be reductive. "I don't think my trauma is the full cause of my FND," she told me. "My brother doesn't have FND, and in some ways his trauma was worse than mine."

The stories that Emma shared with me were awful. Her drunken father crawling into her bed when she was three and assaulting her sexually so that she could not walk the next day. Her mother beating her, when she was little, with her own shoe. Eventually, her father stopped his drinking. Her mother found treatment and her mental health improved. The couple split up when Emma was little, but then got back together. The traumas of her early years were something she neither talked nor thought much about as she grew up to be a gymnast, a math major, a financial analyst, and a mother. The trauma wasn't on her mind that day in 2009 when she was unemployed and engaged to be married and crossing the street when the truck hit her.

Emma's story, for me, encapsulates a whole history of FND—from early biological thinkers, like Sydenham and Charcot, to deniers like Slater and Shorter, to the current science of Hallett and Staab, all of these brilliant minds struggling to define a problem for which we have no good name. Freud is at the center of this history, charting a difficult territory between the symbolic and the physiological. He is no cartoon villain or infallible sage, but a brilliant writer, asking the deepest questions, and striving for—and gaining—power over us all. The first case in Freud's great project was Pappenheim's, and the story he revised all his life was "Anna O."

21

It's unlikely that Bertha Pappenheim's symptoms all of a sudden vanished when she moved to Frankfurt. It's hard to imagine that she never felt pain in her face, never experienced any difficulty with her hands or feet or mouth, and never fell into her "*condition seconde*," what she called "clouds," what Emma A. called "brain fog."

In the mornings she joined her cousins, and together they rode horseback in the woods. She went to the opera. She ran a sewing circle. She made and collected ornate lace collars. At her cousin Anna Ettlinger's house in Karlsruhe in 1889, she performed on stage, acting as King Priam's daughter in something called *Holy Day Eve Play of Troy of 1463*. In Karlsruhe she met Helene Lange, the great German feminist, editor, pedagogue, and politician. Sometimes she went back to Vienna, where she collected porcelain, glass, and lace. Her cousin Paul Homburger reports that everyone in her circle in Vienna knew that she had been ill.[72]

Her cousin Dora Edinger claims to have always known about Pappenheim's secret: "BP knew that I knew, that she was 'Anna O.' but never has she ever made any remark to any one of us concerning her experience."[73] Pappenheim's official JFB biography elides the period of her disability and drug addiction, stating that she moved to Frankfurt in 1882.

She was a Jew, an old maid—if she was going to be respected, she could not let on that she had been a hysteric. Every weekday morning, she walked thirty minutes from her apartment to the Jewish Girls' Orphanage. Every evening she walked home. Her early political interests were in liberation through education. In one of her first newspaper articles, "A Woman's Voice on Women's Suffrage," Pappenheim argued that most women needed more sophistication before they could enter the "large complicated area" of politics and so earn the right to vote. In another, "On the Women's Question a Hundred Years Ago," she wrote: "Teach women to be intelligent and to do their duty, then they will be able also to share in rights to the benefit of mankind." She translated Mary Wollstonecraft's *A Vindication of the Rights of Woman*, and she wrote a three-act play, *A Woman's Right*. In its first act, two prostitutes inform on a group of poor women who are trying to organize politically, and Suzanne, one of the organizers, is sent to jail. Alice Scholl, the wife of an editor, wants to help the poor working women, but her husband won't let her give them any money; Alice's husband, Martin, has in fact impregnated Suzanne. Alice discovers all this and takes responsibility for the child Suzanne bears, and rebukes Martin:

I am supposed to go with you, Martin, and can you believe, after what I've now found out, that everything can remain the way it was between us? No! I'll go with you, but only so far as duty requires as the mother of your child and for the purpose of sparing my daughter my fate. I am no longer your wife. This is my right as a woman.

Suzanne by the play's end is also radicalized.

We have to help ourselves. One lone person can't do it, of course, not even twenty people, and not even the workers from one factory or town. Everywhere in the whole world—in England, in Switzerland, here, and in Berlin—it has to start. The manufacturers have to be shown that they're nothing without us.

Pappenheim visited a Christian home for former prostitutes and found that the deaconess had few Jewish girls under her protection. In a meeting of the Israelite Jewish Women's Association, she took the floor and argued that Jewish women needed to take care of their own, that a "decline in piety increases delinquency," and that Jewish women "might want to learn something from their non-Jewish sisters."[74] In an essay about child-rearing, she argued that Jewish families should not shelter their daughters from the horrors of the world.

> Until now, an axiom of proper education was to keep girls from knowing anything that occurred beyond the confines of their homes. They studied history from books which were "rewritten for girls" but they remained cut off from the enormous demands of everyday life. They do not understand the relation of poverty, sickness, and crime. To them, poverty is a street beggar or a scene in a play, sickness is disgusting, and crime is a sin. Under such circumstances, we cannot be surprised when girls do not understand, or at best, feel fleeting pity for the tragedies of humanity.

In 1902, she founded her first political organization, *Weibliche Fürsorge*, or Care by Women. The group held Monday Meetings, where each week the members would discuss a case, another lost young Jewish girl. In the organization's annual report, Pappenheim wrote:

> If one were to seek an artistic representation for this work, then it could be Jewish woman as the maternal guardian of the vital treasures of the Jewish community, braced by the rock of the commandments, and tradition, and listening into the distance in order not to miss anything in the great world.

That same year, she attended a conference on prostitution and sex slavery at the Frankfurt Hof, a grand five-story hotel, a Victorian castle of a building taking up a whole block and overlooking a public square and fountain. Pappenheim was forty-three years old when:

> the word "*Mädchenhandel*" first sounded upon my ear. I did not know what it meant, and could not at all grasp that there were people who would buy and sell human beings, girls, and children. . . . I did research, listened, and was told things, and learned something which added deep shame to the frightfulness: Many Jews are dealers, many Jewish girls are sold.[75]

The conference elected that she and her colleague Dr. Sarah Rabino-wich, "a lady of great economic knowledge," would travel to Galicia and learn about the conditions of women and girls there. Pappenheim was middle-aged when her career began in earnest, and she took her first train ride out into the East, to see firsthand what poverty looked like. In "On the Position of the Jewish Population in Galicia," she argues that the poor Jews in the East are living in a "state of the deepest moral depravity," and that lack of education and culture had led to sexual and moral degradation.

Pappenheim, child of the Viennese haute bourgeoisie, does not see the Galician Jews' suffering in terms of the complex social, historical, and economic forces that afflicted them. Instead, she writes in moralizing terms, looking down upon their religion, their culture, and their perceived lack of social graces. Pappenheim has contempt for the Hassidic wonder rabbis. She says they prey upon the "superstition and limited intelligence" of their followers, followers who seem docile and of limited piety: "More often than not they only live under the spell of ritual, which they have not dared cast off, because they are superstitious, and afraid of what their neighbors will say." In their religious schools, Pappenheim says, the boys are taught exclusively from Hassidic dogma that "all other knowledge is frowned upon." Her reporting gets still more nasty when she writes about Hassidic women, who, she claims, live "under the spell of absolute ignorance and lack of culture." In Galicia, she reports (exaggerating the facts) that the majority of pimps and prostitutes were Jews. Even "girls who finished school," she writes, "in many families—according to the widespread (mis)practice in the East—sit around doing nothing." She was appalled by what she called the "sad Saturday afternoon 'parade,'" where "throngs of young girls, dressed to the nines, roam the main streets and public gardens of the small towns, flirting with officers and high school students." Those girls were "fresh and pretty," but the women for Pappenheim were "prematurely aged and wilted, often with the demeanor of dull domestic animals."[76]

The sense of beauty among Galician Jews seems to have died, under the pressure and distress of daily life. The women and girls dress strikingly and tastelessly, but they do not adorn themselves. To want to make aesthetic demands on their living spaces, in their hygienic inadequacy, would sound like mockery.[77]

Her word to describe these Galician Jews was "*hungerkünstlers,*" "hunger artists," and she opposed Zionism because she thought the Galician Jews incapable of running a nation. "Certainly it would be nice to give the Jewish people their own country," she wrote, "but in its present state, the Jewish people cannot yet live as a nation. They cannot work yet, and they aren't even mature enough to recognize what they must learn."[78] They lacked "social graces" and "good manners." Her solution was moral and educational: to teach them, particularly the girls, "home economics, childrearing, health and hygiene."

It occurs to me that these women Pappenheim described were very much like my own grandmother—a motherless girl who worked in a bakery in Polish-Austrian Galicia, a bakery crowded with aunts and uncles and cousins, a business run by her grandmother, Brucha, who had founded it on the advice of a wonder rabbi ("bake bread, and you'll have bread"), and where Brucha's husband, Moishidle, sat all day long in the choicest spot, on top of the oven, where it was always warm, and he studied Torah all day, which was a man's job, while young Reisel, my grandmother, never got much education, but worked hard, hauling sacks of flour and tending to the ovens. Young Reisel went (maybe she snuck off without her grandmother's knowledge?) to meetings of Zionist youth, Hashomer Hatzair, meetings where she hiked and sang and danced with boys. My mother tells me that, one time, my grandmother and she were going through Port Authority Bus Terminal in New York, and my grandmother looked at the prostitutes there and said, with an empathy that surprised my mother, "Ach, that's a terrible job." Pappenheim didn't have that kind of empathy. The dominant pitch of her writing, here and elsewhere, is outrage: at Jews, at their circumstances, at rabbis, at Zionists, even at her audience of wealthy Jewish Germans and Austrians, whom she castigates for their prejudice against their poor Galician cousins (a prejudice she certainly shared):

If you are interested in Galicia today for the selfish reason that you are afraid that the dreaded Polacks might leave their country in ever-increasing numbers and inconvenience you by settling down in your beloved and clean corner of the earth or neighborhood—then you can do the same thing to protect against this calamity as someone with purely altruistic motives, who want to help masses of suffering, sinking, intelligent people.[79]

In 1903, as a representative of the Frankfurt committee for Eastern European Jews, she attended a second conference on the *Mädchenhandel*, this time in Lemberg, what is now Lvov. There she railed against the men who dominated the meeting, attacking them for "underestimating the value of women's work, and trifling with their interests by refusing to admit them as equal partners."[80] She initiated a women's section at the conference. "Men," according to Pappenheim, "always and in every situation follow their private interests."[81] This caused a scandal. Rabbi Georg Salzberger wrote that she was "unmarried and a man hater." Rabbi Caesar Seligmann agreed that she didn't "get along well with men who didn't subordinate themselves to her will and leadership." For Elizabeth Loentz, "There may have been a bit of truth to Seligmann's observations."[82]

"She did not like men," Marion Kaplan told me.

In 1904, Pappenheim traveled to Berlin for the International Council of Women. She met representatives of the Protestant and Catholic women's organization, and conceived of an organization devoted to voicing the concerns of German-speaking Jewish women, the *Jüdischer Frauenbund*, or JFB.

Depressive, prone to migraines and fainting spells, with a morbidly neurotic fear of trains, Sigmund Freud spent long days with his patients, and after the publication of *Studies in Hysteria* spent long nights fueled by rockets of cocaine, revising and reworking his "Project for a Scientific Psychology," that ambitious synthesis of neurology and psychology that burst and fizzled and went nowhere. The spring of 1896 must have been depressing for him. His father was ill. He was increasingly intellectually isolated. "I can do nothing right for [Breuer], and should give up trying," he wrote to Fliess. "According to [Breuer], I would daily have to ask myself whether I am suffering moral insanity or *paranoia scientifica*."

In April, before a select group of neurologists, Freud presented a paper, "On the Aetiology of Hysteria," which argues for what has since been called seduction theory, a theory Freud had great hopes for, but which he was forced to abandon almost as soon as he proposed it. "At the bottom of every case of hysteria," Freud told his audience, "there are *one or two instances of premature sexual experience* [italics his]." Freud reported that he had explored eighteen "hysterics" through "psycho-analysis" (this is one of his earliest uses of the term) and in all eighteen he had encountered the same kind of repressed traumatic memory:

> All the singular conditions under which the ill-matched pair conduct their love-relations—on the one hand the adult, who cannot escape his share in the mutual dependence necessarily entailed by a sexual relationship, and who yet is armed with complete authority and the right to punish, and can exchange the one role for the other to the uninhibited satisfaction of his moods, and on the other hand the child, who in his [the male pronoun here stands for both genders] helplessness is at the mercy of this arbitrary will, who is prematurely aroused to every kind of sensibility and exposed to every sort of disappointment, and whose performance of the sexual activities assigned to him is often interrupted by his imperfect control of his natural needs—all these grotesque and yet tragic incongruities reveal themselves as stamped upon the later development of the individual and of his neurosis, in countless permanent effects which deserve to be traced in the greatest detail.

"It seems to me certain," Freud said, "that our children are far more exposed to sexual assaults than the few precautions taken by parents in this connection would lead us to suspect."

No one in the audience could believe this. Many of the attendees' aunts, cousins, sisters, wives, nieces, and daughters had been diagnosed as "hysterical," and if all these women had been molested as children, then (mathematically speaking) sitting in the crowded lecture hall were some likely molesters. Freud went graphically into the horrors:

For the idea of these infantile sexual scenes is very repellent to the feelings of a sexually normal individual; they include all the abuses known to debauched and impotent persons, among whom the buccal cavity and the rectum are misused for sexual purposes.

Freud told his audience that he was finding truth through the talking cure, "in the way described by Breuer's case of Anna O."

While they are recalling these infantile experiences to consciousness, they suffer under the most violent sensations, of which they are ashamed and which they try to conceal; and, even after they have gone through them once more in such a convincing manner, they still attempt to withhold belief from them, by emphasizing the fact that, unlike what happens in the case of other forgotten material, they have no feeling of remembering the scenes.

In his analytic sessions, Freud claimed, he had followed his patients' memories and symptoms backward in time: vomiting at the sight of a rotten apple, to vomiting at the sight of a dead animal, to a deep dark memory of sexual violation.

The chain of associations always has more than two links; and the traumatic scenes do not form a simple row, like a string of pearls, but ramify and are interconnected like genealogical trees, so that in any new experience two or more earlier ones come into operation as memories. In short, giving an account of the resolution of a single symptom would in fact amount to the task of relating an entire case history.

Freud's word for this intersecting skein of memories is "overdetermined," that meaning gathers recursively around certain images, certain symbols.

Breuer was there in the audience. His name and the name of his hysterical patient had been called out—"Anna O." The implication was clear: that she had been molested as a child, and that Breuer had either misdiagnosed her, had missed the central fact of her experience, or was concealing that fact. Krafft-Ebing was dismissive after: "Sounds like a scientific fairy tale." Breuer did not join in the general attack, but neither was he supportive of Freud's theory.

Afterward, in private, he said, "All the same, I do not believe it."[83]

Their relationship further deteriorated. "Freud is a man given to absolute and exclusive formulations," Breuer wrote in 1907.[84] There is a story, told by one of Breuer's daughters, that when the two men passed each other on a sidewalk in Vienna, Breuer opened his arms to his old friend, but Freud walked on.

He had expected to be received as a genius for his discovery of the etiology of hysteria, but he was humiliated and mocked. Friendless in the Viennese scientific community before this lecture, he was exiled from it immediately afterward. "The word has been given out to abandon me," he wrote to Fliess, "and a veil is forming around me." He was, he said later, "despised and universally shunned."

> The expectation of eternal fame was so beautiful, as was that of certain wealth, complete independence, travels, and lifting the children above the severe worries that robbed me of my youth. Everything depended on whether or not hysteria would come out right.

Freud was forced to reject the ideas he had advanced in "On the Aetiology of Hysteria." In September, he wrote to Fliess, "I no longer believe in my *neurotica.*"

That October, his father died. "The most important event," Freud called it in *The Interpretation of Dreams*, "the most poignant loss, of a man's life." In his solitude, he began to look inward, to begin what he called his "self-analysis." He meditated on the abstract, universal churning forces of desire, memory, and imagination. In retreat from the world and relentlessly examining the workings of his own mind, in refutation of the seduction theory, Freud began to glimpse a new possibility. "The great secret of something in the past few months has gradually dawned on me," he wrote Fliess.

He came to agree with the physicians of Vienna and to accept their critique: that it was inconceivable that so many girls had been molested. So he concluded, his patients had only *imagined* that they had been. In "On the History of the Psychoanalytic Movement," Freud declared that the rejection of seduction theory was the crucial step in his journey toward the discovery of psychoanalysis and psychosexuality:

> When ["On the Aetiology of Hysteria"] broke down under the weight of its own improbability and contradiction in definitely ascertainable circumstances, the result at first was helpless bewilderment. Analysis had led back to these infantile sexual traumas by the right path and yet they were not true. The firm ground of reality was gone. . . . Perhaps I persevered only because I no longer had any choice and could not then begin at anything else. At last came the reflection that one has no right to despair because one has been deceived in one's expectations. If hysterical subjects trace back their symptoms to traumas that are fictitious, then the new fact which emerges is precisely that they create such scenes in *fantasy*, and this psychical reality requires to be taken into account alongside practical reality. This reflection was soon followed by the discovery that these fantasies were intended to cover up the autoerotic activity of the first years of childhood, to embellish it and raise it to a higher plane. And now, from behind the fantasies, the whole range of a child's sexual life came to light.

Forever after in psychoanalysis, actual trauma was not the problem. Imagined trauma was—or more precisely, lust and the repression of unspeakable, libidinous urges.

In the arc of Freud's heroic career, "On the Aetiology of Hysteria" was remembered as a stumble, a passing moment of blindness, a mistaken idea he had to reject in order to achieve his complete vision of psychoanalytic theory. For the later Freudians, "On the Aetiology of Hysteria" was an embarrassment. According to Anna Freud, had her father continued to believe his patients' stories of child rape, he would have achieved nothing.

Keeping up the seduction theory would mean to abandon the Oedipus complex, and with it the whole importance of family life, conscious or unconscious phantasy. In fact I think there would have been no psycho-analysis afterward.[85]

For Peter Gay, the argument made in "On the Aetiology of Hysteria" was absurd. Who could believe so many girls were molested?

The seduction theory in all its uncompromising sweep seems inherently implausible; only a fantasist like Fliess could have accepted and applauded it. What is astonishing is not that Freud eventually abandoned the idea, but that he adopted it in the first place.

In the 1980s, debates raged about the seduction theory and its aban-donment. In retrospect, these arguments can feel like the passions of a long-ago religious war. To Freud's followers, like Kurt Eissler, the one-time director of the Freud archives, "Freud was a near perfect man." Eissler's heir and protégé, Jeffrey Moussaieff Masson, turned on Eissler, and in his best-selling *The Assault on Truth*, Masson argued that Freud had known for certain that his patients were being raped, and that Freud concealed the fact in order to advance his career. In response, Freudians attacked Masson. The psychoanalyst Charles Rycroft said that Masson "combine[d] the nose of a trufflehound with an incapacity to distinguish between facts, inferences, and speculation." And he called *The Assault on Truth* "a book that is distasteful, misguided, and silly." Janet Malcolm, in the *New Yorker* articles that were collected into the volume *In the Freud Archives*, insulted Masson's looks and his clothing and wrote pages of di-alogue, for some of which she had no notes. (One jury found that she had libeled Masson, but that was overturned in a case that went to the Supreme Court.) Malcolm placed Masson in Chez Panisse, nattering on about his sex life ("My main symptom was total promiscuity—sleeping with every woman I could meet. . . . I'd slept with close to a thousand women by the time I got to Toronto") and his power to destroy psycho-analysis ("they sensed that I could single-handedly bring down the whole business—and let's face it, there's a lot of money in that business"). "Miss Malcolm does not admit to writing fiction," Masson wrote in the *New York Times*, "yet her main character, myself, exists only in her imagination, invented to serve as the mouthpiece for whatever she happens to disdain." How to get to the bottom of this? Again, it's so many fictions around fictions around fictions. . . .

Freud himself, in *An Autobiographical Study*, casts doubt on "the technical procedure I used at that time" to summon up his patients' memories and wonders if they were only stories "I had perhaps forced on them." His conclusion—"that as far as neurosis was concerned psychical reality was of more importance than material reality"—calcified over the years and across the ocean into rigid analytic dogma.

For much of the twentieth century, many US psychoanalysts in training were taught that sex abuse was not an important factor in patient suffering or mental illness. In 1974, in Freedman and Kaplan's *Comprehensive Textbook of Psychiatry*, a basic educational resource, the kind of rape that Freud describes in "On the Aetiology of Hysteria" is deemed irrelevant to the practice of psychiatry: "Incest is extremely rare and does not occur in more than 1 out of 1.1 million people," they write. Furthermore, according to Freedman and Kaplan, child rape is not particularly harmful. It can even be salutary. "Such incestuous activity diminishes the subject's chance of psychosis and allows for a better adjustment to the external world," they write. "The vast majority of them were none the worse for the experience."[86] In 1974 (when my dad was at the height of his powers), it was respectable in US psychiatry to claim that hysteria was not real, and that child rape was not dangerous.

———◆———

Freud and Pappenheim never addressed each other publicly, but in the German press's wide-ranging arguments about sexual mores and "The Woman Question," they played for opposing teams. She believed that, with education and Jewish values, she could combat sexual promiscuity in young girls. "She was very severe" is how Pappenheim imagined her epitaph. "Controlling sexual love out of the strongest sense of responsibility is moral," she wrote. "Morality is controlling ALL egotistical drive out of a feeling of social consciousness—loving one's neighbor."[87] Freud believed the opposite, that anti-sexual childhood socialization was devastating to the ego. In *Three Essays on the Nature of Sexuality*

(1905), he writes about the dangers of anti-erotic bourgeois morality, about:

> the mental forces which are later to impede the course of the sexual in-
> stinct and, like dams, restrict its flow—disgust, feelings of shame and the
> claims of aesthetic and moral ideals. One gets an impression from civi-
> lized children that the construction of these dams is a product of educa-
> tion, and no doubt education has much to do with it.

"As long as I live," Pappenheim is reported to have said, "psychoanalysis will never penetrate my establishment."[88] As Makari demonstrates,
Freud's work was championed early on in Vienna by writers like Christian von Ehrenfels, who in his *Sexual Ethics* argued for polygamy as a new
scientifically sound basis for the family; by Karl Kraus, who argued for
the legalization of prostitution; and by Otto Weininger, who wrote, "The
disposition of and inclination to prostitution is as organic in a woman as
is the capacity for motherhood." For Pappenheim, these were the kind of
writers "who want the unrestrained, irresponsible enjoyment of sex . . .
[and] regard prostitution as merely a cheerful 'affirmation of life.'"[89] Pappenheim, a middle-aged former "hysteric" (if the public didn't know about
it, Freud did), an "old maid" in a black Victorian dress, with her Shabbat
candles, and her railing against sex and prostitution, must have seemed to
Freud the embodiment of forces that he saw as dark and oppressive.

From 1905 until his death, as he rewrote the story of hysteria and of
hysterical women and of Anna O., his "talking cure" became less and less
a listening cure. The patient was no longer the author of her own story.
The analyst had the authority to compose a story from those things that
the patient could not speak. Every story told by a hysterical woman became a story that a doctor could revise, reinterpret, or ignore.

22

We can see the shift in Freud's thinking about "hysteria," or "hysterical conversion," most clearly in the "Dora" case, which Freud first wrote in 1899, but which he did not publish until 1905—*Fragment of an Analysis of a Case of Hysteria*, his last major work on the disease. As a case history, "Dora" is unreliable in many basic ways. Freud has the dates in which he treated his patient wrong, and also the age of the patient at the time of treatment. His conception of female anatomy is, to say the least, eccentric:

> I had begun to suspect the masturbation when she told me of her cousin's gastric pains. . . . It is well known that gastric pains occur especially often in those who masturbate. According to a personal communication made to me by W. Fliess, it is precisely gastraglias of this character which can be interrupted by an application of cocaine to the "gastric spot" discovered by him in the nose, and which can be cured by cauterization of the same spot. In confirmation of my suspicion Dora gave me two facts from her conscious knowledge: she herself frequently suffered from gastric pains, and she had good reason for believing that her cousin was a masturbator.

The order of events in the story is muddled. These "gastric pains": what was their precise cause? We hear that Dora had appendicitis, but maybe she only imagined it? And when did she get sick to her stomach relative to the other traumas that Freud lists in her life—particularly, sexual traumas? It's not clear. According to Jacques Lacan, even the way Freud conceives of sex is—mechanically speaking—confused. Freud knows that Dora's father is incapable of an erection, so he assumes that her father is having oral sex with his mistress, but as Lacan points out: "Everyone knows that cunnilingus is the artifice most commonly adopted by 'men of means' whose powers begin to abandon them."[90] Everyone, that is, but Freud, who writes delicately about copulation *"per os,"* imagining Dora's father's limp member in his mistress's mouth.

Freud's defenders tend to wave off these problems. "It matters little whether Freud's case histories are called science or art," writes Philip Rieff in his introduction to the Dora case. "The psychoanalytic case history crosses the barrier artificially created between a literature of description and a literature of imagination." But both science and art demand a rigor, and Freud's errors and sloppiness show us not the world as it was, but the world as he imagined it. As Janet Malcolm wrote, "We cherish the Dora case because it proves that Freud, who told us such unpleasant truths about ourselves, was himself just another pitiful, deluded, dirty-minded neurotic. The Dora case shows us a Freud out of control, a Freud whose genius has gone awry."

"Dora" is often described as novelistic. For Steven Marcus, writing in 1974, Freud here "is like Borges—as well as Nabokov," operating "like some familiar unreliable narrator in modernist fiction." But as Malcolm pointed out in the *New Yorker*, this is a misunderstanding of genre: "In the back of every unreliable narrator of modernist fiction stands a reliably artful author." Freud isn't playing with words. He's proposing a way of curing sickness, and he is claiming that the sickness in question comes from the patient's will. "Illnesses of this kind are the result of intention," Freud writes. "They are as a rule leveled at a particular person."

According to the rule which I found confirmed over and over again by experience, though I had not yet ventured to erect it as a general principle, a symptom signifies the representation—the realization—of a phantasy with sexual content, that is to say, it signifies a sexual situation.

By definition, according to Freud, the hysterical patient cannot tell the whole of her own story. So he says he has to understand his patient's words—often—as the exact opposite of their ostensible meaning.

> The "No" uttered by a patient after a repressed thought has been presented to his consciousness for the first time does no more than register the existence of repression and its severity. . . . In such a case, "No" signifies the desired "Yes."

In "Dora," the talking cure is no longer a listening cure. It's a form of narrative combat.

Her name was really Ida Bauer. She was born November 1, 1882, and she lived at Bergasse 32, down the street from the Freuds. Her parents, Philipp and Katharina, were wealthy and cultured Jews. Dora, Freud says, suffered migraines and depression—he calls it *tedium vitae*." Her father had tuberculosis and syphilis. Her mother suffered "housewife psychosis." Dora took ill with appendicitis sometime in early adolescence, around the same time that her aunt died. When she was fourteen, she was sexually assaulted by her father's friend Hans Zellenka, whom Freud calls "Herr K." Herr K. contrived to get Dora alone in his place of business, kissed her, and (Freud surmises) rubbed his erect penis against her.

The story that Dora tells Freud—in fits and starts—is one of constant physical, psychological, and social stress. Herr K. does his best to woo her, "to send Dora flowers for a whole year while he was in the neighborhood, to take every opportunity of giving her valuable presents, to spend all his spare time in her company, without her parents noticing anything in his behavior that was characteristic of love-making." All the while, Bauer's father was carrying on an affair with Zellenka's wife, Peppina, a.k.a. "Frau K."

Dora and Frau K. share a bed, and Frau K. reads to Dora from Mantegazza's *Physiology of Love*. All the while Frau K. is nursing Dora's sick father and pleasuring him orally (or, as Lacan would have it, vice versa), and Dora is tending to the K.'s children, one of whom is dying of a congenital heart defect. According to Freud, Dora falls in love with Frau K.'s "beautiful white body."

Herr K. and Dora take a walk by the lake, when he again makes advances on her. "You know I get nothing from my wife," he says, and Dora slaps him and runs away. She asks her father to break off relations with Herr and Frau K. Her father does not. Dora collapses, falls into a seizure, and writes a suicide note. Her father sends her to Freud, and she tells Freud that her father is engaging in sexual barter with Herr K.—one man's wife for the other man's daughter. Freud is unimpressed:

> When she was feeling embittered she used to become overcome by the idea that she had been handed over to Herr K. as the price of his tolerating the relations between her father and his wife; and her rage at her father's making such use of her was visible behind her affection for him. At other times she was quite well aware that she had been guilty of exaggeration in talking like this. The two men had of course never made a formal agreement in which she was treated as an object for barter.

Why, Freud wonders, did Dora refuse Herr K., who was "still quite young and of prepossessing appearance"? Her disgust at his advances is, for Freud, evidence of her disease. "I should without question consider a person hysterical in whom an occasion for sexual excitement elicited feelings that were preponderantly, or exclusively unpleasurable." Freud tells Dora that her symptoms are not based "in a particular instability in the molecules of the nerves." He tells her that "she had been all these years in love with Herr K.," but "when I informed her of this conclusion, she did not assent to it." Freud has to convince Dora that "his truth is," as Rieff puts it, "superior to Dora's."

> Dora would propose explanations of her wretchedness which Freud criticized, countering with his own; or Freud would spin out his arguments, ending with a fair [Rieff was writing in 1962] challenge to his patient— "And now, what are your recollections to say to this?"

"Where hysteria is found there can no longer be any question of 'innocence of mind,'" Freud announces. Her misery stems from her perversity. "The motive force leading to the formation of hysterical symptoms,"

Freud argues, "draw strength not only from repressed normal sexuality, but also from unconscious perverse activities." Her problems are caused by her lusts.

> It is not to be wondered at that this hysterical girl of nineteen [*sic*] who had heard of the occurrence of such a method of sexual intercourse (sucking at the male organ) should have developed an unconscious phantasy of this sort and should have given it expression by an irritation in her throat or by coughing.

Her desires, Freud discovers, are evident in her history as a "suck-a-thumbs."

> Dora herself had a clear picture of a scene from her early childhood in which she was sitting on the floor in a corner sucking her left thumb and at the same time tugging her right hand at the lobe of her brother's ear as he sat quietly beside her. Here we have an instance of the complete form of self-gratification by sucking.

She doesn't know it, she won't admit it to herself, but she is "poly-morphically perverse." As Freud writes in *Three Essays on the Theory of Sexuality*:

> Prostitutes exploit the same polymorphousness, that is, infantile disposi-tion, for the purposes of their profession; and, considering the immense number of women who are prostitutes or must be supposed to have an aptitude for prostitution without becoming engaged in it, it becomes im-possible not to recognise that this same disposition to perversions of every kind is a general and fundamental character.

Herr K. is a stand-in, in her fantasy life, for her father. Dora wants to be like Frau K., or like her mother. She wants to be her father's lover. "She must have been putting herself in Frau K.'s place," Freud argues. "The in-ference is obvious that her affection for a father was a much stronger one than she knew or than she would have cared to admit." The essay builds to Freud's analysis of two of Dora's dreams. The first and most important dream is described in less than six lines of print.

> A house was on fire. My father was standing beside my bed and woke me up. I dressed myself quickly. Mother wanted to stop and save her jewel-case; but Father said, "I refuse to let myself and my two children be burnt for the sake of your jewel-case." We hurried downstairs, and as soon as I was outside I woke up.

Freud's discussion of the dream then lasts twenty-nine carefully foot-noted pages. The "jewel-case" is a vagina, of course. But the fire?

> I notice that the antithesis of fire and water has been very useful to you in this dream. Your mother wanted to save the jewel-case so that it should not be *burnt*; while in the dream thoughts it is a question of the "jewel-case" not being *wetted*. But fire is not only used as the contrary of water, it also serves directly to represent love (as in the phrase "to be consumed by love"). So that from "fire" one set of rails runs by the symbolic meaning to thoughts of love; while the other set runs by way of the contrary "water," and, after sending off a branch line which provides another connection with "love" (for love also makes things wet), leads in a different direction. And what direction can that be?

Before she can answer, he tells her: bedwetting. From fire to water, from bedwetting (via thumb sucking) to masturbation, to the white vaginal discharge ("catarrh" or "leucorrhea") experienced by both Dora and her mother, and associated (by Dora's mother, Freud says) with her father's syphilis, we see that her symptoms—shortness of breath and palpitations in particular—"are only detached fragments of the act of copulation." Her genitals were on fire for her father. She was "devotedly in love with him." Freud gloats over his own powers:

> He that has eyes to see and ears to hear may convince himself that no mortal may keep a secret. If [the patient's] lips are silent, he chatters with his fingertips; betrayal oozes out of him at every pore. And thus the task of

making conscious the most hidden recesses of the mind is one which it is quite possible to accomplish.

We've moved a long way from Breuer's talking cure. The patient is mostly silent while the doctor examines and attacks. Freud explains what Dora's symptoms mean, and then she fires him. Ida Bauer was not only the first patient with functional neurological symptoms to be treated psychoanalytically, she was also the first one to reject that treatment.

———•———

Freud did not build—or did not intend to build—a barrier between psychology and neurology, between mind and body. He was confident that future advances in neuroscience would eventually render his arguments obsolete.

> The theory does not by any means fail to point out that neuroses have organic basis—though it is true that it does not look for that basis in any pathological-anatomical change, and provisionally substitutes the conception of organic functions for the chemical changes we should expect to find but we are at present unable to apprehend.

Symptoms, he insists, arise initially in the body. "Once again, I have not gone fully into all that might be said to-day about 'somatic compliance.'" But that's not how he was understood thereafter. Freud's ideas about the somatic origins of functional neurological symptoms faded, but his theory about the legibility of those symptoms lingered on. The patients' symptoms represent their repressed urges and flaws: bedwetting, thumb sucking, masturbation, and perversity. If there is a stigma to psychosomatic diagnosis, it's a stigma that was put there, in large measure, by psychoanalysis.

The psychiatrist Felix Deutsch met Ida Bauer in the 1920s and wrote about that encounter in 1957, calling her "one of the most repulsive hysterics" he had ever met. Her husband had "preferred to die . . . rather than divorce her. Without question only a man of this type could have been chosen by Dora for a husband." Deutsch has no doubt that Freud's diagnosis was accurate, and he reports that Ida Bauer accepts the diagnosis and even celebrates it, "displaying great pride in having been written up as a famous case in psychiatric literature." But the diagnosis doesn't help her. She continues to suffer, per Deutsch, "unbearable noises in her right ear and . . . dizziness when moving her head." This, for Deutsch, has to do with her "attitude toward marital life, her frigidity, and her disgust with heterosexuality."[91]

Even as psychoanalytic notions moved away from this kind of misogyny, two fundamental assumptions about conversion disorder remained: (1) that symptoms like Dora's were intentional, albeit subconscious, and (2) that they were interpretable. But the same symptoms could mean different things, depending on the interpreter. For Erik Erikson, Dora's dreams are not primarily about repressed sexual desire; "the symptom language of hysteria," as he puts it, can be understood in terms of ego formation.

> I can propose only most briefly in Dora's first dream the *house* and the *jewel-case*, besides being symbols of the female body and its contents, represent the adolescent quandary: if there is a fire in "our house" (that is, our family) then what "valuables" (that is, values) shall be saved first.[92]

Jacques Lacan agrees that hysteria is one of those "illnesses which speak," but for him they speak in Lacanian terms, endlessly echoing through the mirror halls of symbol. Writing about the Dora case (though it kind of could be about anything), Lacan concludes:

> Thus, analytic neutrality takes its true meaning from the pure dialectician, who, knowing that what is real is rational (and vice versa), knows that all that exists, including the evil against which he struggles, corresponds as it always will to the level of his own particularity and that there is no progress for the subject other than through integration that he arrives at from his position in the universal: technically through the projection of his past into a discourse in the process of becoming.[93]

The thing about words (for Lacan) is that they're unstable, and the thing about reality is that it's made up of words, and so after Lacan, for his followers, an illness like Dora's was less an instance of human suffering and more a moment of symbolic play. In the late sixties and early seventies in Paris, Lacanian thought merged with feminism, and with it came an attempt to redefine the word "hysteria," to remake the epithet as a cry of women's liberation.

"The hysterics are my sisters," wrote Hélène Cixous.

"*Nous sommes toutes des hystériques*," the Parisian radical women chanted.

People like Pappenheim didn't suffer a neurological condition, they were enacting through their bodies the beginnings of a revolution—but even here, the symbol that was her disease could be played with and re-interpreted. Cixous wrote: "I don't give a damn about Dora, I don't fetishize her. She is the name of a disturbing force which means that the little circus no longer runs."[94]

If the (male) Freudians drew Pappenheim as the other, the scary castrating seducer, the feminists drew her as a symbol of themselves. This line of debate and analysis moved across the Atlantic, and in the United States the story of Anna O. was rewritten again. "Although I think the evident oedipal configurations in Pappenheim's encounter with Breuer are significant, I want to focus on the oral dimension of their relationship," wrote Dianne Hunter in 1983. For Hunter, Pappenheim's hysteria is "a self-repudiating form of feminist discourse, in which the body signifies what social conditions make it impossible to state linguistically." Taking a similar view, her colleague Jane Gallop argued that "if feminism is the calling into question of constraining sexual identities, then the hysteric may be a proto-feminist." Mark Micale, in his 1994 *Approaching Hysteria*, argued that the kind of breakdown Pappenheim suffered "is not a disease, rather it is an alternate physical, verbal, and gestural communication." For Edward Shorter, nineteenth-century hysteria was "a classic example of patients who present symptoms as the culture expects them to, or, better put, as the doctors expect them." If Freudians saw somatoform illness as an expression of sexual frustration, if feminists saw it as a critique of power, then academics influenced by deconstruction saw the illness as a language game. "In some ways," wrote the critic Charles F. Rosenberg, in his *Framing Disease*, "disease does not exist until we have agreed that it does, by perceiving, naming, and responding to it."

In the 1980s and 1990s, what was happening in these professors' seminars was analogous to what was happening to patients in neurologists' offices. The pain was not legitimate, it was only a performance. In the eyes of the authorities, the patients' chief problem was that they did not understand their own stories.

———— ·•· ————

Dora fires Freud—he says—not because he was so hectoring and annoying and insulting, but because she was in love with him. *Fragment of an Analysis of a Case of Hysteria* is important for the history of psychoanalysis not just because it is Freud's last major case history of a hysterical patient, but also because it elucidated an important principle of psychoanalytic thought, the concept of *transference*—that is, that patient transfers the object of neurotic repressed desires from the world of childhood into the room with the analyst. In Dora's case, she transfers her love of her father to her love for Freud. Freud defines the process this way:

> What are transferences? They are new editions or facsimiles of the tendencies and fantasies which are aroused and made conscious during the progress of analysis; but they have this peculiarity, which is characteristic of their species, that they replace some earlier person by the person of the physician.

Two weeks after Dora rejects Freud, she returns. She has new symptoms, which she says came about after she saw Herr K. on a street corner—"they had met in a place where there was a great deal of traffic; he had stopped in front of her as though in bewilderment; and in his abstraction he had allowed himself to be knocked down by a cart" (if "Dora" were a novel, it would be a great one)—and after this incident she develops a case of facial neuralgia. This is an echo, Freud says, of the slap she gave to Herr K.'s face when he came on to her in the forest; with the pain in her face, she is punishing herself for slapping Herr K., and also for leaving Freud.

She left Freud, he says, for revenge, "an unmistakable act of vengeance," he calls it. "No one who, like me, conjures up the most evil of those half-tamed demons that inhabit the human breast, and seeks to wrestle with them, can expect to come through unscathed." (He does sometimes write like a deluded Nabokovian loony.) "How could a patient take more effective revenge than by demonstrating upon her own person the helplessness and incapacity of the physician?" Her new symptoms come about (he says) because she wants to hurt Freud, to demonstrate his incompetence. She has a "remorseless craving for revenge," and she has "transferred her feelings of revenge onto me."

In 1923, in his final edition of "Dora," Freud added a footnote, pointing to a new essay he has written on "transference love." This note explains the theory of "countertransference," the idea the physician in turn falls in love with the patient. Freud had privately discussed the problem of countertransference as early as 1908, but it wasn't until after he had included the notion of countertransference into his gospel that he "suddenly remembered" the strange story that Breuer had told him forty years earlier about Anna O.

<hr />

According to Loentz, Pappenheim wrote for about twenty different publications, and she was written about in over fifty distinct newspapers, most of them German-language. In 1907, at the second delegates' convention of the JFB, Pappenheim delivered a speech that, according to Loentz, created a "scandal that spread quickly throughout the German-Jewish press."

"And the woman in the Jewish community?" Pappenheim asked her audience rhetorically. "She doesn't count, she's worth nothing. She learns nothing. . . . She has to mutilate or at least disfigure herself. In the eyes of the Jewish law a woman is not an individual."

In the official publication of her remarks, Pappenheim said that Jewish law regarded women "only as a wife and mother," but her actual words, reported in the papers of the time, were that Jewish law reduced women to "sexual beings."

A leading Frankfurt rabbi, Jacob Horowitz, accused Pappenheim of "defaming Judaism." Berlin's *Die Jüdische Presse* attacked her "appalling, elementary ignorance" and "scant knowledge of Jewish literature." What

Loentz calls "the most scathing attack" came when Rabbi Isak Unna wrote a lengthy essay, *"Fraulein Pappenheim und die Stellung der Frau im Jüdentum."* I doubt Freud was reading the rabbis' articles, but there's no way in the little bourgeois community of Jewish Vienna that Freud's ears didn't catch the whispers about his one-time muse, and his wife's old friend.

While she was provoking her enemies, he was gathering acolytes. In 1908, Freud's followers gathered, as Peter Gay has it, in "a small international congress in Salzburg, the first of many, when a group calling itself 'friends of psychoanalysis' from Vienna, Zurich, Berlin, Budapest, London, even New York, came together." There, Freud delivered, without notes, what's now known as "the Rat Man" case. That was the first time Ernest Jones heard Freud speak. Freud "began at eight o'clock and at eleven he offered to bring it to a close. We had all been so enthralled, however, at his fascinating exposition that we begged him to go on, and he did so for another hour. I had never before been so oblivious of the passage of time." Young Max Eitingon, "one of Sigmund Freud's most devoted and valued colleagues," according to Theodore Draper, attended the conference in Salzburg. According to Draper, Freud "did not take to [Eitingon] immediately, but once convinced of Eitingon's dedication, he received him into his inner circle." Eitingon offered one of the earliest revisions of the Anna O. story, a version very much in line with the new theory of hysteria as propounded in the "Dora" case. He "proposed in a lecture to interpret 'Anna O.'s' symptoms as expressions of incestuous fantasies toward her father, including a fantasy of pregnancy that she supposedly transferred onto Breuer taken as a father figure."[95]

———•———

Was Pappenheim molested as a child? "Were there any early traumatic events," speculated Joseph. D. Noshpitz writing seventy years after Eitingon, "which might have involved exposure to overstimulation—for example, bathing with father, spending a good deal of time in the parental bed, or seduction by some member of the household?"[96] Was that another secret she carried around with her, along with the secret of her hysterical illness? There is no answer.

She may not have been sexually active, but she wasn't shocked by sex—"it is not the worst thing to have made love with a boyfriend in adolescent passion,"[97] she wrote in a letter—and she was in fact a little bit sexy. When she was fifty-two years old, a lighthouse inspector invited her to run away with him for two weeks. "The most enticing thing he had to say was, 'I could show you so much depravity,'" she wrote to a friend. "You can't imagine how much fun I had inside."[98] She was nothing like the stereotypical "hysteric" woman as described by Felix Deutsch. She was fearless. The biggest fight in her life was against the sex trade, but there were so many battles. Her long correspondence with the philosopher Martin Buber began with hostility, when she objected to a letter he had printed in the first episode of his magazine, *Der Jude*. Buber wrote back a conciliatory note and invited Pappenheim to contribute to his magazine. She didn't like the offer.

> Now, if you agree that your article, "From the Front," did more harm than good, and if you uphold the principle of unreserved rectification, then in your next issue you will publish my letter, without cuts or revisions—that goes without saying. Under those conditions, I would grant you the right. I would be pleased if a working relationship were to develop between you and me, at least in the areas where our conscience would allow it. I am an opponent of Zionism and even more so of Zionists.[99]

In the end, Buber became her friend, invited her to teach at his institute. In 1925, she said to a Zionist, "Young man, you are going to the Oriental Jerusalem. Frankfurt is the German Jerusalem. You are traveling to a desolate land. The Promised Land is here." Her feminism put her in conflict with religious Jews; her Judaism could put her in conflict with secular feminists—she even fought with her successors at the JFB. She became as she grew older deeply religious, but there was nothing, and no one, that she wouldn't challenge.

> Dear Daughters! If I might allow myself to critique the Bible, I would say that, from the unjust position that the Bible assigns to women, it follows

that it was composed by a brilliant but male human, and not divine dictate. In other words, her inferior status is not the logical and necessary consequence of the difference of the sexes that was willed by God.[100]

Pappenheim didn't join forces with other people—she was the force around which others gathered. She took wild risks, and she had a natural empathy for those who suffered, and in her best writing, she displays a probing eye for detail. *Sisyphus Work*, her collection of letters describing her investigations of whorehouses and the sex trade, contains this description of life in an odd corner of Jaffa in 1912:

Yesterday I went to . . . Little Rochos Hospital which has 140 beds for female venereal patients—nothing but prostitutes running around the wards half nude and without any supervision at all. Only one nurse, an uneducated female, in a room of 30 patients. I had the feeling I had wandered into an insane asylum.

There was one in the courtyard wearing silver shoes, torn stockings, a chemise and open hospital smock, in a familiar embrace with another, wearing a pink-flowered silk slip, a scarf twisted around her tangled hair. Seated at a table in the ward, a girl with hair piled high, wearing nothing but a lowcut chemise, writing a letter; another one lying in bed wearing a yellow silk chemise with lace, wiping away her tears—yes, tears of laughter; a dark-haired tubercular-looking Jewish girl tugging at her chemise because it keeps slipping off her shoulders, etc. A complete picture of mental and physical depravity in human beings between the ages of 16 and 30, about whom no one in the world cares, except the police—and they in their fashion. A third of these girls are Jewish. I think I must have been the first Jewish woman ever to cross the threshold into those rooms of horror out of concern for their social welfare. . . .

Lectures on the social obligations of the community should be held in every single rabbinical seminary so that all the rabbis, grand rabbis, and chief rabbis, and wonder rabbis might know what is really going on among their flock. I would like to scream in their ears that they have other obligations other than raking in their fees.

In Russia, she traveled with an antisemitic countess around the slums of Moscow.

> We drove to one of the night shelters which Countess B. is attempting to combat. . . . I will spare you all the grim details of what I saw. I need only refer you to [the plays of Maxim] Gorky. . . . Of course, the scenes which Gorky presents have to do with individuals, but to actually see the masses of drunken men and women thrown together, to hear the screaming and laughing and howling from the windows, to feel those insolent fingers pressing against you, to breathe that air, to see that hole of a cellar where they throw the bodies of those who die in the nightly brawls, to know that 4,000 people are crammed together at a given moment in a relatively small room, ready to turn into pogrom beasts in the blink of an eye—my breast felt suffocated in terror.[101]

The same year Freud began to write about countertransference, the same year he began to "remember" about the "hysterical" pregnancy of Anna O., the JFB established a chapter in Vienna.

In May 1924, she was in Vienna again, to attend the First World Conference on Jewish Women. She was then sixty-four years old and struggling to maintain the JFB despite the crisis in the German economy and the rising tide of antisemitism. She was forceful, and busy, and desperate for funds. In the winter of 1924, she wrote a letter to the German-American banker Felix Warburg, a fundraising letter that is also an adventure story, a tale about her attempt to recover an Isenberg child, Irmchen Weingart, from a bad foster home in which she has been misplaced—a letter that shows how desperate she was for money, how hard she was working, and how much her charges needed her help. In the story she tells, Pappenheim travels by train and cart and foot from Isenberg to Frankfurt to Crumstadt, "a small Jewish island of 16 families, six children, three of school age—a dying community." To buy her ticket, she has to go to "a shack in the woods," and she is traveling with a baby in a carriage. "I had a choice to walk through underbrush, roots, holes, fallen leaves, or to take a longer path." The baby, Emmy, gets dropped off in Frankfurt, and then Pappenheim falls in with a desperate, cramped, and dirty crowd of train passengers.

> To understand the conditions in Germany, one only has to look and lis-
> ten in a fourth-class car; tired, worn, angry faces. And what rags, what
> talk! How one has to slave to earn nothing at all. All those millions buy
> nothing. Bread is 600 billions (today, 850 billions). A pale, sickly woman
> sitting next to me seemed not to have learned the price yet. She bobbed
> up, repeating desperately "600 billions!"

After the next change of trains, she meets a "red-haired Galician Jew" who is being harangued by an angry crowd. "He was being battered by violently hostile words as by a hailstorm; his answers in Yiddish evoked furious laughter." When she finishes the last leg of her train ride, she finds that the phone at the station is broken, and she breaks into the back entrance of a Jewish general store, where she is welcomed warmly—the woman inside knows Pappenheim because "I had raised her late hus-band's sister-in-law's cousin at" the girls' orphanage in Frankfurt. She is given soup, and then rides in a horse-drawn potato wagon. "It got dark, the landscape was unattractive. Icy wind and half-freezing rain—rather unpleasant. I wore an old military coat, heavy, stiff, but not warm." Fi-nally in Crumstadt, she sleeps on a couch in another Jewish home, her clothes padded with old newspapers for warmth. In the morning her hostess gives her "ersatz coffee, good bread, homemade jam." She is of-fered a pat of butter and cream, but Pappenheim says, "I definitely had to refuse." She would not take from these people what luxuries they had left. Finally, she recovers the poor girl, Irmchen, from a family that cannot keep her, and travels the reverse route back home.

> But now I would have to walk through the woods with the tired child
> and my many parcels. I was undecided; it was an hour's walk. A good old
> Frankfurt cab driver noticed my problem and, as a talkative widower who
> had raised seven children, he offered to wait for half an hour (still more
> waiting) for passengers from the next train. It was late: no one got off.
> The kind driver took us on. Autos passed us, but our good horse trotted

faithfully: at last, at last, we arrived in Frankfurt, where I left Irmchen with friends for the night. The fare was quite reasonable: only a billion and a half. I walked home.[102]

If in her fundraising she wrote such a letter to Felix Warburg, might she have written something to her old friend Martha, who was now wealthy and comfortable and living in Vienna? A little note, asking for a little cash? Did Martha ever meet with Bertha when Bertha came to Vienna? If Minna Bernays (the sister who lived with the Freuds) or Martha wanted to write a check to the JFB—an organization whose tens of thousands of members were bourgeois Jewish women just like them—would Freud have forbidden it, as he had once forbidden his wife from lighting Sabbath candles?

It is all but inconceivable—as Freud revised his theory of hysteria, and certainly as he repeated and revised his stories about Anna O.—that he was not thinking sometimes of the girl Breuer treated, sometimes of the young woman who was his wife's old friend, and sometimes of the actual Bertha Pappenheim who was crisscrossing Europe, making speeches, making noise. In 1928, Bertha Pappenheim returned to Vienna, arguing for voting rights for Viennese women. Can we believe that Freud didn't notice?

———

Breuer was dead by the time Freud began to spread the story of the phantom pregnancy, the story that there was a mysterious "untoward event" that ended the Anna O. sessions. Breuer "never said this to me in so many words," according to Freud, "but he told me enough at different times to justify a reconstruction of what happened." In 1932, when Freud was in his seventies, he began to put his "reconstruction" down on paper, in a letter to Stefan Zweig.

I suddenly remembered something Breuer had told me in another context before we had begun to collaborate and which he never repeated. On the evening of the day when all her symptoms had been disposed of, he was summoned to the patient again, found her confused and writhing in abdominal cramps. Asked what was wrong, she replied, "Dr. B's child is coming!"

Dora Edinger speculates that it was in 1935 that Pappenheim returned to Vienna, and there destroyed all the last bits of the evidence of her mental breakdown. Pappenheim died of cancer in 1936, soon after a confrontation with the Gestapo.

Freud, living now in London, a refugee from Nazism, continued to tell his stories about the hysterical pregnancy, even when cancer had taken out the top of his mouth, and he wore an uncomfortable prosthesis in place of his soft palate. He still smoked his cigars and still talked. Ernest Jones wrote, "Freud gave me two versions of the story," including, "the theatrical one about grabbing the hat."[103] In a 1951 letter to Jones, James Strachey wrote, "Freud told me the same story with a good deal of dramatic business. I remember very well his saying, 'So he took up his hat and rushed from the house—' But I've always been in some doubt that it was a story that Breuer told Freud."

I've always thought of Groucho Marx as a vaudeville Freud (the cigar, glasses, and double-talk), but with his dirty little story, I imagine Freud in his London home—not long after Pappenheim's death and just before his own—doing Groucho: eyebrows above the glasses, cigar waggling, and much theatrical business about a hat.

A hat is the first example of a phallic symbol that Freud uses in *The Interpretation of Dreams*. In the pregnancy story, Breuer has lost his. Anna O. is reduced to a joke, mouth open, legs spread, transformed to the vagina dentata, the castrating witch of psychoanalysis's dream birth. That's what people were taught about her, about Bertha Pappenheim, for most of the twentieth century.

Her cousin Paul Homburger wrote, "the image of Bertha that should and will survive, is not that of a sick patient but of a person who overcame illness and as a leader in the social ascent of mankind."[104] Maybe a similar charity and sympathy and appreciation should be extended to all the patients who suffered as she did. Maybe we should trust their stories, more than the stories that we've been told about them.

23

By the time I got back to my dad's essay, his manila envelope had, as a talisman, lost its magical power. By then Marcia had received her diagnosis. I longed for the company of my father in those difficult, difficult months, but the man I wanted was not an old guy in his underwear screaming about Bertha Pappenheim. I wanted to be a little boy and I wanted him to hold me.

My dad was very, very smart but maybe not the most coherent writer. He had, as one of Pappenheim's critics said of her prose, "a well-known habit of overshooting [his] mark." He wrote the essay in the early 1990s. He was ahead of most interpreters, but his argument as I read it no longer seemed to me as urgent or original as it may have when he was writing.

When Marcia was first diagnosed, I refused to believe that she could die, and I decided that the narrator of this book lived in some parallel universe to my own, that the woman *he* loved didn't have pancreatic cancer. When the cancer metastasized and all hope was lost, Marcia, in bed beside me with a drain in her side, said, "You're going to finish the book."

I had my marching orders.

But I can't quite do it. The narrator of this book is not the guy who drove back and forth from the emergency room, the guy who spent his days crying and screaming, and his nights imagining tumors. I cannot here describe Marcia's beauty and grace, the tenderness of nursing her, the music of her voice when I came to her hospital room and she sang out my name, the fun we had watching *King Kong vs. Godzilla* in pre-op. It was clear, that final morning, that she was fading fast. She could barely swallow the pills that I put into her hands. I crept in bed beside her, and I found a book to read—*Where the Wild Things Are*—and I started, my face covered with tears, and Marcia said, "Simmer down, Brownstein."

I'm not going to get into all that.

The summer after she died, this is what I did: tended to my kids, took care of my house, and worked on this book. It was compulsive, every morning, as if with this story I could hold my world together, and in this way my grief altered my subject matter.

As contemporary neurologists have it, we should not assume that Pappenheim's symptoms were any kind of symbolic storytelling, nor should we dismiss them as some kind of performance suggested by her doctors or the world around her. She was not necessarily trying to say or do anything—consciously or unconsciously. She was in a "hell hole," as Oliver Sacks describes it, a place from which she could not speak but nonetheless needed to be heard. Breuer sat by her side and listened to her. This was not a talking cure in the way that Freud would later have it, and it was not the kind of partnering that happens in Massachusetts General, where David Perez joins his patients in considering the best understanding we have of the function and malfunction of the brain. What Breuer offered in 1881 was preliminary to all that—a human face, a chunk of time, and someone who would listen, all of it offered as medicine.

For my dad, what Breuer introduced was "free association," and my father in his essay argues that Breuer's technique is or should be the ideal in psychoanalysis: two minds meeting, the doctor giving the patient room for play and self-discovery. Very much the antithesis of the practice as spelled out in the Dora case, this is an interchange in which the patient becomes the writer of her own story, and the doctor the companionable audience. My father imagines "Pappenheim and Breuer working together, stimulating one another's imagination." And this, for my dad, is central to the work of psychotherapy. "We have to wonder how we could ever have overlooked Breuer's contribution to the subject."

> By insisting on free association, we create an expectation of a useful and meaningful outcome, not knowing where we are going but valuing the way we get there. There is always some unconscious anticipation of what a given situation may portend. There are hypotheses about what is coming, even wishful thinking that may make the hoped for become more likely.

FND doctors collaborate on narratives, attending to patients who for decades have been spurned by the medical world. Central to this practice is the simple act of listening, of granting legitimacy to patients and their condition, of normalizing the problem. These doctors are no longer asking if the problem is "real," or trying to interpret what a symptom "means," they are asking how they can help their patients. The work is in its early stages. There is not yet a set of agreed upon protocols for treatment of FND, much less a clear sense of how and why particular sets of brain images correspond to particular expressions of symptoms. Different programs are funded and organized differently. If you go to Mayo, you get a one-week outpatient training to help you learn how to reprogram your brain. If you go to Mass General, you get a doctor who will work for you for years. For many patients, FND can become a manageable condition, but many, even after treatment with the leading physicians, continue to struggle. In some cases, the treatments, the creation of a narrative with healing power, may feel like what my dad said all psychotherapy amounts to, "wishful thinking that may make the hoped for become more likely."

The physicians who are treating FND are as smart and as empathetic as any group of people I have ever encountered. Listening to Mark Hallett talk, even on a video feed, one feels one's mind being led along clear and distinct passageways one could not previously have imagined. These people are pursuing a difficult problem, and their work challenges our most basic assumptions and definitions. Description of the disorder tortures language. "Functional" in this case means almost the opposite of what it usually means—it indicates how something *doesn't* work. In cases of FND, the distinctions between "mind," "brain," and "body" seem imprecise. The story FND doctors and their patients write together forces us to reconsider what we mean when we say "self."

If we are to believe their doctors, FND patients are not performing anything—they aren't malingering, and they are not necessarily expressing any subconscious desires. They have lost the ability to perform. They are violating the script the rest of us follow, a script that says consciousness is separate from the flesh, that says our bodies are tools over which we exert the mind's agency. FND patients—when they fall into tremors and seizures and paralysis—are not performing their own dramas, but failing to go along with ours. It's like they're on stage with us, but they're going off script, they can no longer act their part in the show, and so they threaten to put the lie to our collective performance. That's why we turn away from them in horror and laughter. As soon as we empathize with these people, we admit something frightening about ourselves: that any one of us, under the worst circumstances, might fall apart in just this way.

"Modern physiology is in a position to incorporate successfully the phenomenon of consciousness," wrote Breuer's teacher Ewald Hering in the mid-nineteenth century. In *Studies*, Breuer makes fun of that kind of reductively neurological language:

> If we choose to say "excitation of the cortex" instead of "idea," then the
> former would be meaningful for us only in as much as we see the old
> friend through the disguise and tacitly reinstate the "idea."

A century after Breuer, neuroscientists continue to make the same old promise, that, as Eric Kandel speculated, "consciousness is a biological process that will eventually be explained in terms of molecular signaling patterns used by interacting populations of nerve cells." Maybe. But maybe not. If we could somehow map all the molecular signaling pathways of all the cells in Bertha Pappenheim's brain in the years from 1880 to 1882, would we, with all that raw information, really know her mind? To interpret the data, we'd need to know her life. We'd have to be familiar with the places she lived, the Alsergrund and Bad Ischl and the

Schiffschul, and the languages she spoke. We'd have to know her family's Hungarian-influenced upper-class Viennese Jewishness, her youthful "silent struggle and silent opposition" to that religion, and her escape into "private theater." To really understand her, to empathize, we'd need to know about the pain in her face, the hunger she felt when she wasn't eating, the exhaustion when she did not sleep. We'd have to know the effects of the drugs she took and sometimes abstained from, and the trauma of the violence she endured. We'd have to know her sexual temperament (if Freud was right about anything) and the vexed relationships she had with her father and her mother, and the nights when she tended to her father, and the nights her mother forbade her from doing so. Could all that be one day legible in the workings of a person's brain cells? The breakdown in Pappenheim's mind could have only happened there, in that body, that family, that apartment, in that society, and in that era—the lies she was told and the way she saw through those lies.

Maybe what we call "mind" can't be reduced to the soup in the skull. Maybe the stream of consciousness lies not in the chemical composition of the water, but in the play of the wind upon its surface, the current over the stones, the flashes of sunlight, the shadows of the trees, the changes in season, the shifts in climate, and the gravity of the spinning globe. Pappenheim's suffering, as Marion Kaplan wrote, was "integrally related to the position of women of the day." She was profoundly influenced by the way she was treated, and also by the things she read and saw and talked about: *Hamlet*, a hypnotist's performance, or an obituary for a rabbi who had written about catharsis. To know her, we'd have to know how she understood herself, which is to say, how the people around her described her condition, what they thought of her breakdown—what her doctors described as "hysteria"—and what she in turn thought of them.

We cannot diagnose her; we can't know her suffering. To say that she didn't have "hysteria" but instead had "FND" is to mistake current understanding for absolute truth. No one who studies FND thinks we have come to any final word on the subject. If anything is certain, it's that in twenty years we'll have a new and different vocabulary for this problem— better ways to treat the patients' suffering, I hope, and ways to normalize and accept the mystery of their condition. I have tried to get as close to

Pappenheim as I could, to represent her in all her dynamism and not to reduce her to a cartoon. But her story remains a secret. The various attempts at interpretation and reinterpretation of the "Anna O." case show us how we have tried and failed to know the actual woman. The centuries of argument about FND—call it hysteria, hysterical conversion, or conversion disorder—show us how we have tried and failed to know the human mind.

Acknowledgments

This book could not have been written without a lot of help from a lot of people. I am cutting the list to an essential few, the ones who addressed the actual writing. The names of everyone who supported me over the last few years would fill a second volume.

First, I have to thank the patients who shared their stories with me and collaborated with me, and also those patients with whom I spoke but whose names and stories I could not include here. A special thank-you to Bridget Mildon of FND Hope, who not only told me her own story, but facilitated my connections with a number of patients and doctors.

Second, thanks to the experts who looked at some or all of these pages and offered advice: Marion A. Kaplan, Rebecca Kobrin, Kathrin LaFaver, David Perez, and Jon Stone. A genuine thank-you also to Frederick Crews, who read an early draft and hated it—there's no better time to get a bad review than well before you publish, and his attack made my book better.

I want to thank the friends and family who read the book and offered help and suggestions: Jessica Blau, Daniel Brownstein, Rachel Brownstein, Rafael Heller, Ezra Shales, and Virginia Templeton. I got journalistic advice from Sharon Lerner and J. P. Olsen. My kids (whom I love and admire more than I can say) heard me talk (and talk) about this book, and every time I talked to them about it, they helped me—so thank you, Lu and Eliza Brownstein.

I thank my editor, Ben Adams, and my agent, David McCormick; it's my great good fortune to work with you both.

Mostly, I want to thank my late wife, Marcia Lerner, for everything.

Further Reading

About Pappenheim

Guttmann, Melinda Given, *The Enigma of Anna O.*, Whickford, RI: Moyer Bell, 2001.

Kaplan, Marion A., *The Jewish Feminist Movement in Germany*, Westport, CT: Greenwood Press, 1979.

Loentz, Elizabeth, *Let Me Continue to Speak the Truth: Bertha Pappenheim as Author and Activist*, Cincinnati: Hebrew Union College Press, 2007.

About Freud

Breger, Louis, *Freud: Darkness in the Midst of Vision*, New York: Wiley, 2001.

Crews, Frederick, *Freud: The Making of an Illusion*, New York: Metropolitan, 2017.

Gay, Peter, *Freud: A Life for Our Time*, New York: Norton, 1988.

Phillips, Adam, *Becoming Freud*, New Haven: Yale University Press, 2014.

Sacks, Oliver, "The Other Road: Freud as Neurologist," in *The River of Consciousness*, New York: Penguin, 2017.

About the "Anna O." Case

Appignanesi, Lisa, and John Forrester, *Freud's Women*, New York: Basic Books, 1992.

Borch-Jacobsen, Mikkel, *Remembering Anna O.: A Century of Mystification*, London: Routledge, 1996.

Breger, Louis, *A Dream of Undying Fame: How Freud Betrayed His Mentor and Invented Psychoanalysis*, New York: Basic Books, 2009.

Hirschmüller, Albrecht, *The Life and Work of Josef Breuer*, New York: NYU Press, 1989.

Muroff, Melvin, and Max Rosenbaum, eds., *Anna O.: Fourteen Contemporary Reinterpretations*, New York: Free Press, 1984.

Skues, Richard A., *Sigmund Freud and the History of Anna O.: Reopening a Closed Case*, New York: Palgrave Macmillan, 2006.

Swales, Peter, "Freud, His Teacher, and the Birth of Psychoanalysis," in *Freud, Vol. 1: Appraisals and Reappraisals*, Paul E. Stepansky, ed., New York: Routledge, 1986.

About Vienna and Pappenheim's World

Bristow, Edward J., *Prostitution and Prejudice: The Jewish Fight Against White Slavery, 1870–1939*, Oxford: Schocken, 1982.

Rozenblit, Marsha L., *The Jews of Vienna: Assimilation and Identity*, Albany: SUNY Press, 1983.

Schorske, Carl E., *Fin-de-Siècle Vienna: Politics and Culture*, New York: Viking, 1980.

Wistrich, Robert S., *The Jews in the Age of Franz Joseph*, Oxford: Oxford University Press, 1990.

Wolff, Larry, *The Idea of Galicia: History and Fantasy in Habsburg Political Culture*, Stanford: Stanford University Press, 2010.

Zweig, Stefan, *The World of Yesterday*, Althea Bell, trans., Lincoln: University of Nebraska Press, 2009.

About Hysteria

Arnaud, Sabine, *On Hysteria: The Invention of a Medical Category Between 1670 and 1820*, Chicago: University of Chicago Press, 2015.

Cixous, Hélène, "The Laugh of the Medusa," in *Signs*, 1.4 (Summer 1976), 875–893.

Janet, Pierre, *The Major Symptoms of Hysteria*, New York: Macmillan, 1907.

Micale, Mark, *Hysterical Men: The Hidden History of Male Nervous Illness*, Cambridge: Harvard University Press, 2008.

Scull, Andrew, *Hysteria: The Disturbing History*, Oxford: Oxford University Press, 2009.

Shorter, Edward, *From Paralysis to Fatigue*, New York: Free Press, 2008.

Showalter, Elaine, *Hystories: Hysterical Epidemics in Modern Culture*, New York: Columbia University Press, 1997.

About FND

Carson, Alan, et al., eds., *Overcoming Functional Neurological Symptoms: A Five Areas Approach*, New York: CRC Press, 2017.

FND Hope, fndhope.org.

FND Portal, fndportal.org.

Hallett, Mark, Jon Stone, and Alan Carson, eds., *Functional Neurologic Disorders* (*Handbook of Clinical Neurology*, Vol. 139), New York: Academic Press, 2016.

Hustvedt, Siri, *The Shaking Woman or a History of My Nerves*, New York: Henry Holt, 2009.

LaFaver, Kathrin, et al., eds., *Functional Movement Disorder: An Interdisciplinary Case-Based Approach*, New York: Springer, 2022.

O'Sullivan, Suzanne, *Is It All in Your Head?*, London: Other Books, 2008.

O'Sullivan, Suzanne, *The Sleeping Beauties*, New York: Pantheon, 2021.

Stone, Jon, neurosymptoms.org.

Notes

1. See Bristow, Edward J. *Prostitution and Prejudice: The Jewish Fight Against White Slavery, 1870-1939*, Oxford: Schocken, 1982.

2. Unless otherwise noted, I'm quoting from the Penguin edition of *Studies in Hysteria*, Nicola Luckhurst, translator.

3. Guttmann, Melinda Given. *The Enigma of Anna O.*, Whickford, RI: Moyer Bell, 2001, 3.

4. Hallett, Mark. "Psychogenic Movement Disorders: A Crisis for Neurology," *Current Neurology and Neuroscience Reports* 6, 269–271, 2006.

5. LaFrance, Kurt, and Mack, J. D., in *Functional Movement Disorder: An Interdisciplinary Case-Based Approach*, LaFaver, Perez, Nicholson, and Maurer, eds., New York: Springer, 2022, 267.

6. Stone et al. "The 'Disappearance' of Hysteria: Historical Mystery or Illusion?" *Journal of the Royal Society of Medicine* 101:1, 2008.

7. Lidstone, Sarah, and MacGillivray, Lindsey, "The Biopsychosocial Formulation for Functional Movement Disorder," in *Functional Movement Disorder*, 29.

8. Lidstone, Sarah, et al. "Diagnosing Functional Neurological Disorder: Seeing the Whole Picture." *CNS Spectrums* 26:6, 2020.

9. Hirschmüller, Albrecht. *The Life and Work of Josef Breuer: Physiology and Psychoanalysis*, New York: New York University Press, 1978, 116.

10. Kaplan, Marion A. *The Jewish Feminist Movement in Germany*, Westport, CT: Greenwood Press, 1979, 11, 127, 136, 36.

11. See Bristow, 55, 64, 56, 126.

12. Jakubczak, Aleksandra. *(Sex)Worker, Migrant, Daughter: The Jewish Economics of Sex and Mobility, 1870-1939*. Doctoral dissertation. Columbia University Department of History, 2023.

13. Kaplan, 126.

14. Loentz, Elizabeth. *Let Me Continue to Speak the Truth: Bertha Pappenheim as Author and Activist*, Cincinnati: Hebrew Union College Press, 2007, 219.

15. Perez, Aybeck, Hallett, Nicholstone, Stone, LaFrance, et al. "A Review and Expert Opinion on the Neuropsychiatric Assessment of Motor Functional Neurological Disorders," *Journal of Neuropsychology and Clinical Neurology* 33:1, Winter 2021, 16–17.

16. See Muroff and Rosenbaum. *Anna O.: Fourteen Contemporary Reinterpretations*, New York: Free Press, 1984, 47, 30.

17. Borch-Jacobsen, Mikkel. *Remembering Anna O.: A Century of Mystification*, London: Routledge, 1996, 47, 34.

18. Makari, George. *Revolution in Mind: The Creation of Psychoanalysis*, New York: Harper, 2008, 38.

19. Guttmann, 170–171.

20. Quoted in Schorske, Carl E. *Fin-de-Siècle Vienna: Politics and Culture*, New York: Viking, 1980, 116.

21. Wistrich, Robert S. *The Jews of Vienna in the Age of Franz Joseph*, Cambridge: Littman Library and Liverpool University Press, 2006, 42.

22. Wistrich, 118, 164.

23. Loentz, 28.

24. Behling, Katja. *Martha Freud: A Biography*, Cambridge: Cambridge Polity Press, 2005, 14.

25. Crews, Frederick. "Scattered Comments on Psychoanalysis," email to Psychoanalysis Listserve, May 9, 1996, quoted in Forrester.

26. Wistrich, 64.

27. Gay, Peter. *Freud: A Life for Our Time*, New York: Norton, 1988, 42.

28. Borch-Jacobsen, 66.

29. Benedikt, Moriz. "Catalepsy and Mesmerism," trans. Diana George, in Borch-Jacobsen, 115–116.

30. Kaplan, Marion A. "Anna O. and Bertha Pappenheim, a Historical Perspective," in *Anna O.: Fourteen Contemporary Interpretations*, 104.

31. Maurer, Carine, and Duffy, Joseph. "Functional Speech and Voice Disorders," in *Functional Movement Disorder*, 164.

32. Billroth, Breuer, and Eschenbach, all quoted Hirschmüller, 34, 41, 42.

33. Hirschmüller, 292.

34. Neurosymptoms.org.

35. McLoughlin, C., et al. "Functional Neurological Disorder Is a Feminist Issue," *Journal of Neurology, Neurosurgery, and Psychiatry*, March 28, 2023.

36. Scull, Andrew. *Hysteria: The Disturbing History*, Oxford: Oxford University Press, 2009, 3.

37. Honaker, Gilbert, et al. "Chronic Subjective Dizziness vs. Conversion Disorder: Discussion of Clinical Findings and Rehabilitation," *American Journal of Audiology* 19:1, June 2010, 3–8.

38. Scull, 189.

39. Hallett, Mark. "Neurophysiologic Studies of Functional Neurological Disorder," in Hallett, Mark, Jon Stone, and Alan Carson, eds., *Functional Neurologic Disorders* (*Handbook of Clinical Neurology*, Vol. 139), New York: Academic Press, 2016, 61.

40. Quoted in Hirschmüller, 45.

41. Loentz, 219–220.

42. This news report was broadcast on WSMV Nashville in the week of April 26, 2021. I watched it on YouTube. It has since been taken down.

43. Harrington, Anne. *The Cure Within: A History of Mind-Body Medicine*, New York: Norton, 2008, 22.

44. Correspondence in this section all from Hirschmüller.

45. Quoted in Gay, 504.

46. Hirschmüller, 116.

47. Cranfield, Paul F. "Josef Breuer's Evaluation of His Contribution to Psycho-Analysis," *International Journal of Psycho-Analysis* 39:5, 1958, 319.

48. Hirschmüller, 116.

49. Hirschmüller, 28.

50. Quoted in Crews, 69.

51. Hirschmüller, 27.

52. Makari, 14.

53. Munthe, Axel. *The Story of San Michele*, London: Murray, 1929, 296, 302–303.

54. Gay, 54.

55. Crews, 219.

56. Quoted in Swales, Peter. "Freud, His Teacher, and the Birth of Psychoanalysis," in *Freud, Vol.1: Appraisals and Reappraisals*, Paul E. Stepansky, ed. New York: Routledge, 1986, 4.

57. Quoted in Skues, Richard A. *Sigmund Freud and the History of Anna O.: Reopening a Closed Case*, New York: Palgrave Macmillan, 2006, 35.

58. Skues, 35.

59. Boyarin, Daniel. *Unheroic Conduct: The Rise of Heterosexuality and the Invention of the Jewish Man*, Berkeley: University of California Press, 1997, 338.

60. For an excellent map of Frankfurt, and Pappenheim's life there, see https://www.berthapappenheim.com.

61. Loentz, 228.

62. Loentz, 199.

63. Pristhishkumar, Ivan James. "Ludwig Edinger (1855–1918): Founder of Modern Neurology," in *Journal of Historical Neuroscience* 24:1, 2015, 26–57.

64. Kaplan, 42.

65. Guttmann, 123.

66. Masson, Jeffrey Mousaieff. *The Assault on Truth*, New York: Harper, 1984, 77–78.

67. Quoted in Makari, 107.

68. Makari, 1.

69. Koehler, Peter J. "Freud's Comparative Study of Hysterical and Organic Paralysis: How Charcot's Assignment Turned Out," *Archives of Neurology* 60:11, 2003, 1646–1650.

70. Makari, 147.

71. Appignanesi, Lisa, and Forrester, John. *Freud's Women*, New York: Basic Books, 1992, 113.

72. Loentz, 199.

73. Dora Edinger to Max Stern, October 11, 1959, Dora Edinger Papers, B 86/735 Judishes Museum, Frankfurt. Quoted in Loentz, 205.

74. Guttmann, 136.

75. Guttmann, 139.

76. Loentz, 141–142.

77. Wolff, Larry. *The Idea of Galicia: History and Fantasy in Habsburg Political Culture*, Stanford: Stanford University Press, 2010, 315.

78. Guttmann, 161.

79. Loentz, 132–133.

80. Kaplan, 44.

81. Guttmann, 137.

82. Salzberger and Seligmann, quoted in Loentz, 175.

83. Masson, Jeffrey Moussaieff, ed. *The Complete Letters of Sigmund Freud to Wilhelm Fliess, 1887–1904*, Cambridge: Harvard University Press, 1985, 151.

84. Cranefield, P. F. "Josef Breuer's Evaluation of His Contribution to Psycho-Analysis," *International Journal of Psychoanalysis* 39:5, 1958, 319–322.

85. Quoted in Masson, 113.

86. Quoted in Van Der Kolk, Bessel, *The Body Keeps the Score: Brain, Mind, and Body in the Healing of Trauma*, New York: Penguin, 2014, 190–191.

87. Loentz, 177.

88. Guttmann, 120.

89. Guttmann, 261.

90. Lacan, Jacques. "Intervention on Transference," in *In Dora's Case*, Bernheimer and Kahane, eds., New York: Columbia University Press, 1985, 98.

91. Deutsch, Felix. "A Footnote to Freud's 'Fragment of a Case of Hysteria," in *In Dora's Case*, 35–43.

92. Erikson, Erik. "Reality and Actuality," in *In Dora's Case*, 54.

93. Lacan in *In Dora's Case*, 94.

94. Quoted in Gallop, Jane. "Keys to Dora," in *In Dora's Case*, 202.

95. Draper, Theodore. "The Mystery of Max Eitingon," *New York Review of Books*, April 14, 1988.

96. Noshpitz, Joseph. "Anna O. as Seen by a Child Psychiatrist," in *Anna O.: Fourteen Contemporary Reinterpretations*, 104.

97. Kaplan, 38.

98. Kaplan, 39.

99. Guttmann, 229.

100. Loentz, 91, 161–162.

101. Excerpts from Susyphus-Arbeit, in Guttmann, 195–196, 213.

102. Guttmann, 265–273.

103. Borch-Jacobsen, 39.

104. Loentz, 20.

Index

Gabriel Brownstein is the author of three previous books, most recently *The Open Heart Club*, a history of the struggle to save children with heart defects. For his short stories, he's won a PEN/Hemingway Award and a Pushcart Prize. He's an English Professor at St. John's University in New York City.

PublicAffairs is a publishing house founded in 1997. It is a tribute to the standards, values, and flair of three persons who have served as mentors to countless reporters, writers, editors, and book people of all kinds, including me.

I. F. STONE, proprietor of *I. F. Stone's Weekly*, combined a commitment to the First Amendment with entrepreneurial zeal and reporting skill and became one of the great independent journalists in American history. At the age of eighty, Izzy published *The Trial of Socrates*, which was a national bestseller. He wrote the book after he taught himself ancient Greek.

BENJAMIN C. BRADLEE was for nearly thirty years the charismatic editorial leader of *The Washington Post*. It was Ben who gave the *Post* the range and courage to pursue such historic issues as Watergate. He supported his reporters with a tenacity that made them fearless and it is no accident that so many became authors of influential, best-selling books.

ROBERT L. BERNSTEIN, the chief executive of Random House for more than a quarter century, guided one of the nation's premier publishing houses. Bob was personally responsible for many books of political dissent and argument that challenged tyranny around the globe. He is also the founder and longtime chair of Human Rights Watch, one of the most respected human rights organizations in the world.

•   •   •

For fifty years, the banner of Public Affairs Press was carried by its owner Morris B. Schnapper, who published Gandhi, Nasser, Toynbee, Truman, and about 1,500 other authors. In 1983, Schnapper was described by *The Washington Post* as "a redoubtable gadfly." His legacy will endure in the books to come.

Peter Osnos, *Founder*